WHAT IS LAW?

WHAT IS LAW?

—

The Differing Theories of Jurisprudence

by Surya Prakash Sinha

Paragon House
New York

First edition, 1989

Published in the United States by

Paragon House
90 Fifth Avenue
New York, NY 10011

Copyright © 1989 by Paragon House

Library of Congress Cataloging-in-Publication Data

Sinha, S. Prakash.
What is law? : the differing theories of jurisprudence / by S.
Prakash Sinha.
p. cm.
Includes bibliographies and index.
ISBN 1-55778-082-X. — ISBN 1-55778-192-3 (pbk.)
1. Law—Philosophy 2. Jurisprudence. I. Title.
K237.S57   1989
340'.1—dc19   89-3065
                                                        CIP

Manufactured in the United States of America

The paper used in this publication meets the
minimum requirements of
American National Standard for Information
Sciences—Permanence of Paper
for Printed Library Materials, ANSI Z39.48-1984.

To
Jessica and Sonya
and
to
Aleksander and Maria Rudzinski

Contents

CONTENTS

Contents

1

DIFFERING THEORIES OF LAW

This book presents the theories which have been formulated by jurists and philosophers to define law or explain its nature. It examines them critically. In the end, it attempts to explain why the enterprise of defining law has not been very successful.

While geology has given us theories of origin of the earth, history has given us legends of its creation. These legends are found in four major sources: the epic Enuma Elish of the Mesopotamian cosmology, composed during 1894–1595 B.C.; the theology of Memphis, written in Egypt sometime during 715–664 B.C., but referring to events about 3,000 B.C.; the Vedas of India, created during 1500–500 B.C.; and the Book of Genesis of the Hebrews, composed during the period from the tenth or ninth century B.C. to the fifth century B.C.

The Enuma Elish of Mesopotamia is largely based on the Sumerian cosmology, wherein the god of air, Enlil, separates earth from heaven from the primeval world matter. The Enuma Elish employs the god Tiamet and the Sumerian gods. Tiamet participates in the creation, as do the monsters borne by Tiamet and the winds created by the god Marduk. According to Enuma Elish, Apsu and Tiamet are the parents of the gods. Ea forms the subterranean sea out of Apsu's carcass and Marduk creates heaven, earth, the heavenly bodies, vegetation, and, together with Ea, mankind.

The Theology of Memphis of ancient Egypt borrows many of its ideas from the speculations of the priests of Heliopolis of the previous centuries and presents a new chief god, Ptah, who creates the world through the power of the mind and through speech that expresses his thoughts.

The Vedas of India present two views. In Hymn X, 121 of the Rig Veda, creation occurs through the action of the god Hiranyagarbha. In contrast, Hymn X, 129 presents a highly abstract and logical concept of creation wherein in the beginning there was neither nonexistence nor existence and the universe was developed from the single primordial substance so that "He, the first origin of this creation, whether he formed it all or did not form it, whose eye controls this world in highest heaven, he verily knows it, or perhaps he knows not."[1]

The Book of Genesis of the Hebrews is composed from the "J", the "E", and the "P" sources. The "J" source originates in the tenth or ninth century B.C. in which God is called Jahweh (Yahweh). The "E" source, in which God is called Elohim is later in date. The "P" or Priestly source is set forth by Priest Ezra in the fifth century B.C. According to Genesis, one eternal god effected the creation as a purposeful event, and evil in the world is the punishment for disobedience to God.

However the world did begin, humans and protohumans emerged in it by 500,000 B.C., and fully modern human or *Homo sapiens*, appeared by 30,000 B.C. The development of food production enabled the growth of population and made the emergence of civilizations possible. One of the earliest instances of transition from hunting and gathering to grain cultivation is found in the Middle East between 8500 and 7000 B.C., from where it spread to Europe, India, China, and parts of Africa. It is likely, though not certain, that agriculture emerged independently in the Americas, monsoon Asia, and west Africa. The earliest civilized communities appeared around 3500–3000 B.C. in the valleys of the Tigris-Euphrates and the Nile and soon thereafter in the Indus Valley, although the origin of the Indus Valley civilization is not yet fully known due to lack of sufficient archaeological investigation. A thousand years hence, civilization extended from river valleys to rain-watered land.

Agricultural surplus promoted a distinctive social order. Trade by sea sustained places such as the palace city of Knossos on the Island of Crete. Shortly after 1700 B.C., techniques of chariot warfare were perfected along the northern fringes of Mesopotamia, so that the warrior tribes of central Asia and the Ukraine, in time, overran all of Europe, western Asia, and India. Others, too, acquired the technique and conquered the Yellow River valley of China. The interaction between the indigenous peoples and their new conquerors in Europe, India, and China generated, by 500 B.C., the distinctive European, Indian, and Chinese civilizations in Greece, the Ganges River valley, and the middle reaches of the Yellow River, respectively. In the Middle East the three civilized empires in Egypt, Asia Minor, and northern Mesopotamia competed for supremacy, eventually resulting in the rather unstable unification of the entire area under the Assyrians. Civilized history was thus initiated in these four centers of civilization.

Laws made their first appearance between seven to twelve centuries after the beginning of civilization. The earliest evidence of their promulgation is found in 2360 B.C. in the reign of Urukagina of Lagash. They were adopted in 2300 B.C. in the reign of Sargon of Akkad, and are found in 2100 B.C. in the reign of Ur-Nammu of Ur. These are followed by the more extensive laws of Lipit-Ishtar, the King of Isin, in 1930 B.C.. Then appear the famous laws of Hammurabi, King of Babylon, who reigned from 1792 to 1750 B.C.

Hammurabi's laws are in the nature of amendments and alterations reforming the existing laws, consisting of a heterogeneous series of decisions by judges in a number of separate cases. They exhibit little systematization and do not attempt to cover all possible situations. They are expressions of what Hammurabi desired the law of the land to be; the written text is not an authoritative statute but a memorandum of a decision based on Babylonian notions of justice.

The Middle Assyrian Laws were inscribed on clay tablets during the reign of Tiglath-Pilesar I, from 1115 to 1077 B.C., although they probably go back to the fifteenth century B.C. These laws, too, are amendments and modifications of the existing laws and are even less comprehensive in scope than the laws of Hammurabi.

The Hittite laws were inscribed on clay tablets probably in the thirteenth century B.C., although their original compilation probably dates to the seventeenth century B.C. These laws are a record of judicial formulae and decisions of the royal court at Hattusas, and they do not cover all areas of law in their scope. They were enlarged by more decisions and by certain ordinances of King Telepinus, who reigned from 1511 to 1486 B.C. The Hittite Laws give the impression of an attempt to unite the various classes and groups that composed the Hittite Empire.

The Hebrew Laws, which are neither the decisions of judges nor the ordinances of kings but are claimed to be laws dictated by God Himself, are found in the first five books of the Old Testament, known as Torah (Law) to the Jews and Pentateuch (Five Rolls) to the Greeks. They were compiled from the "J", "E", and "P" sources mentioned above, as well as the "D" source, the Deuteronomic code. And, of course, laws are found in civilizations subsequent to these beginnings.

Over all these centuries, much thought has been devoted to speculation about the nature of law. The present book is not an exhaustive collection of everything that has ever been said about the nature of law. Rather, the theories presented here are believed to be the significant theories, and the measure of their significance has been the originality of their contribution to human thought. This collection is not presented in a historical chronology. Instead, the theories have been classified around their central distinction, the particularity of their thought, their ideational pecularity. The classification itself is not sacrosanct; it is only an aid to the purpose of this book. A cross-classification of the theories is quite possible and not disturbing, although it has been avoided here.

Accordingly, the theories have been placed in ten categories (1) the divine or prophetic theories; (2) the natural law theories; (3) the idealist theories; (4) the positivist theories; (5) the historical theories; (6) the sociological theories; (7) the psychological theories; (8) the realist theories; (9) the phenomenological theories, and (10) the critical legal studies movement.

A study of these theories prompts reflections on the cultural location of the theories, their epistemological incompatibilities, conflicts among them, and the incipience of value preference in many of them.

A. Cultural Location of the Theories of Law

1. The West

Very many, though not all, theories about law have issued from the Western culture, in contrast with the Chinese, Japanese, Indian, or African cultures. This is not because of a higher attainment denoted by law due to some cultural superiority of the West, as erroneously supposed by such thinkers as Sir Henry Maine of England,[2] but because of the fact that law and legal institutions have played a central role in the particular cultural history of the West, a function which in other societies has been fulfilled by other principles of conduct and other institutions of social organization. Since law has been so central in the life of the West, it is only natural that western thinkers would occupy themselves more with thinking about the nature of law than world thinkers in cultures where law has not played as central a role.

Law as playing a central role in social organization is an experience of the historicity of Western civilization, whereas other civilizations have grown each in its own particular historicity. Thus, in the principal stages of early Greek history, the territorial state was the most important political organization, prevailing over all other bases of human association, and it was through the laws of nature that the world was explained. The earliest Greek invaders took to the sea, conquered Knossos in Minoan Crete, and established themselves among the Aegaen Islands as well as on the mainland. For two hundred years following the destruction of Knossos by the Mycenaeans from the Mainland in 1400 B.C., the Mycenaeans carried trade as well as raids into practically all coasts of the Mediterranean, one of the last such raids being against Troy at the mouth of the Dardanelles in 1184 B.C., about which Homer wrote. Shortly after 1200 B.C., the Greek-speaking Dorians came from the north and invaded the Mycenaean centers of power. The displaced refugees went across the Aegean to settlements on the coast of Asia Minor. Since they did not bring with them any pre-existing pattern of governance, they created a viable set of laws and governmental systems to assure cooperation in the new settlement. They thus initiated the earliest Greek city-states or the poleis. Once again, therefore, it was law that became the means for governance and cooperation in these settlements.

On the mainland, the polis developed slowly, as the semi-migratory tribes began to settle permanently and joined with neighbors to constitute a polis. Local chieftains began settling disputes by sitting in council under a high king. When the council could not be held in session, individuals were appointed to look after matters of common concern. These magistrates were appointed for a limited period and were endowed with delegated authority that eventually became legally defined. Law and its institutions thus maintained their central role in social organization. The compelling pull of poleis influenced all areas of Greek cultural activity. The polis was small in size, from 50 to 500 square miles, and had a small population so that men participated in politics directly. Monarchy, oligarchy, tyranny (one-man rule), and democracy evolved variously as forms of government.

Although the polis was generally successful in ordering things, the inquiring Greeks sought learning first from the East. When they found no agreement among the priestly experts of the Middle East on fundamental questions, they, in Ionia, faced these questions themselves and began explaining the phenomena by imaginative reason. Using reason they dismissed gods as the ruling force of the universe and employed natural law in explaining the phenomena.

Greek thought evolved through four stages: the Heroic Mind, the Visionary Mind, the Theoretical Mind, and the Rational Mind. The Heroic Mind based thought on concrete experiences of the physical senses and flourished with fantasy and myths, as in Homer's epics. The Visionary Mind, prompted by the firm establishment of the polis, sought ordering through ideas interlaced with senses. The vehicle of its expression was poetry and drama, as of Pindar, Aeschylus, and Sophocles. The Theoretical Mind, spurred by the emergence of Athens as a metropolis following the Persian wars, called for analytical powers to look beneath the surface. The Rational Mind took to concepts of rational order, as in Plato and Aristotle. It used concepts of *logos, arete*, and *metron* to express its world-view. *Logos*, meaning word, conceptualized the Greek instrument for finding truth and justice by thinking and discussing issues. *Arete* conceptualized man's special worth as a reasoning creature. *Metron*, meaning measure, conceptualized measurement and proportion in order to avoid *hubris*, or excess. Man was thus possessed of reason, freedom of choice, and the ability to make decisions, so that he lived for his own sake rather than for the sake of some other exalted human being or some supernatural power. This individualism yielded the political consequence of independence of the polity whose citizens possessed political and legal rights held in common under the rule of law. Law provided the means for realizing these rights, and, thus, became central to this mode of social organization.

After the end of the Peloponnesian War in 404 B.C., the Athenian dominion yielded to the Spartan supremacy. The sovereignty of the local polis was lost with the Macedonian conquest in 338 B.C. The Macedonian kings embraced Hellenism. Alexander directed it eastward and, in the wake of Alexander's conquest, the Greeks emigrated in large numbers. In fact, the Ptolemaic empire and the Seleucid empire depended greatly upon Greek immigrants.

Meanwhile, Rome began to emerge as a power. It became the leader of the Latin cities in central Italy by establishing an aristocratic republic in 509 B.C., at the end of the Etruscan rule. By 226 B.C., Rome expanded over all of Italy south of the Appenines. Romans drove the Carthaginians from Sicily by 241 B.C.. and conquered Macedonia and Greece in 146 B.C., Seleucid Asia in 64 B.C., and Egypt in 30 B.C..

Involvement with wars of the east and civil war between rival generals resulted in the breakdown of the Republic in favor of a military dictatorship. Emperors followed. The attendant long period of peace witnessed the spread of Hellenistic civilization to Italy, Gaul, and Spain. Although Latin remained the prevailing language, intellectuals such as Lucretius (d.55 B.C.), Cicero (d.43 B.C.), and Vergil (d.19 B.C.) developed it to express Greek philosophy, rhetoric, and poetry. Provinces of the empire were organized into a series of city-states. Beginning as a small city-state on the Tiber, the Romans eventually established an *imperium* which extended from Britannia to Mesopotamia. Thinkers such as Cicero developed the idea that government originated in a voluntary agreement of citizens and that law must be the paramount principle of government. One major consequence, especially significant for our notice here, was the emergence of Roman Law, its codification, and its prominence.

Until about 200 A.D., Christianity and other competing mystery religions offering salvation from tribulations remained more or less obscure. However, eventually Christianity became an important historic force. During A.D. 235–84, the Romans suffered civil war and invasion from the Steppe barbarians. Emperor Constantine (ruled A.D. 306–337) established a new capital at Byzantium, renaming it Constantinople, and made Christianity the state religion. Emperor Theodosius (d.A.D. 395) prohibited all rival faiths. But the Christians did not agree on doctrine. Most of the German kingdoms accepted a version disliked by their Roman subjects, so that Emperor Justinian (A.D. 527–65) launched campaigns into the western Mediterranean to reestablish the unity of the empire.

During the period A.D. 600–1000, the primacy of politics over other bases of human association was reasserted in the disturbed events of this Dark Age. The empire suffered three successive waves of barbarian invasions, the first of which occurred with the Hunnic invasion of central Europe bringing Goths, Burgundians, Vandals, Franks, Anglo-Saxons, and other Germanic peoples into the Roman territory between A.D. 378 and 450. The second wave began with the invasion of the Avars from southern Russia immediately following the death of Justinian. Christendom was culturally and politically divided when the last wave came with the Magyars crossing the Carpathian passes in A.D. 846. Then followed the spontaneous conversion to Christianity of Russia in 989, of Hungary in 1000, and of Denmark, Sweden, and Norway between 831 and 1000.

The formal separation of Latin (Roman Catholic) and Greek (Orthodox) Christendom occurred in 1054. Latin Christendom spread in Europe during the medieval times through conversion and conquest. With Christianity a shift was made from natural philosophy to revelation, although Christianity retained the concept of *logos* as reason and as a principle of cosmic ordering. The power of God sustained both spiritual and secular orders. Human existence became meaningful only insofar as it reconciled man with his Maker, and the European order in these medieval times was sustained by a divinely-ordained unity. The theologian and the scientist alike proceeded to discover inner coherence and harmony to this order.

In the field of law, Gratian (d. 1140) argued the pros and cons of discordance within the laws of the Church. Irnerius (d. 1130) launched a systematic study of Roman Law as a means of sorting out confusions in the local law of Europe. The individual was subordinated to a collective world order. Obedience to authority became the main emphasis. Collective ends became the goal of the work ethic. However, with the Renaissance, man returned to the center of things.

The years 1500–1648 were a period of self-transformation of Europe through the rival movements of Renaissance and Reformation.

The former, dating from about 1350 in Italy, inspired the ideal of giving rebirth to the knowledge, skills and elegance of the ancient past, whereas the latter reasserted religious concerns in the face of rampant secularism in the Renaissance. Although the primacy of God was not disputed, secular measurements were increasingly used to judge events and acts, replacing the divine measurements of God and His commandments.

The humanists and the Christian Platonists reasserted the classical concepts of *logos*, replacing the Age of Faith by a rational status of man. They reasserted *arete* to give man a new intrinsic worth. They reinstated *metron* to determine not only the limits of man but of macrocosm itself. A neoplatonic philosophy surfaced, placing the fundamental relationship of man and his world at the center of cosmology. This it did through its belief in the correspondence of the microcosm and the macrocosm, through its belief in the harmonic structure of the universe, and through its belief in the approach to God through the mathematical symbols of center, circle, and sphere. Individualism asserted itself by insisting, in the manner of the Protestants, on man being his own mediator with God, by challenging the centralized political authority, by legitimizing political needs of the individual rulers, and by instituting capitalism in the economic field. A cultural pluralism entrenched itself as never before. In this individualistic, non-feudal, non-tribal, non-communal, and non-caste frame of society it was law again that provided the technique of social organization.

In the period that followed, gunpowder, printing, and the compass, all invented in China about 756, 1100, and early in the twelfth century respectively, came to the West. They were sufficient to advance it into the era of the national-industrial state.

During the period 1648–1789, both church and state retreated from enforcing conformity to truth, whether theological or otherwise. Passions of Reformation and Counter-Reformation were replaced by the competence of trained professionals in all walks of life. This pluralism of thought was not burdened with the necessity of creating and imposing an overall synthesis of all truth and knowledge. Specialized professions came to flourish, including, for our particular notice here, law. This moderation and balance gave rise to increased professionalism among soldiers and diplomats. It led to the formalization of war—as at the battle of Fortenoy in 1745 when the French and the

English officers offered each other the courtesy of firing the first shot—it promoted international law, which provided the states the technique of reconciling their sovereignty, admitting of no legal limit to their freedom, within the calculations of the balance of power.

Since intellect had been relieved of its preoccupation with the religious debate that had prevailed for more than a century, a start was given to advances in agricultural and manufacturing technology, making Europe rich and advantaged as time went on. Innovations were made in mathematics, science, historiography, empirical philosophy, and political theories that no longer accepted that God intervened in man's everyday affairs. The roots of Europe's subsequent dominance of the world and the seeds for its eventual overthrow of the cultural autonomy of other great civilizations were securely implanted.

During the period 1789–1914, Western civilization was transformed by the Industrial Revolution[3], which had its primary center in England until 1870, and by the democratic revolution[4] which first centered in France after 1789. Western nations expanded enormously in power and wealth as a result of colonization and trade, which had first begun about the year 1000. The Industrial Revolution greatly increased the West's wealth and accelerated the growth of its population, while the democratic revolution established the notion that governments were man-made, and that they therefore could be changed or manipulated. Skilled political leadership could win the support of the majority of the population, the government thereby commanding much greater power than before. In these processes, law played a significant role and provided the social organization with a central mechanism.

During the period 1914–1945, social changes intensified even further with the discovery, through the two World Wars of 1914–18 and 1939–45, that economies could concentrate effort on particular goals and that human societies could be deliberately manipulated for war as well as peace as illustrated by such diverse regimes as Hitler's Germany, Stalin's Soviet Union, and Franklin D. Roosevelt's United States. Society and economy were no longer considered "natural." They were amenable to conscious control. Again, law played a central part in the control and management of these matters, and it continues to do so in the period following 1945. In sum, therefore, it is an incidence of the particular historicity of the Western civilization that law has played a fairly central role in its social organization.

2. China

Such is not the case with the history of the Chinese civilization. Farming began in the Yellow River valley before 3000 B.C. The neolithic Black Pottery people were probably ancestral to the historical Chinese, but the archaelogical evidence from the city of Anyang (about 1400–1100 B.C.) reveals important differences between Anyang and the Black Pottery villages. The Hsia are considered the first rulers of China. The Shang dynasty (1523–1028 B.C.) is the second dynasty recorded in Chinese history, but not much is known about that society or government. The Shang dynasty was overthrown by the Chou in 1051 B.C. In the early or western Chou period (1051–771 B.C.), the rulers may have exerted an effective control over a large area of northern China, but a barbarian attack in 771 B.C destroyed that authority. The later or eastern Chou dynasty (770–256 B.C.) was inaugurated in the following year, and the Chinese civilization expanded rapidly at the end of this period known as the age of the warring states (402–221 B.C.).

The Chou conquerors eliminated human sacrifice and rituals that were prevalent in the Shang religion and explained their own supreme power in terms of a mandate from Heaven. This idea is a crucial one in later political thought and it maintained that Heaven, somewhat of an anthropomorphic diety, granted earthly rule to the specially selected Son of Heaven, the Emperor. The Son of Heaven could rule as long as he behaved piously and properly. Consequently, he could lose Heaven's mandate by impiety or impropriety. The accompanying cosmology maintained that the cosmic order involved a reciprocal interaction between heaven, earth, and men. Earthly affairs revolved around the emperor just as the heavens turned on the pole star. The emperor was responsible for war and politics, as well as for terrestrial phenomena, such as weather that affected human activity. It was the emperor's duty to behave in accordance with the prescribed rites so as to attain the harmony between earth and heaven that was necessary for human welfare. However, the belief that correct observance of traditional rites would bring order and prosperity was challenged by the fact of wars. The Legalists, therefore, repudiated the pieties of the past.

What prevailed in the end, though, was the conservative, though modulated, piety of the sage Confucius (551–479 B.C.). He did not regard Heaven and spirits as proper objects of inquiry, although he

11

did not doubt their reality or power, and he directed attention to the human aspects of things. He looked back nostalgically to the days of the early Chou, the Shang, and the Hsia empires, and even to the divine emperors of the legendary age when, he felt, times had been good because harmonious relationships existed between Heaven and earth. Since that harmony was lacking now, Confucius raised the question what a wise man should do and gave his answer, which his disciples recorded. The Five Classics were compiled during his lifetime. Later, the study of the Classics became essential for a well-educated man and provided the Chinese of subsequent generations a common core from which grew fundamental attitudes and values. While Confucianism emphasized decorum and self-control, other schools, most importantly contemporary Taoism, emphasized human passion and the mysteries of nature. Together, they provided a balanced and stable pattern of thought that, with later changes and enrichment but without fundamental interruption, provided the cement of civilization down to modern times.

During the period from 500 B.C. to A.D. 200, China's unification brought great disturbances among the peoples of the steppe. In 221 B.C., the ruler of the state of Ch'in waged wars against the steppe barbarians, overthrew his rivals within China, and declared himself the First Emperor (Shih Huang-ti) of the new Ch'in dynasty. Among other things, he prescribed a uniform script, completed the Great Wall, embraced the Legalist school, and repudiated anything that set limits to his power, especially Confucianism, which compelled the emperor to govern in accordance with traditional rites. Confucian teaching was prohibited, and Confucian books were burned, except for a single copy of each work retained in the imperial archives.

After the emperor's death in 210 B.C., civil war broke out, ending, in 202 B.C., with the founding of the Han dynasty that ruled until A.D. 220, except for a brief interruption in A.D. 9–22. The Han emperors soon accepted Confucianism and officially repressed rival doctrines. In time, the educated classes developed a remarkable uniformity of outlook.

During the period A.D. 200–600, the Sui emperors and their successors of the T'ang dynasty (A.D. 618–907) successfully met the barbarian threat and reestablished an effective frontier guard against the Turkish confederacy. The Sui organized an efficient and ruthless bureaucracy, completed the Grand Canal linking the Yangtse with the

Yellow River—which became a major route of economy—and succeeded in reconstituting an imperial China even stronger than it had
been during the Han dynasty. Shortly after the reunification of China
by the Sui dynasty in A.D. 589, there was a war and the T'ang came
to power (618–907), followed by the Sung (960–1279).

Strong central power prevailed only until 755, but the disruption
of central power did not disrupt the economic development. Foreign
trade and interregional exchanges did not challenge the traditional
dominance of the landlord-official class whose classically educated
members pursued arts and decorum worthy of gentlemen, the gentle-
manly ideal being considerably elaborated during the T'ang and early
Sung periods.

Although Buddhism practically achieved an official status in the
early T'ang period, it met with systematic persecution after 845 due
to the Confucianist distrust of it. However, it taught the Confucians
how to read new meanings into old texts by analogy and symbolic
interpretation, and it helped them discover new meanings in the Classics by bringing to their attention metaphysical and cosmological questions. The Taoists took from Buddhism not only aspects of doctrine
but monastic organization and schooling as well. Neo-Confucianism
was thus well initiated even prior to 1000, and the policy of the Sung
rulers to preserve things authentically Chinese guaranteed its preem-
inence. During the period 1000–1500, Neo-Confucianism developed
to its heights under the later Sung, especially with philosopher Chu
Hsi (1130–1200) and his followers, who tried to be faithful to the
ancients. Socio-economic changes during the Mongol period took a
toll of the traditional values, but in the end the old Confucianism
reasserted itself.

In the early part of the Ming period (1368–1644), China took to
maritime enterprise but, after the expeditions of the court eunuch
Cheng-ho from 1405 to 1433, the Ming emperor forbade seagoing.
The mercantile class suffered from the Ming restoration of the Neo-
Confucian orthodoxy, but the trading community faded in importance
because of the strikingly great productivity of Chinese agriculture.
Therefore, conservative Confucianism prevailed again.

Printing, invented in 756, was used to disseminate Confucian literature. Gunpowder, invented about 1100, was used to put down
local warlords. The compass, invented in the early twelfth century,
was used to ward off seaborne enterprise. Confucian institutions had

achieved such perfection and inner strength that no upheaval made more than a transitory impression upon them until the massive social breakdown of China in the twentieth century.

During the period 1500–1700, a barbarian war band from Manchuria came to Peking in concert with a Ming general for the purposes of suppressing a domestic rebellion. Soon the Manchus founded their own Ching dynasty and consolidated their hold over China. Although the Manchu emperors distrusted the native Chinese, the civil administration employed both the Chinese and the Manchus and used recruitment examinations based on the knowledge of the Confucian classics. The Manchus secured the land frontier of China against the steppe nomads through a process that began with the Treaty of Nerchinsk of 1689 with Russia and ended with the smashing campaign of 1757 against the Kalmuk confederacy. They settled their problem of sea defenses when Japan abandoned its sea adventures in 1636 on its own, thereby eliminating the main source of raids on the China coast. The activities of the European merchant ships were tamed when the local representatives of the Chinese administration concluded agreement with the Europeans.

The society prospered with the restoration of peace. In spite of the novelties brought by the Europeans, such as new geographical information, improved astronomical skills, pendulum clocks, and the Jesuits, conservatism continued to prevail in the cultural life, which, due to the perfecting of its own inner balance, did not take more than a casual notice of the European novelties. Scholars invented critical methods to establish true meanings of old Confucian texts. The rigorous Han School of Learning discouraged wayward interpretations of the sort indulged in by the Neo-Confucianists of earlier generations.

The Chinese order continued to function quite well until about 1775, when dynastic decay began with peasant grievances resulting from the pressure of population. Revolts started, climaxing in 1850 with the outbreak of the disastrous Taiping rebellion. There were also problems with the European trade, especially when the British government, after abolishing the East India Company's monopoly of China trade in 1834, tried to introduce European patterns of commerce at Canton. British and European traders took to extralegal forms of trade in opium when its import was forbidden by Chinese officials. The Chinese dispatched a special commissioner to Canton to stop these activities. A dispute over the punishment of British sailors for a murder on shore gave the British an excuse for war with the Chinese, in which British gunboats overwhelmed Chinese coastal defenses. At the end of the war the British extracted the Treaty of Nanking (1842) from the Chinese, giving them all they wanted. Promptly enough, other Western countries demanded and obtained similar privileges and more. However, in spite of this affront to power, the old traditional pattern of Chinese life and culture remained uninterrupted until after 1850.

The period 1850–1945 began with the Western adventurers flooding the treaty ports after the opium war of 1839–41. They refused to remain in the humble position appropriate to foreign merchants in the Confucian tradition. Moreover, they always had the guns and diplomacy of their governments behind them. This was immoral and unjust to the Chinese, but they could not bring themselves to abandon the Confucian ways in order to deal effectively with the West. In 1860, the French and the British seized Peking and burned the Imperial summer palace as an act of retaliation for the imprisonment of some of their diplomats. China's stronger enemies began chopping off its territory and its tributary dependencies. The land beyond the Amur River was ceded to Russia in 1860, Indochina (Vietnam, Cambodia, and Laos) to France in 1885, and Burma to England in 1886. Further dents in sovereignty were made with foreign control of customs in 1863, of postal services in 1896, and of railway construction in 1888. China was defeated by Japan in Korea in 1894–95 when the Chinese intervened in Korea, which they had come to consider their dependent kingdom. As a result, they had to withdraw totally from Korea, transfer Formosa and other islands to Japan, concede a base to Japan on the mainland Liaotung Peninsula, and pay an indemnity as well.

Special concessions and advantages were continually ceded to the foreigners. This struck many Chinese as a betrayal of the national interest by the government. Secret societies began to proliferate with the aim of overthrowing the Manchus. When the Boxers, so-called by the Westerners because of their calisthenic exercises, attacked the hated foreigners and missionaries, the Western powers occupied Peking (1900) and made China agree to pay an indemnity. In 1911, revolutionary activity against the discredited Manchu rule became quite overt and a republic was installed in 1912 without much carnage.

New kinds of ideas began to attract the educated class. Legalism reappeared. Codes were adopted on Western models in order to attain freedom from Western domination. However, traditional concepts

15

persisted. The new codes were applied when they coincided with the traditional ideas of equity and propriety and were ignored when they conflicted with them. The increased number of trials resulting from these codes was considered a sign of decadence. However, intellectual and political leaders turned their back upon Confucianism.

Sun Yat-Sen (d.1925) founded the Kuomintang Party despite his intellectual confusions resulting from his hurry to absorb Western culture quickly. The Kuomintang had to subdue local war lords, Japanese puppets, and rival Communists. Its military commander, Chiang Kai-shek, was able to retrieve most of China from local war lords by 1928, but the Kuomintang did not succeed in destroying the Communists, so civil war continued sporadically throughout the period between the two World Wars. When the Japanese had to end their occupation of China with their defeat in World War II in 1945, Chiang Kai-shek and the Kuomintang clashed with Mao Tse-tung and the Chinese Communists, ending in the Communist victory in 1949.

Although radical intellectual change was augured early on with the breakdown of Confucian orthodoxy, the new ideas and techniques did not reach the masses until after 1949. Socialist legality on the Soviet model established itself in the early years following 1949. However, in 1952–53 attacks were made on such concepts of legalism as separation of law from politics, equality before law, independence of the judiciary, limitation of actions, and non-retroactivity of legislation. Nevertheless, Soviet-style socialist legality was adopted in the Constitution of 1954.

The Soviet model was abandoned when relations with the Soviet Union were broken off in 1960. China reverted to a path of its own, where priority was given to social transformation over economic growth. Soviet-style democratic centralism was abandoned, and persuasion was emphasized over force. The adversary was treated as not beyond redemption, and the practice of self-criticism was adopted. The masses were asked to be vigilant of their leaders. The Central Committee itself was invited to practice self-criticism.

There has been a modest return to the ancient traditions, although there are significant departures from the traditional thought. The cosmology of natural phenomena and human behavior has been abandoned. Former methods of mediation such as appeal to the family, clan, neighbors, or local dignitaries have been replaced by mediation of those politically involved, such as the people's mediation committees, of which there are more than 200,000 in the country. The view that each party in a dispute must sacrifice something of his own in order to reestablish harmony has been supplanted by the need to assure success of some policy.

But the principle of legality is repudiated in favor of education and persuasion. Conciliation, not recourse to law, is the honorable course. While law is appropriate for dealing with those counter-revolutionaries for whom reform can no longer be hoped, it is not considered suitable for resolving internal social contradictions. Most conflicts are resolved by appeal to conscience, rather than by pursuit of rights in the courts of law. Law is resorted to when all else has failed. Resort must first be made to *Ch'ing* (human sentiment), next to *Lii* (reason), and only lastly to *Fa* (law). There used to be a legend in China that *Fa* was invented by the barbarous tribe of Miao in the time of the prophet Shun in the 23rd century B.C., whom God later exterminated. Law is for the morally perverse, the incorrigible criminal, and the foreigner who is alien to Chinese values. In sum, therefore, law has not played a central role in the social organization of China due to the particular historicity of its civilization.

3. Japan

Law has not been central in the historical development of concepts of social order in Japan. At the beginning of their civilized history, the Japanese steadily raised their farming to the levels of the Chinese at the northeastern flank of the Chinese center. During A.D. 600–1000, they imported Buddhism, Confucianism, and other aspects of the Chinese culture. The Japanese Emperors of the Nara period (A.D. 645–784) copied the T'ang court of China. (A more rough life-style was sustained by the baronial patrons in their provincial castles.) In the Taika era (beginning in A.D. 646), a system of periodic distribution of rice plantations was introduced in proportion to the number of people to be fed. The society was divided in ranks. Each rank performed a particular task for the regime. The duties for each class were collected in a compilation known as *ritsu-ryō* a series of prohibitions (*ritsu*) and rules of administration (*ryō*). The *ritsu-ryō* were the source of enlightenment for the people, rather than a list of legal rights and duties in the Western sense.

In the ninth and the tenth centuries, the system of sharing of public land was replaced by a feudal system, in which the seigneurial unit of *shō* became a sovereign domain with fiscal privileges, whose master owned all the land within it.

This decline of imperial power did not result in a total disappearance of the courtly culture. However, the militarily expansive warrior barons or *samurai* did not have much appreciation for the antimilitaristic cultural idea that had been imposed from T'ang China. They developed their own warrior ideal in its place, emphasizing such things as courage in battle, loyalty to the leader, and the personal dignity of the fighting man. Although possession of territory taken in wars between these warlords became hereditary, continued vigilance and prowess in battle were needed to maintain it. Disputes between different bands, as well as within a single band, were settled by the sword. The power and position of the Emperor and the courtier class (*kuge*) lost much substance. Although the Emperor was still revered because of his sacred rights, the warrior class (*buke, bushi, samurai*) had its own code of conduct (*buke-hō*) the basis of which was not like any Western concept of law, but instead was based upon the duty of faithfulness to the overlord. Thus, *buke-hō* applied to the warrior class while *ritsu-ryō* applied to others. This dualism continued until the superiority of the warrior over the peasant resulted in the dominance of the *buke-hō* and desuetude of the *ritsu-ryō* during the period of the Ashizaka Shoguns (1333–1573).

After about A.D. 1300, the townsmen and the sailors began to be prominent. The Japanese achieved naval supremacy in the southeast Pacific after China withdrew from the seas in 1430s. The poor *samurai*, without much land, took to piracy and searoving. With their riches brought home, the town life assumed a new importance, giving rise to a warlike, self-reliant middle class that developed an elaborate high culture. That culture manifested itself in drama based on the wars of the *samurai*, in a distinctive Japanese style of painting, and in refinement of *samurai* manners, as in the elegant tea ceremony and the use of silk clothes.

Similarly, Zen Buddhism, although originally imported from China, was mixed with the *samurai* ideal, beginning in about 1200. It developed into the Pure Land Buddhism, whose monasteries defended themselves like a *samurai* clan, for they often were important landholders. Peasant uprisings began to break out against them after 1400, but they did not amount to much. The cult of the Sun Goddess, from whom the imperial order descended, was at one time confined to the imperial court and was patterned after Chinese ancestor worship. After 1400, however, it began to be reinterpreted and acquired its own metaphysical theology under the new name of Shinto.

Japan suffered from civil wars at the beginning of the period 1500–1700. The Portuguese arrived in the 1540s. European dress styles, Christian baptism, and European guns spread rapidly. The increased cost of armaments necessitated large territorial sovereigns. The result was a political consolidation of Japan under Hideyoshi (d.1598). After his death, one of his companions, Ieyasu of the Tokugawa family, succeeded at the end of a civil war and proceeded to protect himself from his rivals, controlling the searovers and eventually forbidding them altogether. With the coming of the Dutch in 1609, a new supplier of arms materialized for the Japanese, so that the Shogun could now safely proceed against the Christian community. Following a Christian revolt in 1637 at Kyushu, almost all Christians, whether European or Japanese, were executed.

The Tokugawa Shoguns ruled from 1603 to 1868. The end of warfare deprived the *samurai* of a meaningful occupation, so they spent their time engaging in ceremonies of their class or amusing themselves in the sensuous life of the towns, bankrupting themselves but giving rise to a bustling market economy. The merchants gladly accepted the assignment of the right to collect rice from the villages, which had belonged to the bankrupt *samurais*. Thus, the vulgar culture of the towns and the decorous culture of the officialdom existed contemporaneously, almost complementarily. The social order was based on a strict separation into the social classes of warriors, peasants, and merchants.

Although the Tokugawa Shoguns had made Neo-Confucianism official and even prohibited the study of other philosophies, a few disaffected Japanese began studying Western as well as Chinese thoughts. Others used Neo-Confucianism and its teaching of obedience to superiors as a reason to oppose the Shoguns' usurpation of authority from the Emperor. Yet others embraced Shinto in place of Neo-Confucianism. Thus, when the Shoguns were forced to abandon the policy of isolation in 1854, there were men waiting in the wings with alternative policies.

During this period, the idea of law was quite absent. Order was based on a series of *giri*, or proper rules of behavior, such as the *giri* of father and son, of husband and wife, of landowner and farmer, of lender and borrower, of merchant and customer, of employee and employer, and so on, and they were observed because violation brought social reprobation.

During the period 1850–1945, it became clear that the policy of rigorous seclusion that had been in effect since 1638 could no longer be enforced against the Western navies. In 1853, the United States dispatched Commodore Perry with four warships and demanded Japan let the U.S. use its ports for trade and as coaling stations for its ships. After initial hesitation, the Tokugawa Shogun accepted the American terms in 1854. This offended the Japanese and they overthrew the Tokugawa government in 1868, restoring the Emperor, and inaugurating the Meiji era.

The Japanese soon realized that the only way to protect themselves from the West and to end the national disgrace of unequal treaties extracted from them in 1858, was to adopt Western technology and political organization. Therefore, feudalism was replaced by a democratic state. Western-style legislation was adopted to link Japanese law with the laws of the West. European-style codes were adopted. Public institutions were modified extensively by establishing freedom of agriculture in 1871, sale of land in 1872, and a Constitution in 1889. The administrative structure of the country was modified by creating departments (kin) and municipalities. An industrial revolution was launched in order to facilitate military strength.

When European powers engaged themselves in World War I in 1914, Japan sought to extend its own special privileges in China by making its Twenty-one Demands in 1915. However, after a period of Chinese protests and American efforts to restrain Japan, the new balance of forces imposed its own general settlement in the Pacific area at the Washington Conference of 1922 and kept Japan away from China.

Although both Western-style industrialization and democratic politics were achieved by Japan during this period, the deep-seated ways of traditional Japanese life continued. Thus, in the industrial field, attitudes deriving directly from the spirit of the samurai clans governed conduct. Rather than seeking profit as an end in itself, factory managers took it as their duty to be of service to the nation, obeying superiors, and disciplining and protecting inferiors. Firms took their goal to be honor and prestige. Private venturers pursued the old warrior virtues of courage, endurance, and loyalty. Human relations within the firm were patterned after the traditional mode that had existed between the *samurai* and the peasant, whereunder managers commanded, the workers obeyed, and the workers were looked after throughout their life. In the political field, universal male suffrage to the Diet was introduced by the Constitution of 1889, but, until the 1930s, behind-the-scenes authority was exercised by an inner circle of elders who descended from the clique of clan leaders.

In the 1930s, ambitious young army officers emerged, through their semisecret patriotic societies, as a rival power to the civil government. Japan, meanwhile, embarked on a course of military conquest, conquering Manchuria in 1931 and most of China in 1937–41. The United States imposed trade embargos against Japan on such crucial supplies as oil and scrap iron in order to check the Japanese moves and secure its own interests in the Pacific. The Japanese attacked the American fleet in Pearl Harbor in 1941 so that they could seize the oilfields in Borneo and construct a "co-prosperity sphere" in Southeast Asia and the Southwest Pacific. However, World War II ended with the surrender of Japan to the U.S. in August 1945. The American occupation ended subsequently.

In modern Japan, the law made in imitation of the West governs a very small segment of social life, under the presupposition of the Western law, namely, middle class individuals fashioning their relations on the basis of freedom and liberty. The majority of the people follow the Confucian idea of hierarchy based on natural order. There is a general dislike for involving oneself in public affairs, and a general preference for leaving matters of government to a powerful minority. Recourse to law is shameful conduct. *Giri-ninjo* are followed for pursuing personal relations. The notion of legal rights is contrary to the Confucian hierarchy and is deemed to depersonalize human relations by putting all persons on an equal basis. Law is considered appropriate only for depersonalized matters relating to business and industry. Disputes are settled preferably through conciliation procedures of *jidan, wakai,* and *chotei*. In *jidan* the parties settle the dispute amicably through mediators; in *wakai* the judge brings the parties to a settlement; in *chotei* the parties request the court to appoint a panel of conciliators, who are charged with proposing an equitable settlement. Resort to *chusai* (arbitration) is avoided in domestic contracts, although it is employed in foreign trade contracts. In sum, therefore, law has not been a central element of social organization in the particular historicity of the Japanese culture.

4. India

The position of law in the cultural history of India is unique. The origin of the Indus valley civilization is not fully known due to insufficient archaelogical investigation. The currently available data puts its establishment shortly after the period of 3500–3000 B.C., when the earliest civilized communities appeared in the valley of Tigris-Euphrates and the Nile. With the transition to rain-watered cultivation, Indus civilization spread toward the south and the east. The Aryan invaders from the West destroyed the Indus cities by about 1500 B.C. Their wandering bands gradually settled down to agricultural life, although they nevertheless kept expanding into southern and eastern India. The Sanskrit poems of Rig Veda and the epic Mahabharata descended from this Heroic age and indicate an aristocratic chariot culture for that time.

The chariot and the aristocratic predominance were displaced by the coming of iron about 900 B.C., yielding to great centralized monarchies of the Ganges Valley. By 800 B.C., the Ganges valley was on its way to civilized complexity in which the centralized monarchies supported courtly centers, artisan skills, and inter-regional trade. Sea trade with Mesopotamia was resumed by about that time.

Caste emerged as the institution of social organization which, with later modifications, continues to this day. A caste is an exclusive group of persons whose customs govern intimacies of dining and intermarriage with each other, and with definite rules of behavior toward members of other castes. Strangers and intruders automatically become another caste, as do wanderers and displaced persons. New occupations create new castes. A large caste is subdivided into subcastes. Exact origins of such organization of the society are not clear. However, three main principles have sustained it: one, the idea of ceremonial purity with its fear of contamination by a member of a lower class; two, the pyramidical structure of castes in which each caste has another to look down upon and thus be satisfied psychologically so that there is no need to compel the newcomers to surrender their ways and be assimilated into the population as a whole; and, three, the doctrines of *varna* and reincarnation, in which *varna* divides all people in four large castes in this descending order: Brahmans who pray and perform rituals; Kshatriyas who fight wars and defend the society, Vaisyas who carry on trade, and Sudras who perform unclean tasks. The doctrine of reincarnation gives a logical explanation of a man's situation in terms of reward or punishment for acts in the former lives of the soul. Since everyone identified foremost with his caste, political and territorial administration became of only secondary importance in this period. Caste also made it easy for newcomers to come within the embrace of the Indian civilization without any radical displacement of their own customs and habits. This went well with India's unique religious evolution wherein the doctrine was passed on by word of mouth from teacher to pupil and which, for that reason, allowed for easy blending of different doctrines.

The Vedas were the handbooks of religious rituals; however, as their language became unintelligible, the priests shifted the emphasis from gods to the act of worship itself and put forth their own claims in texts known as Brahmanas. Since the priestly claims of authority were not widely accepted, a rival type of piety arose in another body of oral literature known as Upanishads, which recommended a godless asceticism. The Brahman priests, in turn, reconciled the Upanishads with their Brahmanas by arguing that the former were suitable for the last stage of a man's life.

The Brahmans were more seriously challenged by the emergence of Jainism and Buddhism about 500 B.C. Jainism remained a faith for an elite, but Buddhism became more popular. It moderated and defined the Upanishadic style of religious life. In the end, however, it gave way to a transformed Brahmanical religion, Hinduism. The *Dharma Sutras,* or the manuals of human conduct, were composed between the sixth and the second centuries B.C.

During the period 500 B.C. to A.D. 200, the kingdom of Magadha had already consolidated itself in the Ganges region by the time Alexander invaded the Indus Valley in 327 B.C. That invasion disrupted Indus defenses and alliances. Chandragupta Maurya of Magadha (reigned 321–297 B.C.) added the Indus region to his kingdom, while his grandson Asoka (reigned 274–36 B.C) annexed central and southern India to the Mauryan empire. Asoka gave official patronage to Buddhism, supplementing it with such innovations as pilgrimages and almsgiving. While the monks found in it a complete way of life, how-

23

ever, the ordinary people resorted to Brahmans for the daily rites of their lives.

The period A.D. 200–600 witnessed a golden age in India. The Gupta empire (A.D. 320–535) extended over all of northern India from the Arabian sea to the Bay of Bengal. The society and culture remained of a strongly apolitical bent, as before. Politics remained relatively superficial for the Gupta rulers, who, for example, allowed the defeated rulers to remain in control of their lands and were content with ceremonial deference from them on state occasions. The Gupta rulers accepted the Hindu notion of authority that put their own edicts last in authority, authority being arranged in the descending order of Vedas, the Brahmana commentaries on Vedas, examples of holy men, and, lastly, personal inclination, including edicts of a king or public official.

The *Dharma Shāstras*, or instructions in the sacred law, were compiled during the Gupta era and became basic for Hindu life ever since, albeit interpreted subsequently to meet contemporary needs. The *Dharma Shāstras* gave the theory of caste its classical formulation, laid down the duties of members of different castes, and asserted that their faithful performance would lead to the salvation of soul, wherein the soul would free itself from the cycle of reincarnation and unite with the Absolute Soul, or God.

During the period A.D. 600–1000, the Muslim invaders conquered Sind in the northwest (by 715), seized control of the Indian Ocean, and separated India from her cultural dependencies in southeast Asia. The Hindus were unable to repel the Muslims due to the caste organization of the society, which kept it politically and militarily weak. They peaceably recoiled to conserving their heritage. Philosophers such as Shankara (788–850) showed why the Muslim criticism of Hindu idolatry had been mistaken for the reason that the practice helped people to achieve a pure and transcendental monism. They even argued for the validity of Muslim rites.

The popular culture, however, rejected everything alien and defended everything its own. Hidden practices came out in the open, such as Tantrism, wherein supernatural powers were sought by magic charms and incantations. Temples became prominent after the collapse of the Gupta rulers, which meant a setback to the more secular aspects of civilization. Hinduism remained firmly rooted. Indian society expanded geographically, but the Muslim threat forced the Hindus to concentrate upon what was Indian and, therefore, reject whatever was alien.

During the period 1000–1500, the Muslim conquest of India brought significant changes. For the Hindus, their conquerors became another class and thus fitted into the Hindu social system, but the universal and missionary faith of Islam resisted the caste system. The egalitarian teachings of Islam, preached by the itinerant Sufi holy men, appealed to the low-caste urban Hindus, as well as to the newcomers to Indian society along the frontiers, especially in eastern Bengal, who had been put in the lower caste. Hinduism itself changed. Driven out of temples due to their destruction by the Muslim invaders, it took to the streets. The ceremonies became more public, with the result that Islam attracted only the fringes of society. Thinkers such as Kabir (d.1518) and Nanak (probably a disciple of Kabir in his youth) attempted a synthesis of what they saw as the common core of truth in both Hinduism and Islam. Nanak even founded the new Sikh faith. Furthermore, the popular Hindu piety replaced Sanskrit as the religious language with vernaculars such as Hindi. The courtly official aspects of culture, of course, became Muslim.

During the period 1500–1700, the Muslim rulers conquered the last independent Hindu state of Vijayanagar in the south (in 1565) and brought almost the whole of the Indian peninsula under their control during the reign of the Mughal Emperor Aurangzeb (1658–1707). Hinduism was deprived of state support, but it was revivified in the streets by the saint Chaitanya (d.1527) and poets Sur Das (d.1563) and Tulsi Das (d.1623). The arguments of both the Muslim and the Christian missionaries failed to overcome the public religious excitement made possible by these new movements. Therefore, although the form of Hinduism was changed by the political submission of the society, the overwhelming majority of Indians remained true to the Hindu faith, Hindu traditions, and Hindu ways of life, including the caste system of social organization. Muslim law, being linked to Islam, applied to Muslims but was inapplicable to non-Muslims, except, of course, in criminal matters.

During the period 1700–1850, the Mughal power began to decline with the revolts of the Marathas and the Sikhs, although the Mughal Emperor survived in name until 1857. The European trading companies began equipping their own armed forces, made up of Indian soldiers (sepoys) under European officers. In the rivalries of the European powers in India, the British won a decisive victory over the French in 1763 after a struggle that had begun in 1756. After the Afghan invasion of India and the defeat of the Marathas at Panipat in 1767, the local princes had to choose between the Afghans and the British. Most preferred the British, so that by 1818 almost all Indian states came under British control. That control was exercised through a resident at court. Part of India was directly administered by the British. After 1818, the British triumphed in the last Maratha war, thereby leaving no military rival.

The official British policy was to leave the social institutions and relationships alone. For example, they kept Persian of the Mughals as the language of administration until 1837. However, initiatives from both the British and the Hindus began to expand the interaction between the Western and the Hindu cultures. Although few Indians became Christians, missionary activity made the knowledge of the European civilization more accessible to the Indians and stimulated efforts, pioneered by Ram Mohen Roy (d.1833), for understanding the British culture. Indian leaders urged the British authorities to reform traditional customs and institutions, so much so that the administrative action failed to keep pace with their demands. However, the great majority of the population remained only vaguely aware of such developments.

During the period 1850–1945, the British succeeded in quelling the revolt of 1857 and installed an autocratic civil service recruited from British universities. That civil service began imposing a long series of reforms. Indian reaction to Western civilization was peaceful, so that new ventures of industry and commerce were largely left with the outsiders, such as the Parsis and the Englishmen. Disruption of supply lines from England during the two World Wars resulted in the strengthening of Indian industries, which proceeded in enterprises wherein the private sector and the government merged. The Indian National Congress was organized in 1885 with the aim of eventually achieving self-government. After World War I, its leadership passed to Mohandas Gandhi. The Muslim League was organized in 1905 and, in 1940, proclaimed its goal of establishing a separate Muslim state of Pakistan. Independence from British rule came in 1947 when India was divided into a Muslim Pakistan and a secular India.

During British rule, the Hindu sacred law of *Dharma* was applied to such matters as marriage, inheritance, the caste system, and religious usages or institutions, whereas other important aspects of the newly reshaped society were governed by a newly created territorial law that applied to all subjects, regardless of their religious status. The idea of a territorial law, in which the law existed as an autonomous body independent of religions, was an alien concept to Indian traditions. A distinction was drawn between the Presidency towns of Bombay, Calcutta, and Madras and the rest of India, known as *Mofussil*. English courts operated in the Presidency Towns and applied English law as it existed in 1726, subject to regulations made by the local authorities and to its applicability to Indian conditions. Originally, their jurisdiction availed in disputes involving an Englishman or for parties who formally accepted that jurisdiction. In 1781, it was extended to all disputes. These courts were authorized to apply Hindu law and Muslim law for matters involving Hindus and Muslims.

The *Mofussil* courts in the rest of India had been established by the East India Company which, in 1765, had obtained the privilege to collect taxes in exchange for an annual payment to the Mughal Emperor. In 1857, these courts passed to the direct authority of the British government. In accordance with Governor-General Warren Hastings' Regulation for the Administration of Civil Justice of 1772, the *Mofussil* courts applied Hindu or Muslim law in matters of inheritance, marriage, caste, and religious usages or institutions, whereas they applied general principles of justice, equity, and good conscience in other matters. The Regulation of 1781 created two superior courts, one the *Sadar Diwāni Adālat* for private law matters and the other the *Sadar Nizāmi Adālat* for criminal matters, for the provinces of Bengal, Bihar, and Orissa.

The Indian High Courts Act of 1861 reorganized the court system throughout the colony. Although the Cornwallis Code of 1793 and the Elphinstone Code of 1827 had already been adopted for India in criminal matters, organized codification began with the Charter Act of 1833, which formally anticipated codification. The first Law Commission submitted its famous *lex loci* report proposing three codes, one for Muslim law, one for Hindu law, and one in the nature of territorial law (*lex loci*) for matters where Hindu or Muslim law was not applicable. These proposals met with serious objections. A second Law Commission was established in 1853 and made its own proposals. However, it was only after the revolt of 1857 that an intensive legislative activity for India took place. Adopted were the Indian Code of Civil Procedure (1859), replaced by a Civil Code (1908), a Criminal Code (1860), and a Code of Criminal Procedure (1861), the Limitation Act (1859), the Succession Act (1865), the Contract Act (1872), the Evidence Act (1872), the Specific Relief Act (1872), the Negotiable Instruments Acts (1881), the Transfer of Property Act (1882), the Trusts Act (1882), and so on.

After the independence of India in 1947, the Constitution of 1950 provided for the maintenance of the former law (Section 372). New legal activity followed. The modern tendency is to replace religious laws with secular law. However, nearly eighty percent of the population living in villages continues to conduct its life through the traditional institutions. In sum, therefore, law in the Western sense is not a product of the historicity of the Indian civilization but was imported by the English rule at a much later stage of its development.

5. Africa

Law is also not a central factor in the historicity of civilizations in Africa, as is evident in the cultures of (1) the Tallensi, (2) the Ashanti, (3) the Hausa-Fulani, (4) the Yoruba, (5) the Ibo, (6) the Tiv, (7) the Ganda, (8) the Lugbara, (9) the Kikuyu, (10) the Nandi, (11) the Arusha, (12) the Nyakyusa, and (13) the Nuer.

The Tallensi had no central authority, no temporal chief, and no council of elders for the purposes of responding to the cues of life, solving their common problems, and resolving their inter-group conflicts. The kinship heads handled these problems. The people sorted their problems between those appropriate for the clan head, those appropriate for the diviner, and those appropriate for the family head. They knew what was to be handled in their world and what was to be settled in the world of spirits. They saw themselves living in the world of tangible substance as well as in the world of ancestors and spirits. The spiritual world operated with real effect in the material world, so that the former had to be propitiated with solemn ritual and display for the latter to prosper. Great festivals and rituals emphasized the harmony of the whole society. Inter-clan wars, as between the Namoos and non-Namoos, were part of the social process that released tensions and preceded ritual affirmation of inter-clan solidarity. They were a stable, unchanging society, fixed in their locality and in their ways. Conflict arising from violation of norms within the clan was

28

handled by measures of self-help by the injured party. Members of the lineage group exerted pressure upon the disputant members of the lesser groups.

The Ashanti, too, believed in the supremacy of the spiritual world. They assumed a particular form of social order because it was the appropriate mode of linkage with the spiritual world. They used the family or lineage as the means for organizing action in the tribe and the nation. The lineage, the tribe, and the nation represented particular spheres of competence. The concept of *ntoro* provided the bond with the spiritual world, while the concept of *mogya* provided the bond with the world of the flesh. The *mogya* made the child the member of its lineage, which was a group descending from a common original female ancestor. The lineage group formed a part of the clan. The clan was composed of matrilineal descendants from a common female ancestor. The senior members of the lineage elected the lineage head or elder, who, among other functions, decided disputes among lineage members.

The Ashanti chief, or the *Asantehene*, performed rituals of propitiation of the spirits and gods and led his tribe in war. The relationship between the leaders of these groups was not that the *Asantehene* was supreme over the chief and the chief over the elder in a scheme of delegated authority, but that the specific competence of the needs of the particular group was laid down by tradition and was called into action when appropriate. The individual was placed both in the world of his ancestors and in the world of his family and clan. Life was a matter of performance of obligations. Land was held with the obligation to use it. Property was held with the obligation to employ it for the benefit of those sharing one's blood. The Ashanti male had obligations to till the land, render services to those who had links with the spiritual world, serve the *Asantehene* in war, assist in performing rituals, pay levies duly imposed, raise the offspring, and so on. Tradition laid down the norms to protect the social order and avoid injury to gods. Violation invited inquiry in the family, in the tribe, and in the nation. Tribal offenses called for severe sanctions because of the great risk of injury to the tribe through gods.

The Hausa-Fulani states and the Nupe state developed from a people with a unique culture who conquered peoples of differing cultures and ruled them by keeping their social distance from the mass and preserving their monopoly of political and economic advantage. The ruling Fulani were also more Islamized than the conquered peoples. The Fulani kept to their image of superior separateness even when they had considerably merged with the conquered peoples through intermarriage. Due to risks of armed attack and slave raiding in the open savanna or orchard bush land, life centered in villages and towns behind walls, and cultivation was carried out in the outlying farms. Families lived in compounds of related households whose members were organized into work units called *gandu*. Although the king in the Hausa state of Zazzau had less power than the king of the Nupe, both represented the most powerful single person in the state, manipulating rewards and deprivations to his followers and opponents. There was a system of control of succession to the kingship. Thus, the Habe state of Zazzau controlled succession from four eligible dynasties, the Habe state of Abuja had a single royal lineage, and the Nupe state used a rotational system among three royal houses.

Social mobility existed among the members of the society, so that the less advantaged could move to positions of greater power, prestige, and wealth. Each occupation had its own standard of *arziki*, which denoted high achievement of admired values and was a composite of birth, prestige, political protection, large family, good farming, money, wealth, greater than average consumption, and so on. The institution of clientage prevailed, so that those seeking advantage sought the protection of a patron. Slaves were used in political office, in armies, in work as fiefs in slave villages, and in household tasks.

Islam, brought by the ruling Fulani, tended to replace the clan and the extended family by the nuclear family and the individual, but it failed to destroy the unity of the family, kin, and tribe and their world of spirits. Traditional custom, not Muslim law, was applied to the pagan disputants, although the role of Muslim law expanded in criminal matters. Disputes were decided by the chief of the village, the *hakimi* or the overlord of fiefs, the *Alkali* court, and the *Salenke* court.

The Yoruba lived in three types of settlement patterns: one, where there was a central town surrounded by farm lands and hamlets with subordinate towns at the periphery of the kingdom; two, where there was plentiful land so that beyond the central town and its short belt of farm lands were numerous independent villages; and, three, where there were central towns peopled largely by refugees, surrounded by farm land, with no subordinate towns, and including widely dispersed hamlets.

The *oba*, or the king, lived in a metropolitan town. The affairs of town and the state were handled in traditional bodies. The domestic family of the man was the smallest group and was part of a larger group composed of descendants of a common male ancestor. This group in turn was part of the *idile* or the *ebi*, the largest lineage group of all, descended from a founding male ancestor.

There were intermediate patrilineal segments in the *idile* known as *isoko*. The *isoko* members cultivated that part of the lineage land that was allotted to them. They pursued a lineage craft and jointly worshipped ancestors and gods. Harmful effects of the supernatural could be lessened through Ifa, the god of divination, and by respecting social norms. Punishment resulted from the reports of Eshu, the messenger of gods, and could be averted by proper behavior. Custom defined offenses and punishment. Decisions concerning the use and allocation of land among the members of the family, the community, and the kingdoms were made by the head of the lineage, the chief, and the *oba*, respectively. Despite urbanization, the social organization remained kin-structured.

The Ibo had as their largest social unit the tribe or village group in a single territory, whose members were descended from a common male ancestor. The members of a village had their own male ancestor, who was a descendant of the tribal ancestor. The basic social unit was *ummuna*, or a patrilineal group that lived together. The lineage groups divided themselves into halves of a larger whole for social and exogamous purposes. There was a wide variety of social groupings of both the associational and the kinship character. There were gods and spirits; oracles and diviners were employed.

The council of elders governed the lineage groups as well as the members of a village, since the latter, too, were descendants of a common male ancestor. This council, as well as oracles, saw to the obedience of norms and settled disputes. Offensive behavior was of two kinds, that which disrupted the harmony of the relationship of a community to the earth goddess and that which did not. Immediate physical deprivations as well as future spiritual deprivations were meted to the offender.

The Tiv were crowded on their land. They migrated to other lands and were torn by conflict within and between groups, with no adequate authority to organize action. Witchcraft and mystical powers were accepted as a part of life. Leadership flowed from the possession of *tsav*, or witchcraft power, as well as personal qualities. *Tsav* and *akombo*, or fetishes, were principal manifestations of spiritual forces. The *mbatsav*, or one who possessed an unusual degree of *tsav*, was able to use it for good or ill. In addition, there was *swem*, an impersonal sacred power.

Ancestors were used to identify lineage groups but did not possess the power of bringing fortune or misfortune. There were two concepts of lineage, the *ityo*, which determined a person's status for the purposes of marriage, performance of rituals, and armed support, and the *tar*, which determined the relationship of a lineage group to the land it occupied and the ways in which the harmony of that relationship was expressed. When an offender disturbed that harmony, the *jir*, or a group of elders, saw that it was repaired.

The Ganda had a number of patrilineal clans, each identified by common descent from a male ancestor and common totems. The clans were a part of the kingdom. Each clan had a special duty to perform for the king, such as supplying the chief herder, or a certain official for the coronation ceremony, or a certain gatekeeper, or the keeper of a certain shrine, or the keeper of the bark cloths, and so on. The head of the clan settled kinship matters such as inheritance, succession, and dowry. Clientage relationships prevailed and were established by the act of *kusenga*, whereby one inferior in status attached himself to a superior.

Offenses such as murder, adultery, theft and so on were redressed by a system of self-help as well as by a system of decision making bodies. Cases were decided by the village headmen or subchiefs. They were appealed to the chief of the *ssaza*, a territorial district, from there to the *katikiro*, or the chief minister of the king, and ultimately to the *kababa*, or the king.

The Lugbara structured their social action through a lineage group. Their homesteads were scattered across the country and were organized into family clusters based on a minimal lineage. The head of the lineage acted as the head of the cluster. Clans were divided in subclans, which in turn were divided into major, minor, and minimal lineages, each lineage being the agnatic core for a territorial group. People's lives were organized through the family cluster. The family head, or the elder, who was the eldest son of the senior wife of his predecessor, possessed complete authority in the cluster. The ancestors responded to the invocation of the living, which was performed by those with legitimate authority to do so.

Conduct that offended or impaired the harmony within a lineage group or with its related lineage groups was dealt with by a scheme whereunder, first, an elder made the determination whether the conduct under scrutiny was offensive to the existing structure of authority. Upon such determination, the elder invoked ghosts against the offender. Next, visitation of sickness by an ancestor occurred as the punishment. After the offender recovered from this, a diviner validated the fact that the sickness occurred from such visitation. Finally, a rite of sacrifice was held to purify the offender and restore the impaired harmony.

The Kikuyu had nine clans, each divided into exogamous subclans. The clans were not territorial in identification but were identified by common ceremonies. The *mbari* was the local kinship group based on common descent from a male ancestor. Its senior elder was its ceremonial head. The *mbari* was the governing structure for the *itoro*, or a group of people living on a piece of land who accepted a particular *mbari* for associational purposes.

The society was organized into age-sets for military and governing functions. The age-sets cut across the society regardless of clan or district. Elders in the age-set settled the disputes. The elders were selected for settling a particular dispute on the basis of family relationships between the disputants. The living constantly interacted with their ancestral spirits, but the supernatural did not figure much in controlling deviant behavior.

The Nandi lived in scattered homesteads organized into groupings called *korotinwek* (singular, *koret*). The members of a *koret* were identified not by lineage relationship but by territorial location. The *tiliet*,[5] or relationship system, provided a means for identifying the interrelationships of persons united by blood and marriage. A council of elders called the *kokwet* (plural, *kokwotinek*) governed the *koret* and was headed by the *poiyot* ap *kokwet*, or the elder of the council. Its decisions were obeyed because of the force of public disapproval for noncompliance, fear of the power of the spirits, and private acknowledgement of guilt by the offender. *Karuret*, or custom, provided a general standard of approved behavior.

A larger territorial grouping was of warriors called the *pororiet*, of which there were sixteen, each with its own council, whose principal concern was war. The largest territorial grouping was the *emet*, of which there were originally six and eventually five, but it was not much more than a means of referring to a defined region, rather than an integrated unit of social organization. The living, the ancestral spirits, and the supreme god Asis were joined together to reinforce moral standards.

The Arusha were a pluralistic people concerned more with the preservation of peaceful relations among themselves than with the prosecution of norms of conduct. They organized themselves into pairs of units. The polygynous family was divided into two units or *ilwasheta* (singular, *olwashe*). The whole people were divided into two clans, each clan into a pair of clan sections, each clan section into a pair of subclans, and each subclan into two *ilwasheta* composed of various maximal lineages. Each maximal lineage consisted of several inner lineages, each of which was divided into *ilwasheta*. The *ilwasheta*, however, were not divided into two parts but consisted, instead, of a number of families. Of course, each family was divided, as mentioned above, into two *ilwasheta*. Lineage relationships were determined by descent from a common male ancestor. The maximal lineage was based on descent from the earliest known male ancestor and the inner lineage consisted of heads of families who were sons of the same dead father.

Territorially, the Arusha were divided into two subtribes which were divided into territorial local groupings of family homesteads. Their male heads were organized into age-groups or age-sets for the purposes of performing the functions of war and governance. The assembly of the territorial local grouping settled public affairs and disputes among its members. The goal in dispute settlement was the elimination of the dispute by an agreement between disputants and the performance of that agreement. Compromise and reparation were valued not for achieving harmony but for reducing violence within the community.

The Nyakyusa organized themselves in age-villages in which men of closely contemporaneous ages lived from boyhood until death. Their headmen were selected at a coming-out ceremony, which was held every thirty-three or thirty-five years. At that ceremony, new chiefs were elected and new age-villages were created. The old chief was replaced by two new chiefs and their respective chiefdoms, each of which consisted of four age-villages. These, in turn, were divided into two age-villages.

Witches were active in bringing sickness and misfortune as well as in protecting persons from the evil use of witchcraft. Wrongdoing was dealt with by the institution of "breath-of-men," whereunder the men of the village murmured about the violation of the norm and invoked supernatural punishment on the offender. The offender was punished by illness or misfortune, leading to his reformation. A commensal feast was given thereafter, at which he and his neighbors openly acknowledged the guilt and the punishment. The medicine man present at the meal administered a medicine designed to prevent a repetition of the violation. Disputes were settled by a senior relative or a respected neighbor. Men used force to protect their rights from violation by others.

The hut of a wife and her children where sometimes the husband also lived was the smallest unit of social organization of the Nuer. The homestead of huts and a cattle byre formed the polygynous family. The family lived in the village during rains and in the cattle camp during the dry season. Relationship to the dominant clan in the village determined membership in the village community. The community was not made up exclusively of the members of a single lineage, and there was a mixture of attached elements and lineage.

A bunch of villages or camps engaging in regular social relations formed a district of the tribe. There were fifteen tribes. A tribe had distinctive sections, the tribal segments being divided into primary, secondary, and tertiary segments.

Although the age-set system defined the social status of seniority and indicated the appropriate behavioral patterns, it was not a significant means of social organization. Conduct was perceived as *cuong* (right) or *duer* (wrong). Compensation was provided for a wide variety of injuries resulting from wrongs. Self-help and duels were deemed justified measures against wrongs. The aggrieved person was assisted by his kinsmen in these measures. Spiritual punishment did not have a place in this scheme. The wronged person could seize the cattle of the offender. The owner would take no further action if he considered the seizure right. If not, he would either negotiate the dispute or resort to force. Disputes of killing were settled with the intervention of the leopard-skin priest.

The cultures of the thirteen African societies surveyed above demonstrate that law and its institutions have not played a central role in African social organization. Africa began experiencing powerful

35

changes in the middle of the nineteenth century. An extremely vigorous activity of state building began as a consequence of (a) a substantial increase in food production that supported larger populations due to the success of the American crops of maize, peanuts, and sweet potatoes—although it is unknown when they were first introduced there, (b) the suppression of slave trade by the British by 1833 in west Africa and by 1897 in central Africa, and (c) the increase in demand for African products, such as ivory and palm oil, traded in exchange for European machine-made cloth and other products. Guns and more efficient firearms made shambles of older military systems, such as that of the spear-wielding Zulu war bands of Natal and the armored horsemen of Bornu in west Africa.

While Muslim influences were exerted upon Africa from the north and east, Europeans pressed upon it from the west and south. Both the Muslim movement and Christian missionaries added their own dimensions to changes in Africa. The first Muslim missions came to Africa almost at the inception of Islam. Through the nineteenth and the twentieth centuries, Muslim ideas of law became very helpful to the rulers in much of east and west Africa in extending their power, as exemplified by the Ashanti kingdom, although these ideas did not displace the traditions and customs of the land in the villages. When the Muslim movements came in conflict with the European Christians, they took on extremely zealous forms, such as the dervish brotherhood of the Sanusi founded in 1837 near Mecca by a native of Algiers, or the declaration in 1881 by Mohammed Ahmed in Sudan that he was the Mahdi, the restorer of Islam. His rebellion against the Turkish-Egyptian authorities of the upper Nile valley was crushed by the British forces in 1896–98. The Christian missionaries brought schools, hospitals, and knowledge of Western civilization that produced Africans educated in Western ways. However, the Europeanization of the sub-Saharan Africa remained insignificant, except in Algeria in the north and the Boer Republic in the south. The interior remained for a time under the control of the ancient kingdoms such as that of Bornu near Lake Chad or the new regimes such as that of the Zulu founded in 1817 by Shaka (1787–1828).

By 1914 the native rulers throughout Africa, with the exception of Ethiopia, had become colonial subjects of foreign imperial administrations. The Europeans replaced slave labor with wage labor for their projects in Africa, although the fine distinction was lost to the natives.

France and England were the major contestants for the African soil. Late arrivals included Germany, which took over Tangkanyika, south west Africa, and Cameroon in 1884; Italy, which had some successes in the Red Sea region but was defeated in Ethiopia in 1896; Belgium, which organized an international association in 1876 to explore and civilize the Congo basin; and Portugal, which revived its claims in Angola and Mozambique. Inevitably, clashes arose among the imperialist powers. Between 1875 and 1914, the European colonial administrations grew rapidly but remained superficial in most of Africa. The native Africans resented the European activities on their soil. For example, the Berbers of the Atlas mountain region rebelled against the French for decades, the Ashanti kingdom of west Africa battled against the British four times and was not annexed to the Gold Coast (modern Ghana) until 1902, and the Zulus of South Africa did not submit to British rule until subdued in battle in 1879. The Africans were defeated in all their wars against the colonizing powers, except for Ethiopia, whose Emperor Menelik II defeated Italy in 1896. However, the social structures of the African societies continued in their traditional ways.

World War I (1914–18) did not cause much disruption in Africa, for German colonial possessions were easily taken over by the British and the French. During the inter war period, rebellions were minimal and so were clashes between the colonial powers.

South Africa, Liberia, and Ethiopia existed as independent states. The Union of South Africa was set up in 1908 as a self-governing dominion under the British crown that gave full political autonomy to the white Boer and British populations. Liberia was established in 1847 as a republic offering homeland for former slaves of America. Ethiopia remained independent until attacked and made part of Italy's imperial domains in northeast Africa in 1934. The British granted independence to Egypt in 1922 and promised in a treaty of 1936 to withdraw British troops.

The exposure of the Africans to the European experience resulted in the movement of hundreds of thousands of persons to an environment in which old customs did not fit. When people of different tribes began living together in mission schools, mines, and towns, they had to find some other basis of mutual accomodation than old kinships and tribal patterns. The two models that competed in this search were the Islamic and the Western models. The Islamic model prevailed in parts where it had been established for many centuries. However, the Western model competed strongly with the Islamic model in most of sub-Saharan regions.

After independence, following the end of World War II in 1945, the new nations of Africa have demonstrated a tendency for modernization along European principles. New legislation has been adopted to change the traditional ways. However, despite this modernization, eighty to ninety per cent of the population continues to live by traditions and customs, generally unaffected by the reform legislation, and largely unaware of the laws and institutions of the cities.

In sum, therefore, law has not been central to the social organization of African societies in the historicity of their cultures.

The above examination demonstrates that while law and its institutions have played a central role in the historic development of Western civilization, such has not been the case with Chinese, Japanese, Indian, and African civilizations. It is only natural that thinkers of a civilization would employ their intellect in speculating about the nature of a phenomenon that has been central to its growth and not about something that has not been so. That is why almost all of the theories about law, though not all, have issued from the Western cultures.

B. Jurisprudential Aspects of Cultural Development

Jurisprudentially, there is a more fundamental point to be made here concerning civilizational pluralism. We shall make this point by using three examples, namely, the Western civilization, the Chinese civilization, and the Indian civilization.

At the most fundamental level, *nomos*, *li*, and *dharma* represent the essential principles of life for the Western, Chinese, and Indian civilizations. The most fundamental principle of the Western way of life is *nomos*. The word *nomos* first appeared in Hesiod (c. eighth century B.C.) to denote law laid down for men. Although the word does not appear in Homer (c. eighth century B.C.), either in the *Iliad* or in the *Odyssey*, there is the concept of *themis* (that which is laid down and established) in both Homer and the later compositions of Hesiod. *Themistes* (plural of *themis*) were divine ordinances of Zeus granted to man for his benefit. The king was entrusted with *themistes*. With the growing self-consciousness of man, the emphasis shifted from *themis* to *dike* (order, right, judgment, that which is right) and eventually to *nomos*. The king had to exercise his power in light of *nomos*. In Hesiod's *Theogony* and *Works and Days*, *nomos* appeared in three aspects: an entity ordained by Zeus in place of Homer's *themis*, an independently established practice or usage, and that which conformed to nature's regulations. Thus, there was in *nomos* a notion of preexisting natural phenomenon the regularity of which governed man's actions as well as a notion of the given way of life, whether given as divine directives or human usages.

Mythos and *logos* appeared in man's efforts to achieve results that gods and men would appreciate. Virtue was a matter of concrete *arete* (excellence or goodness) and not abstract truth. Soon *nomos* assumed the meaning of *thesmos*, or law authoritatively laid down for the benefit of the community. Gradually, its divine aspect faded with the growth of the rule of *logos* and abstract reasoning. Pre-Socratic thinking moved toward searching for an *arche* (first principle), i.e., what *is* at its beginning? For example, Anaximander (611?–547? B.C.) proposed that whatever existed did so in being exposed to the order of time. Heraclitus (540–475 B.C.) distinguished between *nomos theios* (divine *nomos*) and *anthropeioi nomoi* (human *nomoi*). *Nomoi*, thus, comprised the cosmic totality, inclusive of both man's usages and nature's phenomena.

There was an organizational scheme that underlay all occurrences. *Nomos* was the dominant constitutional element of the polis. *Nomos theios* was the basic structure that sustained all the *human nomoi*. It was now very much of this world, not of the domain of gods. For Pindar (522?–443 B.C.), *nomos* was the supreme ruling authority. The poets Aeschlus (525–456 B.C.), Sophocles (496?–406 B.C.), and Euripides (fifth century B.C.) extolled the ancient custom, in effect, referring to an unwritten *nomos*. The substantive meaning of *nomos agraphos* was a constitution of the polis that pleased the gods, deviation from which resulted in the decay of good order (*eunomia*). However, in the sixth and fifth centuries B.C., unwritten customary rules (*nomos agraphos*) and equity rules lost ground to codified laws.

The Sophists of the mid fifth century held that neither customary regulations (*nomoi agraphoi*) nor written regulations (*nomoi gegrammenoi*) provided sufficient foundation for an order of justice. The divine *dike* (order) was replaced by the abstract conception of *dikaiosyne* (righteousness, justice). *Nomos* was contrasted with *physis*, a concept that had already been introduced by such pre-Socratic thinkers as Xenophanes (sixth century B.C.) and Heraclitus. *Physis* (nature, natural form of a person or thing) denoted not a product of culture but an elementary phenomenon. For Democritus (460?–362? B.C.) *physis* was real and *nomos* was unreal in our everyday knowledge of the world. *Nomoi* was arbitrary and conventional, *physis* necessary and grown (as distinguished from being conventional). *Physis*, as the real order of things, had the ability to disclose the true basis for justice for moral and legal conduct, or, in other words, for *nomos agraphos* (ethos) and *nomos gegrammenos* (statute law). Thus, the *nomos physis* controversy produced the natural *nomos*. Democritus, for example, thought that men must obey *nomoi* for their own welfare because of their natural tendency to hurt each other. Plato (427–347 B.C.) considered *nomos* as participating in the idea of good and justice. The divine *nous* (intellect) was, for him, the *physis* wherein *nomoi* participated. Aristotle (384–322 B.C.) rejected the position that Plato granted to *nous* as a participation in good and justice, but he, like Plato, considered *nomoi* inevitable for man in order for man to exist differently from wild beasts. He distinguished between the *nomos idios* (special) and *nomos koinos* (universal). *Nomos* became natural law. For him there was a general idea of just and unjust in accordance with nature. Man-made conventions were just insofar as they were not in contravention of the universal (*koinos*) unwritten *nomos*, *i.e.*, the natural order of things present under the rule of god (*theos*) and reason (*nous*). *Nomos*, in its final development, came to denote a constituted order of society comprising individual rights and duties. This idea is basic to the Western way of life.

That which is called Confucianism is an expression of *Li*, the essential principle of Chinese life. *Li* originated in the course of a period of 350 years, beginning with the early years of the Western Chou dynasty (1122 B.C.) through the Shu Ching (Book of History), the Shih Ching (Book of Poetry, 1122–600 B.C.), and Tsao Chuan ("Spring and Autumn" Annals, 770–464 B.C.). It attained its full meaning through the Lun Yu (Analects) of Confucius (551–479 B.C.), the works of his successors and followers during the Warring States period (463–222 B.C.), and the Li Chi (Book of *Li*) compiled during the early part of the Former Han dynasty (206–8 A.D.).

In the Shu Ching (Book of History), *li* translated as ceremonies or religious ritual and indicated sacrifices usually connected with ancestor worship and attributed with magical powers. In the Shih Ching (Book of Poetry), *li* indicated correct and proper behavior, which propriety was essential to man himself and his relations with others. It pointed to man's proper way of life.

The imperative of *li* was that human order must correspond to the nature's order. In the "Spring and Autumn" period of the Eastern Chou kings, *li* expanded to cover all aspects of human existence, as is evident in the later documents of the Shu Ching and the Tsao Chuan ("Spring and Autumn" Annals). It became the particular responsibility of the ruler, called the Son of Heaven, to govern in accordance with *li*; failure to do this led to imbalance and confusion.

T'ien (heaven) represented a totality of cosmic events with which man's way of life had to be harmonized. Therefore, conforming with the *t'ien-ming* (the appointment of heaven) was considered the primary concern for the king. Harmony between heaven (*t'ien*) and earth (*ti*) was ensured by cultivation of *te* (virtue in character, excellence). Thus, although there was some belief in the supernatural, the crux of belief was in the interdependence of nature and human behavior. Consequently, it was up to man to follow that conduct that would maintain harmony between him and nature. *Hsiao* (filial piety) was the virtue that maintained harmony in the family and, consequently, between human and nature's events. Thus, although *t'ien-ming* issued directives on various matters, there was no all-powerful personal lawgiver controlling man's destiny.

The society was ordered in *wu lan*, or five relationships: the relationships between father and son, ruler and subject, husband and wife, elder and younger brother, and between friends. *Li* was observed through the *wu chiao*, or the five respective lessons of behavior. This, in turn, provided the particular *li*; in Shu Ching there are three *li* for observances in the worship of the spirits of heaven, the earth, and men and five *li* for worship, calamity and mourning, state guests, war, and festivities.

Disregard of one's duty invited appropriate action for restoring the harmony between the human and non-human spheres that was lost due to that infraction. Consequently, there were five punishments (*wu hsing*) corresponding to the five *wu chiao* within the five relationships mentioned above.

Fa (law) was always regarded with suspicion and antipathy. The personal relations of *li* and its practice in a spirit of benevolence and harmony were preferred to *fa* and *hsing*. For example, *Chih* (new enactments) were condemned as an omen that the state was about to perish.

In contrast to *fa, li* remained uncodified for most of the Chou dynasty. It was preserved orally and transmitted through example and education. Thus, it is significant to note that *li* was something internal to human conduct, not something imposed from above by a human or divine agency. Its practice was internally enforced as a demonstration of man's personal ability to contribute to the universal harmony and to the cultivation of his being and his society.

Li acquired further meaning with Confucius as described above. It became a principle of social organization and control. *Hsiao* (filial piety) constituted the moral essence of *li*, especially in family life. This principle derived its effectiveness from the moral impetus of *te* (virtue or excellence in character) directed toward the expected cultivation of *jen* (benevolence or humaneness), *i* (righteousness, in the sense of that which is right to do as one's duty), *chih* (wisdom or practical knowledge), and *hsin* (confidence). *Fa* was considered hideous.

Confucius insisted on a positive motivation of the people to avoid misconduct detrimental to social relations and to conform to *li* and avoid litigation *(sung)*. His successors added further meaning to the concept of *li*, especially Mencius (371–289 B.C.), Hsun Tzu (298–238 B.C.), and Mo Tzu (about 470–391 B.C.). Finally, the *Li Chi* (Book of *Li*), compiled in the early part of the Former Han dynasty (206 B.C.—8 A.D.), gives a full expression of *li*. It contains 3,300 rules of behavior made concrete in customs, habits, and ceremonies, devised to maintain an all-embracing social harmony in accordance with the highly valued ancient way of life. Failure in one's duty calls for a socially agreed corrective or disciplinary sanctions, or moral education for securing proper conduct in the future. This education includes both exhortation and punishment. In non-criminal matters, too, reliance is placed on the self-regulating procedure of *li*, so that prevention of litigation is considered better than taking recourse to it.

The essential principle of individual and communal life of most Indians is *dharma*. The word *dharma* is untranslatable and the term, experts agree, has defied definition, but the concept certainly is not that of law in the Western sense. *Dharma* originated at the very beginning of Indian civilization, when the Aryan tribal community assigned the governmental leadership to the king *(raja)* and the spiritual leadership to the priest *(brahman)*. By the end of the Rg Vedic period a four fold traditional division of society came to prevail along the lines of the four *varnas* (social divisions). A mode of order had thus been achieved wherein men engaged in actions in a regular and constant manner to ensure the support of the gods.

Rta denoted the universal cosmic order, which was immanent, preexistent, and independent of any other force; *Vrata* denoted the notion of laws laid down by gods; *Dharma* denoted that which upholds or sustains. *Rta* offered an order to apprehend man's phenomenal surrounding and to structure irregular phenomena into a form of regularity. Gods gave examples of *dharma* to uphold that which existed in order (*Rta*), thereby making man conscious of his own active, though ordered, way of life.

The Vedas expressed *dharma* as an example of action, conduct, ordinance, and principle of regularity in various existential situations. As such, it had three aspects; an expression of nature's most active parts, an expression of natural and human phenomena, and an expression of abstract as well as concrete relations of pure knowledge and human affairs.

The Upanishads shifted the emphasis to the life of man in all its aspects. While they recognized *dharma* as the supreme force of the world, they transformed it into an all-embracing support of life in the world. The Vedic imagination of *dharma* was thus related intimately to practical necessities of everyday life.

The principle of *karma* (act; the causal principle connecting actions with actor's destiny) operated within the all-embracing function of *dharma*, thereby elaborating *dharma* into the many precepts and rules for human affairs. *Karma* sustained by *dharma* led to *moksha*, or release from the cycle of life, death, and rebirth. The basis for a life of good actions lay in man's efforts to conform to his duty. The Vedas, Brahmanas, Aranyaka, and Upanishads constitute the *shruti* (trans.: heard) literature. The subsequent *smriti* (trans.: remembered) literature further elaborated *dharma*, adapting it to the changing conditions of life.

The earliest *Smriti* literature on *dharma* consists of the *dharmasutras*, which were in the nature of manuals of the precepts of *dharma* stated in the form of aphorisms. The subsequent *dharmashastras* presented more detailed compositions in verse form, the most important of which was named after the ascetic Manu as the Manu-Smriti, usually translated in a misleading fashion as the Laws of Manu or the Code of Manu. These *dharmashastras* also included the secularly conceived *Arthashastra* of Kautilya. All the various teachings of *dharma* addressed themselves to the issue of how to follow a way of life that would be in accordance with *dharma*.

The sources of *dharma* were *shruti, smriti, achara* (good custom), and *atma-tushti* (self-satisfaction). We have mentioned *shruti* and *smriti* above. *Achara* consisted of widespread and unambiguous practice followed by the virtuous upon a firm belief in *shruti* and *smiriti*. *Atma-tushti*, or self-satisfaction, was considered unimportant by the authoritative mode of interpretation (*mimansa*).

Varna, mentioned above, and *ashram* (the four stages of life: student, householder, ascetic, renouncer), were the existential constituents of *dharma*. There were three kinds of *dharma*: *svadharma, sadharana dharma*, and *purushartha*. *Svadharma* consisted of one's individual duty as determined by his *varna* and *ashram*. One must perform one's own duty in order to move toward salvation (*moksha*). Breach of this duty was also a social offense, since performance of it served social stability for the present as well as future generations. *Sadharana dharma* guided man's conduct for the benefit of the community as a whole and, in turn, as part of the whole, it benefitted his own being. Its most cardinal virtues were *ahimsa* (non-violence or abstention from injury) and *satyam* (truth). *Purushartha* related to attaining the ends of man, which were *dharma, artha* (wealth or material possessions), *kama* (pleasure), and *moksha* (salvation). All modes of existence, if preserved in *dharma*, led to *moksha*.

Thus, *nomos, li*, and *dharma* are three different principles of life in these three civilizations. The contrasts and disparities among them are significant. There are concepts in them that do not have their counterparts in others. For example, the principle of *karma* in Hindu *dharma* or the Confucian connection between the Chinese *li* and *jen* (humaneness) are non-existent in the Western principle of life, whereas the Western *nomos* containing the potential for man-made law is non-existent in *dharma* or *li*. The *Rta* conception of order of the Hindus is totally incompatible with the *nomos* idea of divine agencies creating the universe and gods issuing commands for governance. *Dharma* produces in man a conviction of duty to comply with the pre-existing order of *rta*. *Li* gives the idea of order wherein ways of conduct regulate man's worldly existence in harmony with nature. Thus, order is granted from outside in *nomos*, granted from within in *li*, and pre-ordained in *dharma*. Consequently, while *nomos* laid the ground work for an idea of law from outside, *li* became the social obligation directed toward the harmonious state of the world, and *dharma* produced authoritative texts to teach man his duty to support the *dharmic* state of the world.

Accordingly, while *dharma* and *li* produced a general and all-persuasive way of life as an organizational principle of existence, *nomos*, especially *nomos gegrammenos* (written *nomos*) proceeded along the basis of specific commands. While the validity of the precepts of *nomos* depended upon the authoritative statement thereof made publicly available, the validity of the precepts of *li* never depended on such a statement.

While *nomos* was attributed to a divine lawgiver, such an attribution is non-existent in either *li* or *dharma*, although *dharma*, as distinguished from *li*, has a sacred literature of eternal validity, namely, the *shruti* literature of Vedas, Brahmanas, Aranyakas, and Upanishads.

While *li* is concretized in the five *wu lan* relationships, *nomos* moved on to an abstract way of thinking, producing speculations about laws of the natural. Discovery and speculation about the ways of the non-human nature did not interest the Hindu *dharmashastras*, either. The task of the authors and teachers of the *dharmashastras* was to show man his duty and guide him in close adherence to *shruti*, not articulation and distribution of individual rights typical of the Western legal ethos. *Li*, too, does not dispense individual rights, for the rights approach, with its antagonistic behavior of those claiming those rights, is excluded from the conception of seeking an all-embracing harmony within all human relations. Where the source of obligation is from outside, as in the Western legal order, a need arises to justify rights and duties, but where the source of obligation is from inside, as in *dharma* or *li*, the important task becomes not the justification of laws and individual rights and duties thereunder but the discovery of that obligation and apprehending its hidden sources. The internal coherence of duty-bound ways of life, whether it be pre-ordained as in *dharma* or socially created as in *li*, is quite incompatible with institutionalization of rights as in the Western legal order. Consequently, Western legal order offered a fertile ground for thinkers to speculate about the nature of law.

C. Epistemological Incompatibilities of the Theories of Law

Epistemology is that branch of philosophy that studies knowledge. Its concern is with the nature of knowledge, its scope, its presuppositions, its laws, and the general reality of claims to knowledge. Its concern is not for what psychological reasons people hold beliefs, but whether the beliefs are based on good grounds or whether they are sound. Its concern is not whether or how we can be said to know some particular truth that is delivered by some branch of knowledge, but whether we are justified in claiming knowledge of a whole class of truths, or even whether knowledge is possible at all.

Three types of theories of knowledge are seen at the basis of the theories of law: the metaphysical-rational, the idealist, and the empiricist.

The metaphysical-rational epistemology claims that all knowledge, therefore the knowledge of law as well, is contained in nature and is discovered by reason. This is the theory of knowledge that underlies most theories of natural law, such as the theory of Lāo Tsze of China[6], which views natural justice as paramount; the theory of Aristotle of Greece, which views natural law as justice by nature; the theory of Cicero of Rome, which views natural law as law of right reason; or the theory of Aquinas of medieval Christianity, which views natural law as the law of God.

The idealist epistemology is grounded in the view that the mind and the spiritual values are fundamental in the world as a whole. The term idealism came to be used in philosophy in the eighteenth century with Leibnitz, who characterized those who, like himself and Plato, held an anti-materialist metaphysics.[7] With Berkeley (later in the century), the term came to be used to denote the view that nothing existed but the ideas in the mind of the percipient, although Berkeley called his view "immaterialism" and not idealism.[8] Holders of such views were called egoists, and today we call them solipsists. Philosophical idealism can therefore be classified into immaterialism (Leibnitz, Berkeley, Collier), transcendental idealism (Kant), absolute idealism (Fichte, Schelling, Hegel), and neo-Hegelianism (T.H. Green, F.H. Bradley, B. Bosanquet, J. Royce, J.M.E. McTaggart, M. Oakeshott, B. Blanshard, etc.).

Kant called his own view of idealism transcendental idealism[9] or critical idealism.[10] It is the Kantian (transcendental) idealism that concerns us here in the context of legal theories. According to it, it is not possible to gain knowledge of the world either by rational thought alone or by mere sense experience. Our perceptions have to be organized within the pure *a priori* intuitions of space and time in terms of rational principles. These principles require that our perceptions refer to things in causal relation with one another. The *a priori* intuitions of space and time and the categories of understanding, such as substance and causality, quality and quantity, and so on, make knowledge possible, without which there would only be a manifold fluctuating of sensations. We do not know if there are things-in-themselves, but we cannot have knowledge of an objective world unless we place everything in spatio-temporal contexts and synthesize our sensations according to the categories of understanding. This process is carried out not by our empirical self but by our transcendental self. Nothing can be known of the transcendental self, since it is a condition of knowledge and not an object thereof.

Thus, the idealist theories of law proceed from some fundamental ideas discovered through an inquiry into the human mind. They include the theory of Kant, which views law as conditions for harmonizing voluntary actions, the theory of Hegel, which views law as evolution of the idea of freedom, the theory of Stammler, which views just law as the unity of methodical adjustment of individual purposes in accordance with the final purpose of the community, and the theory of Del Vecchio, which views law as the priniciple of legal evolution guiding mankind toward greater autonomy of man.

Finally, the empiricist epistemology holds that the source of knowledge lies in experience rather than reason. As commonly believed by philosophers, experience is the as yet unorganized product of sense perception and memory, memory being the device to retain in the mind that which is perceived. An awareness of that which is discovered in this way is experience. There is, of course, another sense of the term experience which indicates sensations, feelings, etc. However, crucial to empiricism is the view that knowledge depends on the use of senses and on what is discovered through them.

There are three main ways in which the empiricist theory is held. The first is the claim that all knowledge comes from experience, in the sense that it is directly concerned with sense experience or derived from it by experiential means of learning, association, or inductive inference. The second is the claim that all knowledge is dependent on experience; though not all knowledge is derived *immediately* from experience, all the materials for knowledge are ultimately derived from experience, so that all concepts are *a posteriori*. The third is the claim that while there are ideas that are *a priori* and not derived from experience, we have knowledge of them only upon the general precondition of having experience.

A variety of legal theories have issued from the empiricist epistemology. They include: (a) the positivist theories, (b) the historical theories, (c) the sociological theories, (d) the psychological theories, and (e) the realist theories.

The positivist theories include the ancient theories of Kautilya (India), Shang Iang (China), Shuen Tao (China), and Han Fei Tzu (China); the utilitarian and command theories of Bentham, Mill, and Austin; the normative theory of Kelsen; and the rule theory of Hart. The historical theories include Savigny's theory of law as manifestation of the spirit of the people in history, Maine's theory of law as development in history of personal conditions from status to contract, and Marx and Engel's theory of law in the historical context of economic determinism.

The sociological theories include those which view law in sociological aspects, such as Ihering's theory of law in the social purpose, Kohler's theory of law in the evolution of civilization, Ehrlich's theory of law in the inner order of human associations, Duguit's theory of law in the objective conditions of social solidarity, and Timasheff's theory of law as the specific interaction of individual group-members; the jurisprudence of interests of Heck and Pound; and the free law theories of Ehrlich and Kantorowicz. The psychological theories include Petrazycki's theory of law.

The realist theories include those of American realists and of the Scandinavian realists. The American realist theories include Holmes' theory of law as prophecies of what the courts will do, Gray's theory of law as rules of conduct laid down by judges, Llewellyn's theory of law as what certain officials do about disputes, Bingham's theory of law as generalizations of potential legal effect and considerations weighed by courts in the decision of the cases, and Frank's theory, which views law from a psychoanalytical point of view. The Scandinavian realist theories include Hagerstrom's theory of law as a conative impulse, Olivecrona's theory of law as independent imperatives, Ross' theory of law as a scheme of interpretation for a set of social facts that constitute the counterpart of the legal norms, and Lundstedt's theory of law as determined by social welfare.

The metaphysical-rational, the idealist, and the empiricist epistemologies are irreconcilable. One cannot maintain that knowledge is contained in nature discoverable by reason *and* that it is gained from an inquiry into the human mind *and* that it lies in experience. Consequently, the legal theories based upon these epistemologies are respectively irreconcilable as well. It is important to recognize the epistemological foundations of these theories in order to appreciate their own fundamental irreconcilability and assess the depth of differences among them.

D. Conflicts Among Theories of Law

Conflicts among the theories about law appear on three levels. One, and the most fundamental, is the epistemological level, as discussed above. Next, there are conflicts among different schools of jurisprudence within the same epistemological family, such as differences among the positivist, the historical, the sociological, the psychological, and the realist theories, all of which are based on the empiricist theory of knowledge. Finally, there are conflicts among the theories within the same school, such as conflicts between Austin and Hart, both positivist, or between Savigny and Marx-Engels, both historical.

E. Incipience of Value Preference in Theories of Law

It is useful to keep philosophy separate from ideology, the former being a description of objective truth, the latter a statement of value preference. Both are legitimate exercises, but it is important to maintain the distinction between the two in order to distinguish what is being perceived as truth from what is being promoted as preferred value. The distinction is often abandoned in many theories of law. Examples abound of the incipience of value preference in a philosophy of law. Thus, as will be shown in Chapter III, the very methodology of natural law lends itself to such use, so much so that one critic has likened it to a harlot.[11] But natural law is not the only culprit. For example, in Kant we proceed from an inquiry into the human mind to learning his philosophy of law and find dumped in our laps his ideology about maximization of man's freedom and his maxims of moral law. Or, in Hegel, we proceed along the unfolding of the Idea through his dialectics and end up with glorification of the state. Or, in Stammler, we are led through an analysis of just law but are simply given his principles of just law dogmatically asserted. Or, in Bentham we find the assertion of the ideology of his greatest happiness principle. Or, in Savigny we follow the empirical method of his historical approach but discover preference for values of conservation rather than change. Or, in Marx and Engels, we find a condemnation of ideology but in turn an advocacy of their own materialist ideology. Or, in Duguit we proceed with a scientific positivism and end up facing his postulate of social solidarity that substitutes the dogmas of individualism, subjectivism, and moralism with the dogmas of collectivism, objectivism, and realism, leaving open further use of social solidarity for whatever content one wishes of it. Or, American realism gives a framework in which any preferred ideology can be promoted and, even at that, the range of ideologues permitted is limited to those who become judges. Or, phenomenological theory of the surfacing of immanent values provides a convenient disguise for any ideology. Such examples will become more clear in the following chapters. "When ideology is disguised as philosophy, philosophy is discredited and ideology is made suspect."[12] One has to be on guard against such incipience.

We have attempted in this chapter to locate law in civilization and to present certain reflections that have resulted from a study of the various theories about the nature of law. These reflections concern the cultural location of the theories, their epistemological incompatibilities, the levels of conflicts among them, and the incipience of value preference in many of them. We shall examine the various theories about law in depth in the following chapters.

2

DIVINE AND PROPHETIC THEORIES OF LAW

A. Aspects of the Theories

The divine and the prophetic theories of law are found in some of the ancient legal systems, such as the Babylonian laws, Hebrew laws, and Laws of Manu, as well as in the Islamic law. The essential aspects of such a perception of law are that it is created by God for governance of man, and that it is transmitted to the humans through the agency of a prophet or a ruler.

Thus, it is explained in the Laws of Hammurabi that Hammurabi, the king of Babylon, set forth truth and justice throughout the land when the god Marduk commanded him to give justice and good governance to the people of the land. Or, the Hebrew Laws claim in the Book of Exodus of the Bible (24,31,32,34) that the Lord summoned Moses to Mount Sinai and gave him two tablets of stone that contained the law written by the finger of God. Or, the Laws of Manu,[1] in contrast to the Dharma Sutras, profess to be of divine origin, in that the Supreme Being revealed his Sacred Law to Manu, the father of mankind, at the time of the creation of the world.

The Islamic law, or the *sharia* (the way to follow), also professes the prophetic theory in a large measure. The sources of this law are, hierarchically, the *Koran, sunna, hadith, qiyas*, and *ijma*. The *Koran* is the scripture composed of the inspired utterances of the Prophet Muhammad (570–632 A.D.), written a few years after his death. *Sunna* consists of the way of life and conduct of the Prophet, his practices, acts, and behavior. *Hadith* is the story of an eyewitness concerning the Prophet and his tradition. *Qiyas* is the analogical deduction from the principles laid down in the Koran. *Ijma* is the unanimous consensus of the legal scholars of Islam (*fukahā*) whose task it is to discover and reveal the law. Thus, the *Koran* is purely prophetic, and *sunna* and *hadith* are closely linked to the Prophet. *Qiyas* and *ijma* are employed to discovering the meaning of the prophetic law.

B. Criticism

The success of the divine and prophetic theories of law in pulling the people together and effectuating a system of legal management in their times, and in our times in the case of Islamic Law, is not to be denied. However, jurisprudentially, such a theory suffers from three major defects. Firstly, it requires faith in a divine being, such as God. The consequence is that it thereby puts itself outside the scope of rational analysis. Secondly, it requires acceptance of an agency as the spokesman for God, whether it be a prophet, as in the Hebrew or the Islamic theory, or a ruler, as in the Babylonian theory. Finally, it provides the person interpreting, specifying, and applying the law an escape from the responsibility for making law through these acts since, arguably, the resultant law is the law of God and not a product of his own act.

3

NATURAL LAW
THEORIES

The jurisprudential thinking that is denoted by the term "natural law" has occupied the human mind for several thousand years, beginning with the theory of the Hindu *dharma* developed in the Vedic period of India during 1500 B.C.–500 B.C., and continuing into our own times. It is, therefore, not possible to make a generalization about its nature that would be sufficient to comprehend various theories about it. Nevertheless, one might suggest, for our purposes of collecting these theories in the category of this chapter, that they do not accept the law posited by man as the true law, that they point to something other than the positive law as the true law, and that they ascribe an axiologically superior status to the latter over the former.

These theories may be broadly classified as early and modern.

A. Early Theories of Natural Law

Early theories of natural law include theories that view it as law of virtue, as justice by nature, as law of right reason, and as law of God.

WHAT IS LAW?

1. *Natural Law as Law of Virtue*

The *dharma* of India and Lāo Tsze and Confucius of China point to a law of virtue to be followed by the rulers and other members of society.

a. Dharma *(India, Vedic Period: 1500 B.C.–500 B.C.)*

Dharma is the divinely ordained norm of good conduct. It prescribes duties of man as a member of his caste as well as his duties in a particular stage of life. Thus, there are duties of Brahmin (priest and teacher), Kshatriya (warrior), Vaishya (artisan and businessman), and *Shudra* (servant). On the other hand, there are duties of *brahmcharyin* (student), *grahastha* (householder), *vanaprastha* (forest dweller), and *sanyasin* (wandering ascetic). The sources of these duties are not the edicts of rulers but (1) the Vedas (holy scriptures), (2) the *smritis* (the tradition and practice of those who know the Vedas), and (3) the customs of virtuous men.

b. Lāo-Tsze (China, b. 604 B.C.)

According to Lāo-Tsze, the system of law most conductive to welfare is one that gives a full play to the inarticulate dictates of nature. The ruler must enforce his laws within the bounds of natural justice. Justice and reason, he argues, are the only legitimate judges and executioners. A ruler usurps the function of the law of nature when he replaces justice and reason by his caprice. He thereby condemns himself.

c. Confucius (China, 550 or 551 B.C.–478 B.C.)

Confucius argued that if a ruler directs people to the practice of virtue and regulates them to that practice through the medium of moral discipline, they will naturally have a strong sense of personal honor and will be orderly in their conduct. However, if the ruler emphasizes laws and resorts to punishment for their violation, the people will try only to live to the minimum requirements of law and will be destitute of a sense of personal honor.

54

Confucius, accordingly, maintains that the paramount function of a judge is to see that under his jurisdiction there are no occasions for going to law. In order to qualify for a public office, a man should know how to avoid the four vices of tyranny, violence, oppression, and mechanical administration of law; to elaborate, he must avoid punishing people without educating them (tyranny), requiring them to conform to laws without first bringing these to their notice (violence), punishing the breaches of those ordinances and laws that people believe to be in disuse due to the ruler's laxness in executing them (oppression), and dealing with people in bargain-making so as to stick to the exact letter of the laws without looking for justice and mercy (mechanical administration of the law).

2. *Natural Law as Justice by Nature*

The Greek philosopher Aristotle (385 or 384 B.C.–322 B.C.) is the most prominent formulator of the theory of natural law as justice by nature. The Greek philosophers began to conceive of natural law as an order when law emerged as a concept separate from magic and holy rituals. In pre-Socratic philosophy (approximately 600 to 400 B.C.), the philosophers of the Milesian School consciously rejected the mythical and religious tradition of their ancestors, particularly the belief in the agency of the anthropomorphic gods. Thriving in the uninhibited atmosphere of Miletus, which encouraged generalization, abstraction, and bold hypotheses, they installed a construct of universal and discoverable law in place of the mercy of gods who possessed human passions and unpredictable intentions.

Heraclitus[1] discovered the essence of being contained in the rhythm of events. The rhythm was destiny, order, and reason of the world. Nature thus moved from being a substance to a relation and an order of things. This made it possible for the Sophists[2] to see the human elements behind the laws and use nature to oppose tyranny of men, although they continued to see nature as something outside man. With Socrates (470–399 B.C.), Plato (428–347 B.C.), and Aristotle (385 or 384 B.C.–322 B.C.), man's reason became part of nature, so that nature existed not only outside of man but inside of him as well. The decline of Athenian democracy in the aftermath of the Peloponnesian War (430–404 B.C.) prompted a preoccupation with justice in the legal philosophy of Plato and Aristotle. However, while Plato derived his conception of justice from inspiration, Aristotle developed it from an analysis of rational principles perceived from a study of political communities and laws.

For Aristotle, man has a dual character in his relation to nature. On the one hand, he is subject to nature inasmuch as he is a part of the universe and, therefore, subject to the laws of matter and creation. On the other hand, he is the master of nature inasmuch as he dominates it by his spirit, which enables him to will freely and, therefore, to distinguish between good and evil. Proceeding from this fundamental doctrine, Aristotle proposes that what we are looking for is not only what is just without qualification but political justice. Political justice exists among free and equal men sharing their lives with a view to self-sufficiency and whose mutual relations are governed by law. Political justice is of two kinds: natural and legal. Natural justice exists everywhere with the same force and is not dependent on the people's thinking in any particular way. Legal justice is originally indifferent, but does not remain so when laid down, e.g., that a prisoner's ransom shall be a mina. Laws are passed for particular cases. The things that are just by convention, expediency, or human enactment are not everywhere the same, whereas there is but one that is everywhere by nature the best.

Aristotle distinguishes the legally just from the equitable and regards the latter as superior to the former, so that the equitable is the correction of legal justice. Such correction of law is needed where law is defective. This defect or error results from the fact that while law must of necessity speak universally, it is not possible to do so without error.

Law binds both magistrates and the people. Aristotle argues that the rule of law is preferable to that of any individual. Although there must be magistrates in order to determine those matters that are left undetermined by law, law is reason unaffected by desire and passions that pervert the mind.

Laws, according to Aristotle, are of two kinds: particular and universal. The particular law is the one that each community lays down and applies to its members and that is partly written and partly unwritten. The universal law is the law of nature, since the law of nature is binding on all men, even those who have no association or covenant with each other. The universal law does not change, for it is the law of nature, while written laws often do change.

3. Natural Law as Law of Right Reason

According to Marcus Tulius Cicero (Rome, 106 B.C.–43 B.C.), true law is right reason in agreement with nature. It is of universal application, unchanging and everlasting. To alter it is a sin. To repeal any part of it is not allowable. To abolish it entirely is impossible. No senate or people can free us from its obligations. There is one eternal and unchangeable law valid for all nations and all times. There is one ruler, God, who is this law's author, promulgator, and enforcing judge. Moreover, Cicero argues, we need not look outside of ourselves for an expounder or interpreter of it.

Law, according to Cicero, is the highest reason, implanted in nature, which commands what ought to be done and forbids the opposite. This reason, when firmly fixed and fully developed in mind, is law. Law is intelligence whose function is to command right conduct and forbid wrongdoing. Consequently, the origin of justice is to be found in law, i.e., the supreme law, which existed before any written law existed. It is foolish, he points out, to believe that everything is just that is found in the customs or laws of nations. Justice is one, binds all humanity, and is based on law, which is right reason applied to command and prohibition. The difference between good laws and bad laws are perceived by referring them to the standard of nature.

Law, in this view, in not a product of human thought or enactment of peoples. It is something eternal that rules the whole universe. Therefore, it is the primal and ultimate mind of God. Although commands and prohibitions of nations have the power to summon people to righteousness and keep them away from wrongdoing, that power is coeval with God. Since divine mind cannot exist without reason and since divine reason has the power to establish right and wrong, this reason did not first become law when it was written down but, rather, when it came into existence with the divine mind. Just as divine mind is the supreme law, so reason perfected in man is also the law. This perfected reason, according to Cicero, exists in the mind of the wise man. Law is thus the distinction between things just and unjust, made in agreement with nature, which is primal and the most ancient of all things.

4. Natural Law as Law of God

The Christian theological natural law, as expounded by St. Thomas Aquinas (1224–1274), is the most prominent theory of natural law perceived as the law of God. The idea of natural law continued in Europe during the dark period between the demise of ancient civilization and birth of the medieval order, but the Fathers of the Church during this period (most notably Ambrose, Augustine, and Gregory) linked it with the Christian doctrine of original sin, so that political society and the state became institutions of sin. The medieval political and legal thought that began in the twelfth century made a break from this approach of the Fathers. Political society and the state came now to be regarded not as institutions of sin but as the embodiment of moral purpose and instruments for justice and virtue.

Feudalism and the Christian Church were the two foundations for the new European Civilization, which had already begun to form in the ninth century. The Christian religion, which became the religion of all Europe, was organized in an international institution called the Church in the hierarchical pattern of a political society wherein the Pope, in Rome, was its acknowledged head. Since this religion was adopted both by the spiritual and the worldly orders, the new theory of law had to proceed along the lines of accepting Christianity as the supreme legal value. Consequently, the Fathers of the Church began replacing the reason of the earlier natural law with the Christian faith as the supreme law of the universe.

This new hierarchial society of medieval times now needed a hierarchy of laws. With the *Decretum Gratianum* of the twelfth century, the law of nature no longer remained content with being identified with reason but became part of the law of God. The Church was taken to be its authentic interpreter, for the state had already been condemned by Augustine as an institution of sin. The conflict between the spiritual lawgiving authority and the secular lawgiving authority was to occupy Europe for centuries, during which both sides invoked natural law. The result was the scholastic system of law most thoroughly formulated by St. Thomas Aquinas.

Aquinas explores the question of the essence of law through four propositions: whether law is something pertaining to reason; whether law is always directed to the common good; whether the reason of any man is competent to make laws; and whether promulgation is essential to a law. As to the first proposition, he maintains that law is a rule and measure of acts whereby man is induced to act or is restrained from acting. Since it belongs to the reason to direct to the end, it follows that law is something pertaining to reason.

As to the second proposition, he sets forth four premises, namely, that law belongs to reason by virtue of reason being a principle of human acts; that practical matters are the object of the practical reason; that the first principle in practical matters is the last end; and that the last end of human life is bliss or happiness. These premises lead him to the conclusion that law must in the end regard the relationship of itself to happiness. And, he argues, since every part is ordained to the whole, the law must regard the relationship of itself to universal happiness. Thus, every law is ordained to the common good.

As to the third proposition, Aquinas argues that a law's foremost regard is to the common good. Since ordering for the common good belongs either to the whole people or to a public personage who has care of things, it follows that the making of a law belongs either to the whole people or to such a public personage. As to the fourth proposition, he maintains that for a law to have the binding force appropriate to it, it must be applied to those who are ruled by it and that such application is made by the law being notified to them by promulgation.

These four propositions lead Aquinas to define law as an ordinance of reason for the common good, which is made by one who has the care of the community, and which is promulgated.

Aquinas gives a hierarchical scheme of law in which divine law is supreme, since the whole community of the universe is governed by divine reason. Not all of divine law is intelligible to man. The intelligible part reveals itself through eternal law (which is the incorporation of divine wisdom) and the *lex divina* enacted by God in the Scripture. Principles of eternal law are revealed in natural law, from which are derived all human laws. The hierarchy appears as follows:

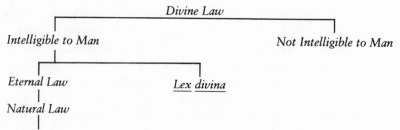

Eternal Law
Natural Law
Human Law

Proceeding with his elaboration of natural law, he maintains that, firstly, natural law is not a habit, since natural law is something appointed by reason and habit is that by which we act. If the term "habit" is applied, he suggests, to mean that which we hold by a habit, the natural law may then be called a habit inasmuch as sometimes the precepts of natural law are in the reason only habitually, as distinguished from being considered by reason actually. Secondly, the precepts of natural law are many, but they are based on one common foundation, namely, that good is to be done and evil is to be avoided. This is so because the first principle in the practical reason is the one founded on the notion of good. Thirdly, natural law prescribes acts of virtue, since each one's reason naturally dictates to him that he act virtuously. Of course, not all acts of virtue are prescribed by the natural law, since there are things done virtuously to which nature does not incline at first but which have been found conducive to well-living through the inquiry of reason. Fourthly, natural law, in its general principles, is the same for all, since truth or rectitude regarding the general principles of reason is the same for all and is equally known to all. However, as to certain matters of details, which are to be likened to conclusions from those general principles, it is the same for all in the majority of cases. In some few cases it may fail both as to rectitude, by reason of certain obstacles, and as to knowledge, due to the reason being perverted by passion, or evil habit, or an evil disposition of nature. Fifthly, while natural law can be changed by addition, since both the divine law and the human laws have added many things over and above the natural law for the benefit of human life, it cannot be changed by subtraction, since it is not changeable in its first principles. Finally, as to the question of whether the law of nature can be abolished from the heart of man, Aquinas continues to make his distinction between the most general precepts of natural law, or its first principles, and its secondary and more detailed precepts (conclusions drawn from first principles), and he maintains that while the latter can be blotted out from the human heart by evil persuasions, vicious customs, and corrupt habits, the former can never be so blotted out.

5. Criticism

The natural law theory gives rise to many crucial points of criticism.[3]

a. Dubious Ontology

There is a misleading ontological dualism in the theory of natural law. There is in it the existence of the empirical world, but there is also the reality of the transcendental that operates under this theory as an existential world and not merely its epistemological antecedent. The transcendental is claimed to have real existence because of its universality and pure rationality. An instrumentality of the cognitive process is thus converted into an object itself of human understanding. The epistemological device becomes reality itself. The postulates of reason become ontological facts that exist independently of understanding. This results in a thorough confusion of deontology and ontology, of value and reality, of the ideal and the factual. This artificial duality imposed upon a single object of understanding produces paradoxes that cannot be solved without recourse to the factual unity of the original problem, but—and here lies a reason why the theory fails to help us with solutions—a truer reality is assigned to the transcendental. The transcendental is not merely a cognitive focus but is the reality or the substance itself from which norms are to be derived. Since the variety of the experiential world obviously cannot be denied, the desired comfort of unity and coherence in the world is thus achieved by turning the cognitive schemata into facts themselves. We are left wondering how a legitimate theory of understanding can be anchored on such an ontology. For natural law under this theory is not merely a quest for ideal laws but the right law itself.

b. Inability of Abstract Reason to Schematize Historical Experience

Abstract reason is, under natural law, the true reality. But however detailed a scheme one might attempt to construct of the content of that reason and of natural law, it seems that the complexity of the

61

historically developed needs, interests, conflicts, and institutions is too vast to be comprised under or approximated to that scheme. If one nevertheless persists, all one will get are precepts that are too general and too vague to be of assistance in solving problems.

c. *Logically Defective Procedure for Deriving* ought *from* is

The procedure of the natural law theory is to derive norms from the ontologically ascribed facts of natural law. This raises a central problem in the relationship of *is* and *ought*, namely, whether *ought* can be derived from *is*. Since the issue of the logical relation between *is* and *ought* is of crucial importance in evaluating the methodology of natural law, it warrants a close scrutiny.

The logic of norms is much more complex than the question of logical relation raised here by the method of natural law. Moreover, it is possible to use it for a descriptive statement of values (*ought*). Values themselves may be teleological (relative to purpose) or absolute (as in natural law). It may, furthermore, be well argued that, ontologically, values belong to the human world and, being part of that human world, are facts. Therefore, it is important to clarify that the proposition at issue here is whether natural law's absolute values or norms (*ought*) derive from nature that exists (*is*), as claimed. Denial of that claim does not mean a denial of other relationships between norms and facts that do, in fact, exist. For example, in a judicial decision both *is* (facts of the case) and *ought* (norms of law) are combined in a logical scheme to produce a normative conclusion (judgment).

It is a basis of deductive logic that one cannot derive a conclusion from that which is not explicitly or enthymematically contained in the premise. In inductive logic, which is a process of generalization of the nature of a whole class from the characteristics of a number of instances belonging to that class, it is basic that there can be no induction from the property of a thing to that which is other than it. That *ought* cannot be derived from *is* has often been called Hume's law[4], even though David Hume (1711–1766) was not the first philosopher to think about the relationship between *is* and *ought*.[5] Even his famous passage on "is-ought"[6] can be interpreted in a variety of mutually contradictory ways: that *is* and *ought* are not related logically at all; or on the contrary, that they are related both deductively and inductively; or that *ought* cannot be derived from *is*, or, on the contrary, that it can be so derived or even entailed by *is*.[7] However, we shall not dwell upon Hume and examine these interpretations here. Instead, we shall move on to considering the maneuvers that have been made to reduce *ought* to *is* and to deduce *ought* from *is*.

Reduction of ought to is: Attempts to reduce *ought* to *is* or to make it identical with *is* have proceeded in two ways; (1) replacement of *ought* statements by *is*-supportable statements, and (2) entailment of an *ought* statement by *is* statements concerning desires and beliefs.

It is claimed that all that can be achieved by *ought* statements can be achieved by *is*-supportable statements, that is, statements that are knowable and believable and, therefore, are in the realm of facts. Consequently, it is argued, *ought* statements can be dispensed with.[8] For example, instead of it being the case that a judge ought to sentence a criminal, the case is that the judge wants to sentence him, we want the judge to sentence him, and we believe the judge will sentence him because we believe that the judge wants to stay a judge and will not remain so if he does not sentence the criminal. It is argued under this thesis that the use of *is*-supportable statements leads no more to the arbitrary result of making the punishment depend upon how the judge, or we, happen to feel at the time than the appeal to *ought* statements leading to the arbitrary result of some saying we ought because we ought or others saying we ought not because we ought not.

The general or universal agreement about *oughts* (ethical and moral standards) that makes the latter indispensable arises, it is claimed under this argument, not from the fact that there is a general or universal agreement that we ought or ought not to do a certain thing, but that we do or do not do it, we do or do not want to do it, we want to try to persuade others to want or not to want to do it, and so on, all of which are is-supportable statements. The objective of making someone do what he does not want to do or wants to do is achieved not by the mere use of *ought* statements but by the use of *is*-supportable statements. Therefore, replacement of *ought* by *is* or want would not result in the odd situation of telling someone that he ought to do something which he wants to do. The replacement may seem to eliminate an important body of ethical and moral truths for those who use intuition, insight, or non-natural qualities for discovering what ought or ought not to be done, rather than arriving at it deductively or inductively from *is*-supportable statements, but, it is argued, the important thing is not that we could know these things but would do or refrain from doing them. That is determined by what we want to do, which is an *is*-supportable statement. If reason-giving is appropriate for what ought to be done, it is equally appropriate for what we want to do.

The fallacy of the above thesis lies in the dual character ascribed to *is* statements, namely, the factual and the evaluative, and in the interchangeable use made thereof. When used in the evaluative sense, the *is* statement amounts to an *ought* statement. If we transcribed the statement that we want to do a certain act but we ought not to do it (the ought-not-ness arising from that act's propensity to violate a rule of behavior), substituting 'want' for 'ought', it would read that we want to do a certain act but we do not want to do it, and that would make sense only if the latter use of the word is in its evaluative sense. The evaluative thus has not been reduced to the descriptive as claimed by the above thesis. Furthermore, discussing reasons or justifications for wanting is justified only when the term evokes evaluation.

Entailment of an ought statement by is statements concerning desire and beliefs: The claim of this thesis is that an *ought* statement or *ought* belief is entailed by *is* statements of facts about desires and beliefs. Thus, that X believes that he ought to do Z logically follows from the facts that X, a rational and normal amoralist, wants to achieve Y, that he believes that doing Z is a necessary and sufficient means of achieving Y, that he believes that doing Z involves a choice between alternatives and carries a price in terms of effort and constraint on his part, that he believes that doing Z is in his power, and that he does not believe that there is any superior counter-consideration to his achieving Y or doing Z. The logical entailment, and not a contingent prediction, occurs, it is argued, because the use of an ought statement is simply the way for a rational and normal person to show his awareness of the constraints or requirements involved in what he believes he must do to achieve that which he wants.[9]

One of the grounds upon which this thesis has been criticized is that it implies the identification of the moral norm with the prevailing conduct while the truth is that the predominant behavior in the community is not always accepted as a moral standard. Moreover, if one is to behave like others in a heterogeneous society, it is difficult to determine who the others are to whom he must be related for resolving his moral question.[10] However, since it is difficult to accept that the thesis under consideration would be so crude as to misunderstandingly believe that morals are to be identified with the prevailing conduct, this criticism may not be justified.

But there are other difficulties with this thesis. First of all, under this thesis the rational and normal person is essential to achieving the claimed reduction. However, it seems quite clear that rationality and normality are evaluative. By using the means of the rational and normal person you have not reduced *ought* to *is* but, instead, you have made him perform the evaluative (ought) task itself. Secondly, while one might accept that mere knowledge of facts may yield a prediction of a determined form of conduct, such knowledge cannot merely prescribe the conduct. Thirdly, the determination of constraints and requirements called for in this form of reduction itself demands criteria as to whom among all of the members of the community, babies and lunatics included, are to be counted for the purpose. That, once again, is an evaluative task. Fourthly, it is not always for moral reasons that people adopt moral attitudes. The reduction of *ought* to *is* wipes out the motives that inspire a specific form of conduct. Finally, this reduces the moral sense to a mere process of adjustment to the prevailing behavior, rather than evaluating that behavior itself.

In addition to the maneuvers for reducing *ought* to *is*, attempts have been made to deduce *ought* from *is* through the notions of performative aspects of ought, constitutive rules of institutional facts, reason for acting, ideal-observer, and underlying commitment.

DEDUCTION THROUGH PERFORMATIVE ASPECTS OF OUGHT.—If you want to achieve Y and the one and the only way to achieve Y is to do Z, then you ought to do Z. From the two factual premises, the non-factual conclusion has followed. This is because, the argument goes, the relevant sense of wanting is not merely desiring, wishing, or aspiring, but being in a state of taking steps necessary to achieve what is wanted. If this is the meaning of your wanting, then given the other factual premise, the *ought* conclusion necessarily follows. The claim of this argument is not that the correct conclusion is factual, that is, that your best course of action is Z or that the one and the only way of achieving Y is for you to do Z, but that the imperative follows from the premises themselves and not by reduction of the *ought* to its factual implications. This is because, it is explained, the ought statement has a performative aspect, something more than truth value. It is argued that the *ought* here does not involve evaluation on the part of the maker of the statement as to the selected action being preferable or obligatory, giving him a reason for urging his addressee to that action; he may still do the urging even without having a reason to back it up. Nor does the *ought* here involve the presumption that he wants the addressee to do what he says in his statement, because he may give advice without wanting it to be followed. The imperative of the ought statement consists in the bare incitement to action, which is not merely a restatement of the factual conditions of the premise. The thesis denies that there is a possible enthymeme in its argument-form to the effect that everybody should do anything that is the one and only way to achieve what he wants to achieve, because it regards this premise as analytic (i.e., being guaranteed correct by virtue of the meanings or functions of the terms contained therein), and therefore, unnecessary. Furthermore, the ought conclusion here is claimed to be categorical, not conditional or hypothetical, because, it is argued, the ought statement is made in context and the use of *ought* and its normative cognates is made plain by the nature of the context. Saying that you should do Z has the force of saying that you should do Z given that you are, say, facing a problem in chess to which the question relates.[11] Thus, given the truth of the factual premises concerning your end and the necessary and sufficient condition for attaining it, the only possible conclusion is that you *ought* to do Z. The truth of the premises is claimed to restrict the conclusion to a single possibility.[12]

There are several difficulties with this thesis. In the first place, the conclusion arrived at in such situations as exemplified by chess, above, is hypothetical and not normative. It is predicted upon the acceptance of the game of chess. Secondly, the facts of the premises lead to the single moral possibility, as claimed above, only for those who share a certain morality that provides the context for the alleged deduction. Therefore, the facts in that context have a moral content, and the case no longer remains that of deduction of the moral conclusion from non-moral or non-evaluative factual premises. Thirdly, it is claimed that the end and the necessary and sufficient conditions for attaining that end lead to a moral conclusion, not merely to an amoral experience. However, it seems that a moral conclusion is reached when the end and the means for attaining it are both moral. Even then, it is quite possible to propose several moral courses, rather than a single possibility, and the moral advice would be different yet outside that particular moral viewpoint.

Fourthly, truth considerations normally are crucial to deductive logic in the sense that deduction indicates relationship between the truth of the premises and the truth of the conclusion, the latter being guaranteed by the former. However, the above thesis denies truth value to the ought statement. Of course, the performative aspect does not necessarily exclude truth value, and it may very well be additional to truth value. But since the above argument denies truth value to the ought statement of the performative aspect, this claim of deduction appears rather odd. Finally, under this thesis conventions concerning advising would determine the content of the advice given. So, the advisor would make the ought statement if he knows the factual premises, but he would do that only if he is to give advice. This process, while descriptive of the performance of the advice, speaks nothing of the logical relationship between the ought conclusion and the factual premises. Moreover, the facts contained in the premises give no reason for the advice. That advice, both in the aspects of whether it should be given and, if so, what kind of advice should be given, would depend on the advisor's desires, values, and interests. Consequently, the facts of the premises may result in no advice, or advice to do a certain thing, or advice not to do it. The case is not that of a single possibility from the truth of the premises. The claimed deduction has, thus, not occurred.

DEDUCTION THROUGH CONSTITUTIVE RULES OF INSTITUTIONAL FACTS.—One way of comprehending facts is along their classification as brute and institutional.[13] Brute facts are understood through essentially physical concepts; empirical observations recording sense experiences provide the basis for the knowledge of them, as, for example, in natural sciences. Institutional facts, on the other hand, presuppose certain human institutions and the statement of their properties. For example, promising means what it does only given the institution of obligation, or certain forms of behavior constitute A marrying B only given the institution of matrimony. A system of constitutive rules makes up an institution, and it is only in terms of these rules that an institutional fact can be explained or comprehended. The existence of the activity that is the subject of these rules depends on these rules. Now, give an utterance which is a brute fact (for example, the utterance "I promise to pay you a certain sum of money"), invoke the institution involved (namely, the obligation here), and, by virtue of the constitutive rule (namely, to make a promise is to undertake an obligation), the deduction of *ought* allegedly follows (namely, I ought to pay you that certain sum of money). A more detailed version of this deduction appears in the following example.[14] Take the statements given below in a series:

1. Jones uttered the words "I hereby promise to pay you, Smith, five dollars".
2. Jones promised to pay Smith five dollars.
3. Jones placed himself under (undertook) an obligation to pay Smith five dollars.
4. Jones is under an obligation to pay Smith five dollars.
5. Jones ought to pay Smith five dollars.

Although, as these statements stand, a subsequent statement is not entailed by its antecedent, the additional statements needed to make the entailment are claimed not to be evaluative. Thus, the needed statements for 1 to entail 2 are: 1(a) that under certain conditions [C] anyone who makes the utterance under discussion promises to pay Smith five dollars and 1(b) that such conditions [C] obtain. These conditions are empirical, not evaluative; that is, they are necessary and sufficient conditions for utterance to constitute the performance of the act of promising, such as conditions for intelligible speaking and understanding, beliefs of the speaker, his intentions, and so on.[15] The needed statement for 2 to entail 3 is: 2(a), a tautological premise, that all promises are acts of placing oneself under (undertaking) an obligation to do the thing promised. The needed statements for 3 to entail 4 are: 3(a) that other things are equal, in order to provide that things do not happen to release the promisor from the obligation, and 3(b), a tautological premise, that all those who place themselves under an obligation are (at the time they so place themselves) under an obligation. The needed statements for 4 to entail 5 are: 4(a) that other things are equal,[16] and 4(b), a tautological premise, that if one is under an obligation to do something, then as regards that obligation, one ought to do what one is under an obligation to do. The *ought* thus deduced is claimed to be a categorical ought, not a hypothetical ought, and is claimed to have been made without importing any evaluative premise in the structure of the argument.

It is difficult to accept this claim of deduction for several reasons. Firstly, the ought conclusion follows only if the prescriptive principle contained in the constitutive rule of the institution invoked is accepted, not if it is not accepted. The conclusion, therefore, does not follow as a necessary logical deduction from non-evaluative premises. The acceptance involved here is an evaluative premise. Secondly, an *ought* within an institution is relative to that institution, and, consequently, it can only be a hypothetical imperative, not a categorical imperative as claimed.

Thirdly, there is a distinction between identity and conditions of justification.[17] While there is no doubt that some, probably not all, duties, obligations, or oughts do presuppose the existence of certain institutions, these institutions only provide the conditions of justification, conditions that make an act morally obligatory, but not the conditions that must exist in order for that act to be of any given sort, or in other words, the conditions of identity. Enjoining conditions are not the same thing as defining conditions. The obligatoriness to follow the requirements of a human institution cannot arise from that institution itself. It, rather, must arise from sources outside that institution, sources that address themselves to the issue of obligatoriness.[18]

Fourthly, the above argument appeals to a constitutive rule of linguistic usage whereby a fact of the institution is asserted in turn to generate a value of that institution. Facts and values are thus comprised in a system of constitutive rules. However useful this construct may be for explaining the institutional imperative, it does not demonstrate that in logic the evaluative (ought) is deduced from the descriptive (is). The concept of institutional fact contains the institutional value, and it is from there that the evaluative conclusion is obtained.

Fifthly, words like "promise" have both normative and descriptive elements in their meaning. The descriptive element in the example under question consists in the utterance made; the normative element consists in the commitment to the institution. The ought conclusion results from the latter, not from the former. To suggest otherwise is to commit an equivocation over the word. One defense that may be proposed against this criticism is that making the utterance in certain conditions is promising, and the description of these conditions does not need any normative element. The difficulty with this defense, however, is the fact that although the normative element does not appear in the neutral description of these conditions, it does assert itself in the commitment made to the institution while using the word "promise" in an unqualified manner. Another defense may be that there is no literal meaning of the word in which it is not an undertaking. Consequently, there is no lexical ambiguity in the word "promise." However, if that is so, then the case becomes not one of deducing the evaluative from the descriptive but, rather, quite the opposite of the claim made above, for the word itself is now claimed to have no other meaning than the evaluative.

Sixthly, by employing a factual sense of evaluative terms the argument amounts to an anthropological statement about the behavior of those who are involved, and not a deduction of the imperative. It has been suggested in defense[19] that the fact that such an anthropological statement can be made does not affect the validity of the deduction, that it is irrelevant. However, it seems that the force of the criticism is not that the deduction is invalid just because it is possible to construct a parallel statement, but because the imperative of the conclusion does not obtain without granting the normative sense of these terms, the argument merely amounts to an anthropological statement and not to a statement of the imperative.

Seventhly, a statement about morality or law may be made from two distinct points of view, namely, internal and external.[20] It is internal when made from the viewpoint of someone both in and of the system. It is external when made from the viewpoint of an outside observer. When used externally, it cannot yield a prescriptive conclusion, only a description of the state of normative affairs. Hence it is used internally in the above example in order to achieve the prescriptive conclusion. Thus, committing oneself to accept the institution of promise means undertaking to use the word in accordance with the sense determined by the internal constitutive rules of the institution. The argument of deduction in the above example is made possible by taking the internal viewpoint connotative of the subsumed commitment. However, in doing so, the process necessarily imports an evaluative premise: in uttering the words of promise the imperative that precedes the uttering constitutes the justification for its imperative, for only then the internal viewpoint would connote commitment. Therefore, it no longer remains the case that the descriptive premises alone have yielded the prescriptive conclusion.

Eighthly, the claim of the above deduction is that the necessary conditions [C] of the supplementary premises 1(a) are empirical conditions. However, first of all, if these conditions are of commitment to the institution invoked, they would seem to be normative to that extent and not empirical. However, even if we grant that these conditions are empirical, it does not mean that if the conditions under which the promise is uttered are empirical, 1(a) is not a moral statement. The crucial supplementary premise (1(a)) in the above scheme of deduction, thus, remains evaluative in its essential character.

Ninthly, the deduction depends on the principle that one ought to keep his promises, and this is claimed to be tautological, not evaluative, on the ground that it is no more than a derivation from the two tautologies: (1) that all promises are (create, are understakings of, are acceptances of) obligations and (2) that one ought to keep (fulfill) his obligations. The failure to see this tautological character arises from (a) a failure to distinguish between the internal and external viewpoints about the institution and to recognize that a promise is, from the internal point of view, that which ought to be kept, (b) a failure to see that even if the obligation to keep a promise is overridden by some further considerations, it does not mean that the obligation did not exist in the first place, and (c) a failure to see that the speech act of promising is performative, a speech act that is different from describing, a feature of which is, among other things, the undertaking of an obligation. However, it appears that the statement that one ought to keep his promise is not necessarily tautological. It is *tautological* if the absence of obligation is accepted as an insufficient reason for withdrawing the word promise; it is *substantial* if it is taken to refer to certain descriptive conditions and to maintain that, if these conditions obtain, certain things ought to be done; and it is *equivocal* if it is taken to insist that granted these conditions those things ought to be done necessarily. The suggestion that the failure to see the tautology arises from the failure to see the internal viewpoint is untenable because the very viewpoint is predicated upon the acceptance of the institution, which is something other than a purely descriptive condition. It is, further, difficult to see how the remaining two failures mentioned above account for the failure to see the claimed tautology. For the tautological character vanishes and the normative imposes at the point where the performance is characterized as a promise. It is not that the constitutive rules of an institution may not contain tautologies, but that they cease to be so to the extent they prescribe that someone act in certain ways and not in others. If one accepts that words like promise have meaning only within their respective institutions, then the consequence of this is that their linguistic reception becomes possible only with the help of synthetic, not analytic or tautological, propositions about how we ought to act. In other words, while the proposition of obligatoriness gives meaning to the word promise, the truth of this proposition is not a function solely of the meaning of the word promise. Moreover, if the contended supplementary premise is merely tautological, then that should render the invocation of conditions [C] unnecessary, but that is not the case. It is only certain, and not just any, conditions that are invoked. What is involved in the supplementary premise is not merely saying the words or merely a word-usage statement (analytic proposition or tautology) but saying the words and placing oneself under an obligation (synthetic proposition).

Finally, the *ceteris paribus* (other things being equal) clause used in the example[21] is claimed to provide the effect that unless we are actually prepared to give some reason because of which the obligation is void or the promisor ought not to keep his promise, the obligation holds. The evaluative circumstance is claimed to occur only when these reasons are found to exist, since only then the evaluative exercise of determining their sufficiency for voiding the *ought* is called for, but not when these are not found to exist. However, it seems that evaluation occurs in the very use of *ceteris paribus*, whether it is asserted or denied, except, of course, in cases where all that is involved is merely a straightforward reporting of the absence of those reasons. For even where it is asserted, what is claimed is that there is no reason to deny it, and that is an evaluative exercise. Of course, it would be ungenerous to suggest[22] that what is meant in the claim that 'unless we are prepared to give reasons . . .' is the literal sense of not being prepared to do so even though such reasons do exist. For, then, the ought deduction would be trivial, if not contrived. Furthermore, if the meaning of the *ceteris paribus* clause in this example is that those considering it know of no reason for promisor not to pay, this does not entail that there is none. Consequently, the result cannot be the deduction of ought. If the meaning ascribed is that other things are equal only if there is nothing sufficient to make the proposition that the promisor ought to discharge the obligation false, it is evaluative. The result, in that case, in not that the *ought* is deduced from non-evaluative premises. It has been argued in defense of the proposition that *ceteris paribus* is non-evaluative; that, given a clearly structured hierarchy of moral institutions, all *ceteris paribus* does is to perform the non-evaluative function of ensuring that normal conditions for the existence of these institutions and their hierarchy obtain.[23] The fallacy of this defense lies in the fact that, even if we do not dispute the fact of a clearly structured hierarchy of moral institutions, evaluation occurs at the point of accepting the given of this argument, namely, the hierarchy. So, while this argument may in a very narrow sense save the *ceteris paribus* from giving the appearance of evaluation, it substitutes for the evaluative aspect of *ceteris paribus*, shown above, the evaluative concept of hierarchy. It does not help the deductive claim of the example in question. It is for these reasons that the attempt to deduce *ought* from *is* through constitutive rules of institutional facts, ingenious as it is, fails to be convincing.

DEDUCTION THROUGH THE NOTION OF REASON FOR ACTING.—The function of an ought judgment is to state that there is a reason for acting.[24] Consequently, it is implied by a proposition that is a reason for a certain kind of acting. Ought is thus claimed to be deducible from that empirical proposition, the crucial characteristic of which is being reason for an act of a certain kind. The reason may be of one kind or another, depending on whether the judgment is prudential or moral. For a prudential judgment, for example, the kind of reason is conclusive in terms of one's interests alone. That someone ought prudentially to do something rather than anything else is claimed to be the logical equivalent of saying that there is a conclusive reason in terms of his interests alone for his doing that thing.[25]

The above argument has been criticized on the ground that it makes two assumptions about *ought* that are incorrect.[26] Firstly, it assumes that *ought* has a personal subject, whereas there are uses of *ought* which do not have a personal subject, for example, in the statement that the bread ought to be baked under the heat. However, this criticism appears to me a bit ungenerous, since the obvious context of discourse is moral judgment and not matters that do not involve the personal subject. Secondly, the above argument is said to assume that ought judgments are judgments of action or choice, whereas the truth is that there is a whole class of ought judgments involving passions, emotions, or feelings (one ought to be ashamed, grateful, etc.) that are not of action or choice. This criticism, too, can be met by simply extending the argument of the above deduction to passions, emotions, and feelings. But the fatal difficulty with the thesis is that if a fact is a reason for doing something, it does not follow that the imperative (ought) is logically deducible from that fact alone. The description of a reason for an act is in itself no reason for performing that act. Ought conclusion can result only when an imperative premise is conjoined with this descriptive premise or imported indirectly as a conditional rule of reaching a goal.

DEDUCTION THROUGH IDEAL-OBSERVER THEORY.—The ideal-observer theory[27] holds that value predicates (a valued or disvalued object, or right or wrong action) and moral predicates (the liking or disliking, or approval or disapproval of an ideal or normal observer) designate a casual relation between them, the former being the cause and the latter being the effect produced thereby in human consciousness. They both have a subjective and an objective component and must be interpreted relationally. Consequently, what is subjectively valued and what is objectively valuable can only be construed phenomenologically, not ontologically, as what evokes liking or disapproval in human consciousness. The primitive data of value experience are considered reactions, the primitive data of morality are considered desires that motivate acts. This theory supplies the cognition of values and the morality of conduct by providing a normal or ideal-observer, which is simply a formal construct of criteria to determine what is to be taken as objectively valuable and morally acceptable. It regards general statements of such claims as lawlike in nature. What we ought to do is discovered by deducing the most rational choice available to us as moral persons from general causal laws applicable in the circumstances. Such is the ought-deduction under this theory, which is claimed to be a better explanation of the actual moral practice than the descriptive-prescriptive distinction model, for, under that model, if laws are essentially either descriptive or prescritive, descriptive laws could not be used to prescribe or *vice versa*. Under the ideal-observer theory, the rational determinants suggest the most efficient means of achieving the desired end, the moral determinants suggest conduct appropriate to the moral person, and they both govern the decision of what we ought to do. Reliable moral knowledge arises upon becoming a moral person and not from intellectualistic presuppositions of the is-ought distinction. Descriptive laws no doubt describe a cause-effect relation, but the same laws also tell a person the means of achieving the effect desired, and to that extent they are prescriptive as well. So, it is not the case, the argument goes, that they are descriptive laws, but, rather, that they are simply laws that may be used either descriptively or prescriptively. Moral laws are descriptive of the conduct, under the assumed conditions, of the class of moral persons, but, for that reason, it is argued, they do not cease to be prescriptive. Moreover, since they state what is to be expected of moral persons, they may, like any descriptive statement, be regarded as true or false.

This is an interesting explanation of moral practice. It may even be a more satisfactory theory of morality than some of the theories based upon the distinction of *is* from *ought*. It may also be a valid criticism of the attempts to propose the is-ought problem as the central problem of moral philosophy, a criticism with which I tend to agree. But to say that what we ought to do is discovered by deducing the most rational choice available to us as moral persons from the general laws of causal relationship between value predicates and moral predicates is no proof that an ought conclusion is deduced from *is* premises. For the evaluative premise is very much operative in choosing from among alternative courses of action the one that would be most rational to us as moral persons. Both the rationality of the choice and the morality of persons under the above scheme are evaluative.

DEDUCTION THROUGH UNDERLYING COMMITMENT.—It is claimed under this argument that a normal member of society moves from factual premises to an ethical conclusion not because of any hidden ought premise or any special rule of inference, but simply because of his moral concern for others, his sympathy, or his commitment to the moral point of view. This inference is argued to be justified because any rational human being sharing the same concern or point of view will accept either.[28]

However, while it may be true that the commitment to the moral point of view leads a person to take a certain ethical position, this does not mean that, when the operative premises and their conclusion are analyzed in terms of logic, the ought conclusion becomes deducible from *is* premises. Moreover, the rationality or normality of the human beings, so crucial to this claim, is indeed evaluative.

Thus far in this section we have examined the maneuvers that have been attempted to reduce *ought* to *is* or deduce *ought* from *is* in order to prove that evaluative conclusions can be drawn from factual premises, a methodology that natural law adopts, and we have attempted to show the failings of these methodologies. In addition to these maneuvers, an argument is made that the distinction between *is* and *ought* disappears in an interpretation of events that treats what is observed as purposive, as, for example, in law.[29]

A clue to purpose is deemed necessary to interpret what is being observed. It is suggested that there are two aspects of understanding of events, the control of events and the prediction of events. It is claimed that understanding in these aspects cannot be achieved without knowing the purpose of the activity being pursued. Value inheres in a purely factual account of a prediction that a certain course of action will be followed or given up. For this prediction is possible only given the knowledge that that course of action is good or bad for the purpose or, in other words, that it possesses or lacks value judged in light of the purpose. This value element is thus claimed to be intrinsic to the facts of the purposive activity. What is claimed by this argument is not that a concurrence of the observation of events, the perception of the purpose, and the provisional acceptance of this purpose have created an illusion of the merger of fact and value, but, instead, that the course of happening can be understood only if we participate in a process of evaluation.

There are several difficulties with this argument. Firstly, the argument is predicated upon the very distinction it denies, inasmuch as the value description is made only upon something that is otherwise valueless. The distinction remains between value (ought) and the fact (is) to which the value is being attributed. Secondly, when, in order to interpret a purposive activity, we inquire whether a given set of acts achieves a certain goal we indeed are making value judgments. We are not merely stating something that is intrinsic to the facts of the behavior under inquiry. Thirdly, what follows from the fact that a behavior is purposive is an is-statement that the actor has that purpose, not an ought-statement that he should have it. Fourthly, the knowledge of the actor's purpose may assist us in organizing the observational data in a certain manner and may inform us of his dispositional characteristics,[30] or his permanent possibilities of performance,[31] or even the purposive criteria for evaluation of his actions.[32] But it does not inform us of the moral (as distinguished from teleological) oughtness of his purpose. Fifthly, while it is true that whether a description is an adequate account of what is being described can be judged only with reference to the purpose for which the descriptive account is made,[33] the account itself does not become intrinsically evaluative for that reason. What is evaluative is the judgment of whether the account rendered is adequate, and not the account itself.[34] Finally, the claim of the above argument is that *is* and *ought* merge when an activity is purposive. However, what perhaps may be happening is the merging of the purpose and the action, but not of *is* and *ought*.

Certain phenomenological theories of law have attempted a fusion of *is* and *ought* as well.[35] Generally speaking, their claim is that facts constitute values *per se*. The argument goes that man cannot exist or act without values and, therefore, human existence is deemed a value by its very ontological structure. Values are objectively realized in the factual activity of man so that they can be understood or observed through the practical activity of man at a given place and moment of history. *Ought* is only an essential particularity of the structure of certain phenomena that express a thing to be realized, and it is not an autonomous sphere of phenomena. There is an immanent sense of the real whose totality is made up of both fact and value. The fact and the value are made one in the factual relationships of immanent value.[36]

However, it is difficult to accept this surfacing of the immanent as the abolition of the distinction between fact and value. Adjustment of values to facts does not demonstrate that the distinction between the two has disappeared. Moreover, the claimed merger of fact and value in the nature of things means that certain inevitable values would surface. However, such is not the nature of moral decisions, which involve choices to be made between conflicting values and are not just a recognition of the inevitable. If one claims this inevitability, one is only disguising his preferred ideology or value under such characterization.

The above examination has been intended to demonstrate that values cannot be derived from facts. When the natural law theory pretends to derive norms from its ontologically ascribed facts of nature, abstract reason, or God, it merely offers us an illusion. Values result not from facts but from the infusion of values made in those facts.

d. Failure to Recognize the Distinction Between
Natural Laws and Normative Laws

It is a criticism of the natural law theory that it does not recognize the distinction between natural laws and normative laws as fundamental. Nature exists. Regularities exist in it. One may even admit that laws in nature exist independently of man's perceptive act, although there are epistemological theories in the philosophy of science that maintain that laws of nature or scientific laws are only logically necessary and not physically necessary, necessity arising from the definitions and axioms from which we start and not in the sequence of sense impressions; thus it is illogical to transfer necessity from the world of conceptions to the world of perceptions.[37]

Such laws, however, are not norms of behavior. Normative laws, whether moral or legal, are outside the competence of laws of nature, for they are produced by human decisions and not by regularities of nature. They are man-made. Therefore, they, unlike the laws of nature, can be altered by human act. Moreover, when a law does not obtain in nature it ceases to exist, but when a norm is violated it does not cease to be a norm. While it is true that we use standards to determine the goodness or otherwise of the existing norms and institutions, these standards are made by humans and not by nature outside humans.

It is sometimes argued that there is no distinction between laws of nature and normative laws since it is not true, as asserted above, that laws of nature cannot be broken or altered by human acts.[38] The argument goes that the laws of nature are rationalizations of the physical world and could be nullified when fresh facts compel it. The fallacy of this argument lies in the confusion it makes between a regularity in nature and the man-made statement thereof. We make a hypothesis about a supposed regularity, and we accept the hypothesis as long as it has not been falsified. When fresh facts contradict it, the result is that what we supposed to be the law is not law and is replaced by a more adequate statement of it. The case is not that the law of nature has been broken or altered but that the supposed statement did not correctly formulate it. By creating the hypothesis about a regularity in nature we do not create the regularity itself.

It is further argued in support of the contention denying distinction between natural law and normative law that as natural law cannot be broken so the normative law cannot be broken, either.[39] One might concede for the sake of argument that a normative law, say, a criminal law, cannot be broken since the consequence is punishment, but punishment is not the necessary consequence since the authorities may decide not to prosecute the offender. That decision is fundamentally different from formulation of a hypothesis. These arguments do not appear convincing enough to establish the proposition that there is no fundamental difference between natural law and normative law.

It may well be that norms may have to be limited by the constraints of nature (*e.g.*, limited resources) or they may have to be compatible with nature in order to be effective, but that does not mean that they are made by nature. On the contrary, it is we who impose our standards, our norms, our ideals upon nature and thereby introduce morals into the natural world, despite the fact that we are part of it. Nature has its facts, its existence, its regularities, but not morals for the use of humans. Man's moral world is fashioned by his own ideals. The facts of nature are neither moral nor immoral. The distinction between natural laws and normative laws is fundamental indeed.

e. Removal from Man of His Responsibility for Moral Decision Making

This brings us to what is probably the most serious danger of natural law. By claiming to provide certainty and guidance to moral conduct, natural law responds sympathetically to man's yearning for such certainty. But that is an illusion; no such certainty exists in moral decisions. Moral decision is the painful task of choosing among alternative values. Pure obedience to nature was given up by mankind the moment man began to improve his condition in the wild, whether it was by means of husbandry and plow or steam engine, surgery, and space shuttle. Much less can nature provide answers to moral dilemmas faced by man. The danger of natural law lies in the disguise that it provides to the need to make a decision between alternative values. There exist deep and abiding conflicts of values and a choice has to be made among them. That choice is made by man, who must consequently take the responsibility for that moral decision rather than escaping into nature. By providing that disguise, that escape, that illusion, natural law removes the burden of that decision from man, who indeed makes that decision.

f. Insensitivity to the Historicity of Man

The trans-temporal absoluteness of natural law goes against the historicity of man. By arguing that a certain value is innate in nature, its realization becomes a process of unfolding of that innate essence. The formal structure of this process is provided by the historical time; necessity in history provides the law of its manifestation. Such an account of that value readily lends itself to a deterministic view of history that ignores its contingent aspects. If that value is a matter of the above unfolding, all efforts on our part become irrelevant to its realization except to await the unfolding of the fate.

Analyzed from yet another perspective, this account generates an assumption that the process of development of that value is autonomous, that it is determined only by its internal law. The truth, however, appears to be quite to the contrary. Values have resulted from social relations and the institutional forms of these relations, both of which have existed in the context of historical times. Taking the example of human rights in our times, this context is provided by such conditions as the state form of social organization, the impersonal character of industrialization, the particular technology available in our times, the particular welfare expectations from the state that exist today, and the particular needs experienced by the modern man. Looking at the history of human rights in the West, these have had different contents at different times, the difference being characterized by three major factors: the dominant value at the time, the public choice process, and the ideological commitment. Thus, in the eighteenth century liberty was the dominant value, market was the public choice process, and the rightful basis of limited political authority was the ideological commitment, all of which produced civil liberties, such as property rights, liberty of contract, free expression, right to travel. In the nineteenth century equality was the dominant value, group bargaining was the public choice process, and the ideological commitment moved toward ameliorating stratified social inequities through admitting new groups into the civic life, and all of that produced civil and political rights. Welfare became the dominant value in the twentieth century, centralized planning became the public choice process, and the need for universal sharing of the risks of industrial development was recognized by the ideological commitment, all of which have produced socio-economic rights. It is not correct to say that these conditions are merely incidentals to the unfolding of an autonomous system of human rights, for, rather, these are the very conditions that generate human rights and provide them their specific character. It may be that some sort of connection does exist between human rights at various historical times, and the historiography of human rights may well reveal such connection,[40] but the nature of history is not that of unfolding of an autonomous system. The advent of man in the world is historical. He is not a passive incident in the unfolding in history of his trans-historic impersonal essence. He is, instead, a personal being whose active dynamism makes history.

g. Non-universality of Its Universals

Beliefs in the facts of natural law, such as a belief in an innermost being of man, or God, or abstract reason, which are taken as self-evident in the natural law theory, are not held as generally in the world as its adherents tend to believe. This being so, the theory becomes unsuitable for constructing upon it a universal system of a particular value, such as, for example, human rights. It is interesting to recall that when the Universal Declaration of Human Rights was being drafted, proposals were made to secure for human rights the protection of the Divinity or, at least, acknowledge the divine origin of man. These proposals were debated very fiercely and ultimately rejected. For instance, a proposal introduced by Lebanon at the Second Session of the Human Rights Commission sought to include language to the effect that human rights were granted by the Creator, and the proposal was rejected. Or, an amendment to Article I was moved by Brazil in the Third Committee of the U.N. General Assembly that tried to include in the Article language that man was created in the image and likeness of God, and it was also rejected. Rejected, too, was the Netherlands' amendment to the Preamble to the effect that the equal and inalienable rights are based on the divine origin and immortal destiny of man.[41] The beliefs of natural law that constitute its premises are not shared universally, or even generally. That being so, such beliefs can hardly hold promise for serving as a basis for a universal value program, such as that of human rights.

h. Inadequate Consideration of Cultural Pluralism

The natural law theory claims that its values, absolute and universal, exist in nature *a priori*. The claim of universality is made not sociologically but *a priori*. Before launching upon the criticism of natural law in this aspect, it must, in fairness, be pointed out that the origins of the idea of a universal moral unity among men lie in a very laudable desire to dismantle the particularist barriers among nations and peoples. Thus, the Stoics assimiliated natural law with the general cosmic law that governed the universe so that all subjects of natural law were, by submitting to the universal cosmic law, held together in one harmonious society. However, the *a priori* claim fails to take an adequate account of cultural pluralism and denies the relativity of ethics, which is a point of particular significance for programs such as human rights since its concern is with the condition of the individual in the culture in which he actually lives and his treatment by the authorities to whom he is subject.

An unilinear idea of civilization dominated European thought until the Europeans began to attain knowledge of the civilizations of India, Persia, and China during the period between the late eighteenth century and the late nineteenth century. When confronted with this knowledge, many European thinkers dismissed these civilizations as merely backward societies, while others perceived them as distinct shapings of human mind that disproved the unilinear idea of civilization. This intellectual tension resulted in three distinct concepts of culture: that culture is a process of universal idea in the embodiment of universal and absolute values; that culture is the different ways of conceiving the notion of perfection and finding meaning and value in life; and that culture is a body of artistic and intellectual work.[42]

If one paid some attention to the history of mankind, it becomes quite evident that in any particular period since the growth of civilized communities in the valleys of Tigris-Euphrates and the Nile between 3,500 and 2,000 B.C. and the Indus Valley shortly thereafter (although recent archeological discoveries in the Indus valley would push the date back) there have contemporaneously existed four civilizations in the old world and three in the new world. Moreover, various cultures have created their own particular ideas about the social order as a result of their particular historical circumstances.[43] Each culture produces its own values, whether they are characterized in the sociologist's terms of the inner order of human beings,[44] or the anthropologist's terms of the pattern of a culture,[45] or the behavioral psychologist's terms of high-frequency, spatio-temporal behavior of the people in question.[46] Man is engaged in a continuous task of generalizing his own view of his environment and in imposing his constructions and meanings, which characterize one culture in distinction from any other. These norms can be determined or ascertained in a homogeneous culture as well as in a heterogenous culture.[47] In any case, the normative content of the societies in the world is pluralistic and particular to its respective culture.

The natural law theory's response to the empirical diversity of values is that this diversity reflects the multiplicity of error against the singleness of truth: *error multiplex, veritas una.* However, since this theory does not provide an adequate criterion for deciding what is truth and what is error,[48] this theory at best deserts us when we are faced with the question. More dangerously, it lends itself, for the same reason, to providing the disguise of universality to any particular philosophy that wishes dogmatically to so generalize.

However, the point about ethical relativity made here needs to be protected from the miscarriage that it precludes moral criticism of other people since "no definite answers are available or achievable",[49] or "contradictory ethical views [may be asserted] without either being mistaken",[50] or mankind has carved for itself "coexisting and equally valid patterns of life".[51] Recent anthropology, psychology, and sociology have shown that while there are differences among people, there are similarities as well that help us construct universal ethical yardsticks without relapsing into the *a priori* dogmatism of natural law. As I pointed out elsewhere in the context of human rights, we must distinguish between what is universal and what is particular, so that while the universal part of the concept of human rights consists of the imperative that there must be a minimization of injustice by states in the fulfillment of the physical and spiritual needs of human beings, the particulars of international accountability of states in this respect must be drafted differently for different cultures.[52] So, the extreme relativity of ethics that argues "anything goes" is untenable in light of contributions made in this regard by psychology, sociology, and anthropology. Psychologists have pointed out that it is possible to speak about good and bad, right and wrong, desirable and undesirable when granted that there is reliable knowledge of what man can be under certain conditions that we call good and granted that he is at peace with himself when he is engaged in becoming what he can be,[53] that individuals and cultures do not differ widely with respect to what they consider the ultimate ethical goals,[54] that cultural differences are compatible with identity in values in that judgment of the value of an act takes into account the particular circumstances under which it occurs, with the consequence that the same act may be right if it fits one set of conditions and wrong if it violates another set of conditions.[55] Sociologists have suggested that society, culture, symbolic interaction, and the potentialities of biological organism interacting in the basic process of socialization have been the basic field conditions for the emergence of the human psyche and that it is probable that there may be certain identical basic structures and functions in the psychic systems of the world.[56] They have pointed out that the pluralistic value-universe is not limitless and that all patterns of moral standards are interdependent with all the other factors operative in the determination of action.[57] Some have suggested the limitation of possibilities due to the facts that human infants are invariably dependent, that they confront the emotional problems of sibling competition, and that they are possessed of similar neurological defense mechanisms.[58] Anthropologists, too, have debated whether the variety in ethical codes is basic or superficial, whether the variations relate to means or ends, whether there are universals or near-universals that cut across cultures, and so on. They have examined these issues both conceptually and empirically.[59] They have investigated environmental, technological, and economic constituents of cultural similarities.[60] Some have pointed out that social life is molded by the same dynamic forces as those thousands of years ago,[61] that there are cultural constraints of family, religion, war, communication, and the like, which are biopsychological frames variably filled with cultural content,[62] that there is a fundamental uniformity underlying the diversity of cultural patterns,[63] that the likenesses are primarily conceptual and variations exist concerning details (prescribed behavior, instrumentalities, sanction),[64] and so on. In pointing to these studies in psychology, sociology, and anthropology the intention here is not to uncritically endorse the theories canvassed, but to show that while there are cultural differences there are similarities as well that may provide certain universal yard-sticks, so that by rejecting the *a priori* universals of the natural law we are not condemned to the radical relativism that precludes moral criticism of other people and compels acceptance of anything that goes.

i. Problems with the Criterion of Truth

A natural right or norm is discovered under natural law theory by such procedures as insight, intuition, evident contemplation, or reason. There may be something, some feeling to this evidence, some comfort, some psychological satisfaction. But what is at issue is the criterion of truth, and the feeling of evidence cannot be that criterion. Evidence guarantees the truth of a proposition only when the feeling of evidence is accompanied by a state of affairs that makes the proposition true, for a feeling of evidence may as well accompany a fallacy as a true assertion. Belief in the truth of a proposition is not enough; what is needed is justification. Belief cannot be its own justification. The natural law theory contains no objective criterion of truth other than faith.

Necessarily, therefore, it is subject to any interpretation inspired by any insight, intuition, or evident contemplation. Such in fact has been the history of natural law theories. While, on the one hand, natural law has justified slavery in Plato, Aristotle, and the southern states of an earlier America, it has, on the other hand, justified equality of humans in the Sophists and in Rousseau. It has provided sustenance to the conservative legitimatists in rationalizing the existing legal order (Bodin, Hobbes) as well as the reformist monarchomachs for over-throwing it (Buchanan, Languet, Althusius, Milton, Sidney).

Natural law has accommodated moral individuality of man so that his personal rights become the final limitation of all political power, as in the Sophists, the Stoics, and the Epicureans, or in the revived nominalism and voluntarism of Occam, Marsilius of Padua, and Duns Scotus' followers in the fourteenth century, or in the revived Epicurean thought of Laurentius, Buchanan, and Gassendi in the fifteenth, six-teenth, and seventeenth centuries.

Natural law has, as well, accommodated the social nature of man so that social solidarity becomes preeminent even to the extent of abolishing man's personal rights, as in Plato's interpretation of natural law as an organic teleological harmony in which each individual and each class has an appointed function, or in Aristotle's identification of natural law with the established order of society necessitated by man's physical or moral nature, or in the Church Fathers' (particularly St. Augustine's) placement of natural law in the spiritual unity of man through Christ (*corpus mysticum*), or in the subsequent reformulation of *corpus mysticum* into solidarity when natural law became secularized (Auguste Comte and others).

Since the natural law theory's claim to universality of its values is *a priori* in nature and not sociologically observed, it has made possible for merely provincial philosophies of nature and culture to generalize for the entire world. Witness, for example, the claim to universality made by the Hindu *dharma*,[65] or by the Chinese Confucianism,[66] or by the Roman Catholic natural law.

To put it another way, natural law theories have varied with various exponents thereof. However, if norms of natural law or natural rights are deduced from an absolutely uniform natural law, there arises a need in the theory to account for variations in these normative catalogs. The theory fails to account for these variations, except to admit that they exist, whether such admission be in terms of Aristotle's distinction between universal justice and particular justice or in terms of Aquinas' distinction between reason and reason led astray by passions.

The natural law theory's answer to this wide variety is that reason can be led astray by passions, as argued by Aquinas, but when we raise the question as to which position is the example of reason and which position is the example of reason led astray by passions, we find no objective criterion of truth in this theory to settle the issue. All we come down to is faith, and if faith is held as justification of itself, which indeed seems to be the essential nature of faith, then we return starkly to the dogmatism made possible by this theory.

j. Undue Distrust of That Which is Man-made

The natural law theory suffers from a misapprehension that what is man-made is wholly arbitrary, that convention implies arbitrariness, that freedom given to man in choosing a system of norms would mean that one system is equally valid as another so that anything goes. This is a mistake. Man has created normative standards, and he lives by them. These may be the artifice of man, but that does not deprive them of normativity. Nor does that make these norms necessarily arbitrary. There even exist transcultural standards, not presumed *a priori* but evident empirically, as we have attempted to show above by soliciting theories of psychology, sociology, and anthropology,[67] and these standards test the rightness or wrongness of other people and their systems as well, such as, for example, extermination of Slavs, Jews, and gypsies of Indian origin in gas chambers of the Third Reich. This, of course, does not mean that man has not produced arbitrary or capricious values, but he has also produced the standards by which we can call them arbitrary or capricious.

k. Mistaken Mixture of the Metaethical with the Normative

Natural law theory insists upon the mixing of the metaethical with the normative as necessary. Metaethically, it gives ontological description of moral concepts. Normatively, it prescribes conduct. However, it insists that the metaethical is necessary to the normative. This, too, seems to be a mistake. For it is quite possible to accept a normative prescription without having to accept its metaethical description. There is no logical, necessary linkage between the two. Conversely, other metaethical theories (*e.g.*, utilitarianism) could very well be compatible with the same normative ethics.

Natural law theory affirms the metaethical theory of value-cognitivism that intrinsic value judgments can be objectively validated. However, it is possible to affirm value-cognitivism and deny natural law, as, for example the Utilitarians (Bentham, Mill) do when they regard utility as a demonstrably valid principle of morals and legislation. Having committed himself to value-cognitivism, the natural law theorist has the burden of proving the validity of his norms but, instead, he merely proclaims them.

l. Problems with the Nature of Nature

There are difficulties in natural law theory with what is nature and with drawing normative consequences from what is found as nature. The exponents of natural law have used nature to denote a variety of things, such as something original, objective, not man-made which exists by itself and for itself, or the inner essence of man and things, or the harmonious totality of all that exists.

Whichever way nature is conceived, the further problem arises as to whether this nature is the paradigm of order yielding ethical imperatives or a set of limitations upon man's capacities within which he must build his normative structure. The conception of naturalness—that the universe is governed by laws of rationality and that man, having been given the capacity of choice between obeying or disobeying the laws of nature, acts in accord with his reason only insofar as he obeys them (Stoics Zeno and Chrysippus, and later Montesquieu and Blackstone)—suffers from the criticism: law that is the formulation of regularities in nature is not the same thing as law that is conceived as norms to which behavior must conform (Mill, Huxley, Pareto). To resolve this discrepancy by an argument that both are expressions of a divine will results only in taking resort to a metaphysical premise that is fraught with its own problems.

There is a further difficulty with nature, namely, of distinguishing between those aspects of it to which normative significance can be attached from those to which it cannot be attached. Aristotle paved way for a solution to this difficulty by invoking nature in a more specific sense, in which every kind of species has its own end the characteristic excellence of which is realized in performing that which is conductive to this end. Aquinas grasped upon this teleological concept of nature to provide the solution that laws of nature are known equally to all through their use of reason. But, again, there are metaphysical assumptions in this solution that are outside the scope of common-sense belief, namely, that phenomena are divided into natural kinds, that each of these possesses an essence, that this essence stipulates an end, and that virtue lies in realizing that end.

m. Difficulties with Purpose of Human Life as Evidence of Natural Law

The purposive behavior of man is given as an evidence of natural law so that one would comprehend natural law by discovering the need of human life. One could see, the argument goes, that human life has purpose and, therefore, we must accept that there is natural law. This is a very dubious evidence for natural law. While it is true that there exists purposive behavior of man inasmuch as he acts for an end, goal, or aim, it is not clear at all that there is a purpose to his life, that there is an end to it, and that virtue lies in realizing that end.

n. Difficulties with the Human Attribute of Reason as a Distinguishing Basis for Natural Rights

The peculiar position assigned to reason in the natural law theory is hard to accept. We have been told for ages that man is a rational animal. While an adequate theory of what is rational is still missing, reason, at its best, is conceived as a capacity to comprehend abstractions. This capacity is claimed to be peculiar to man and, therefore, the basis for equality of man, and, hence, the foundation for natural rights. This is a very shaky foundation. First of all, men are not equal in their reason, that is, in their capacity to understand abstractions. That capacity varies among them as their sense perception. Reason, consequently, does not provide an argument for equality of men as claimed by the theory. Moreover, reason alone does not constitute the only distinguishing feature of man or his only specific nature. It is only one among his many distinguishing features. Even more devastating for natural law theory's treatment of reason is the fact that living beings other than humans possess reason, too. Admittedly, animals are not capable of verbal expression and linguistic articulation as humans are, but some of them, such as chimpanzees, dogs, and cats do possess reason, albeit rudimentary. If this is so, it takes away from natural law its basis (viz., human-peculiar reason) for ascribing men their equality and their human rights as above.

This type of equality argument has found an interesting version in recent literature. A distinction is made between human worth and the merit of persons. Merit is said to be all kinds of valuable qualities of performance that are acquired, in the sense that they represent what their possessor has made of his natural endowments and environmental opportunities; the argument is made that although merit of all persons is unequal their human worth is equal. Thus, it is contended, well-being and freedom are worth the same to all persons. The intrinsic value of all persons' enjoyment of goods is the same where they are capable of enjoying the same goods. This is contended to provide the foundation for natural rights.[68] However, the proposition that each person's intrinsic value of his well-being is equal to any other person's seems to be of doubtful validity. It has been argued by the proponents of this proposition that since the denial of the opportunity to experience the enjoyment of goods enjoyable by all results in a denial of full and satisfactory life, it goes to prove that their intrinsic values are equal for all. But this kind of proof is hard to accept. For while it may well be objectionable to preclude someone from enjoying these goods, this does not mean that their intrinsic values are equal for all. The proponents sometimes concede to the difference in these values, but they argue that these differences are not discoverable or measurable and that is a good basis for natural rights. This argument, however, amounts to nothing more than an appeal to opt for the egalitarian morality over any other competing morality, and my option for it does not prove any logical necessity for it issuing from the premises used in this argument.

One argument that has caught a great deal of popular fancy in this respect is that all men are created free and equal and their natural rights flow from this fact.[69] Again, the proposition is not factually isomorphic, but even normatively the necessity for natural rights does not flow from the supposed equality of man's birth, from which it can very well be argued that since all men are born equal we must respect that fact of nature so that they must not be treated preferentially.

It perhaps ought to be made clear that my intention here is not to argue against equal and humane treatment of human beings but to show that the natural law theory does not provide a satisfactory foundation for it.

o. Difficulties with the Position Assigned to Human Nature

Finally, an appeal is made in the natural law theory to the concept of human nature, and the morality of acts is judged by their relationship to a common human nature. Every man is human by nature. An essential human nature determines his natural status. Norms or natural rights are claimed to follow from this status. Natural rights are owed to man because he is man. Morality is thus grounded in human nature.

However, confusions abound in this sort of thinking. In the first place, there is a circularity in this reasoning. Essential human nature is coextensive in this theory with human being, that is to say, it is constituted by the properties expressed in the concept of human being. The argument of the theory is not that its concept of human nature is a preferable one among many others but that this concept has as its ultimate basis the real essence of man. In order to show that this concept is the real concept, it must be shown that certain activities are essentially human. Here lies the circularity, for reference cannot be made for this purpose to the criteria used for applying the concept of human being because whether these criteria should be used is precisely the question at issue. Secondly, the presupposition of the theory is that human being is a natural being from which norms can be derived. However, although he is part of nature to the extent he is actual to himself, he is not identical with his natural being since this being awaits upon him to give it its meaning. Therefore, his being not being a natural being it cannot constitute that nature from which the theory derives norms. Thirdly, human nature is not a specific quality possessed by man but a potentiality for a certain range of qualities and activities. His perceptual apparatus and his potential ability for reasoning make it possible for him to possess this potentiality. However, nothing normative can follow from this potentiality. It is sometimes said that the normative does follow from man's rationality and his capability of free choice.[70] This suggests that the essence of man is self-determination. But this is just a moral preference which may prevail in some cultures and not in others,[71] and not a norm that necessarily derives from human nature.

In sum, thus, there is a misleading ontological dualism in the natural law theory. Its precepts, too general and vague, do not adequately comprehend the complexities of needs, interests, and conflicts. It adopts the untenable procedure of deriving *ought* from *is*. It does not recognize the distinction between natural laws and normative laws as fundamental. It provides a dangerous disguise to the need to make painful decisions between alternative values. Its trans-temporal absoluteness goes against the historicity of man. Its beliefs, proclaimed self-evident, are not held generally in the world. Its *a priori* values deny the relativity of ethics and take an inadequate account of cultural pluralism. It contains no objective criterion of truth. It suffers from a misapprehension that man-made norms are wholly arbitrary. It unduly mixes the metaethical with the normative. Its views of nature and the use to which it puts nature are objectionable. Its teleological view of human existence is not easily acceptable. Its peculiar treatment of reason, too, is hard to accept. Finally, its view of human nature is fraught with serious difficulties.

B. Modern Theories of Natural Law

In the past few decades there has been a resurgence of natural law thinking in jurisprudential thought that has provided the theory with new formulations. These modern formulations include viewing this law as objectively given (*donné*) value (*Gèny*), as morals (*Dabin*), as deontology (*d'Entrèves*), as related to sociology (Selznick), as based on anthropology (Mead, and Edel and Edel), as ethical jurisprudence (Cohen), as a relationship between moral truths and general facts (Brown), and as the inner morality of law (Fuller).

1. Natural Law as Objectively Given (donné) Value: François Gény (1861–1944)

According to Gény, judicial interpretation of law is an activity much more creative than applying strict logical principles to the code and it requires an investigation of the reality of social life. The sources of law are not merely the written law but, additionally, (a) custom, (b) authority and tradition as developed by judicial decisions and doctrine, and (c) free scientific research. Free scientific research bases itself on three principles, autonomy of will, public order and interest, and just balance of conflicting private interests.

Gény maintains that there are principles of justice higher than the contingency of facts, so that beyond the positive nature of things there are rational principles and immutable moral elements. This absolute justice is necessary to give strength to legal interpretation, but it can indicate only a direction, which the consideration of the facts and the positive nature of things alone can specify. It is an illusion to think that the interpreter of law can find a ready solution for the problems of life in the revelations of reason and conscience, since the just in itself cannot be applied directly and immediately. The just is a goal and the interpreter has to discover the means for materializing it under the given conditions. Thus, while there are principles of justice revealed by reason or conscience that exist outside the world of phenomena and contingencies, they receive their positive imprint only from the various dynamic factors in the life of the community.

Gény applies to law the classical distinction between thought and will, or knowledge and action, or science and technique. Science is the objective knowledge of those social realities that furnish law with its social material. Technique is the specific art of the lawyer and, therefore, a field of creative action. Law is not restricted to the form that regulates change but includes the social situation in which the lawyer operates. Gény's theory of natural law is placed within the framework of the social, which provides the material for legal action. Natural law consists of those immutable and universal factors with which the law operates. These factors are divided into four categories, which he calls *donnés* (givens): (1) *donné réelle*, or the environmental data, which consists of physical and psychological realities, such as sex, climate, religious traditions, social habits, and so on; (2) *donné historique*, or the rules of law historically shaped by the environmental data, that is to say, those facts, traditions, and circumstances that give a particular shape to the physical or psychological facts of the *donné réelle*; (3) *donné rationnel*, or the universal principles of justice that can be rationally derived from the historical-positive norms, that is, principles derived from the reasonable consideration of human relations, and these embody most of the principles of the classical natural law; and (4) *donné ideal*, or the total ideals underlying a legal system that is based on all the physical, psychological, moral, religious, economic, and political considerations, and thus embodying the moral aspirations of a particular civilization at a particular period.

Gény considers his distinctions a general working basis for explaining the unfolding of the legal process, and he maintains that at every stage of this process there must be creative activity. In a conflict between natural law and positive law, the lawyer is bound by positive law but Gény provides for disobedience in those extreme cases where the law is contrary to good sense and would result in flagrant injustice.

2. Natural Law as Morals: Jean Dabin (b. 1889)

Dabin defines natural law as natural moral rule. He raises the question whether natural law is the directing principle of morals or of law;

he explains that historically what one has always sought of natural law are principles of moral conduct. The treatises that have applied natural law to different matters are nothing but treatises on special ethics. Natural law and special morals dictate the same rule and found the same institutions. There is no difference between inter-individual natural law and inter-individual morals, or between family natural law or family morals, or between political natural law and political morals. Even in its most narrow sense, natural law, being the expression of requirements of nature, represents the source for the solution of moral problems in various matters. Dabin argues, there is no distinction between morals of individual action and institutional morals of social life, since morals govern everything human, social arrangements. Thus, natural law is the moral rule taken in its homogeneous totality.

Natural law thus defined is related to the law established by the state in that, on the one hand, civil law comes to the aid of natural law in order to force people from engaging in evil, and it completes natural law by providing conclusions derived from first principles. On the other hand, natural law gives civil laws their foundation as well as the justification for obedience to them. Civil laws contrary to natural law are bad laws. From the fact that civil law borrows a number of its precepts from natural law it does not follow either that natural law does not belong to the category of morals or that the civil law has lost its proper nature.

In Dabin's scheme, therefore, there exists a moral natural law which is fundamental to all domains of moral conduct, whether of individuals or of social institutions. There exists, too, a political natural law based upon the political instinct of man, which is dependent upon moral natural law for the reason that morals govern everything human. But, he maintains, there exists no juridical natural law in the sense of solutions or directions given to the authority charged with the establishment of the civil law. There may be principles commonly accepted in the laws of certain countries at the same level of civilization but these general principles of law are not principles of natural law, since, (1), they are heterogeneous, commingled rules of morals, common sense, and social utility, and, (2), they lack the necessity and universality inherent in the idea of nature.

This analysis leads Dabin to claim that one must not speak of relationships between natural law and positive law but between morals and law (*i.e.* civil law). Natural law signifies morals and does not cover all values, however they may be of interest to the jurist.

3. *Natural Law as Deontology: A.P. D'Entrèves (1902–1985)*

Borrowing the idea from Giambattista Vico, d'Entrèves argues that every law has two facets, *certum* (the element of authority) and *verum* (the element of truth, which is discoverable by reason). It is a factual proposition about authorivy as well as a statement about values. The ground of obligation of law lies within the law itself and must be sought in the interplay of the *verum* and the *certum*, that is to say, in the ideal principle at work in every law despite its material circumstances. Each law is a normative translation of a particular value. The ultimate ground of validity of the law, or the *verum* thereof as distinct from *certum*, is values and not facts. The notion of natural law as a deontology finds its justification in the intersection between the legal proposition and the value that underlies it, or, more precisely, in the ascertainment of the element of obligation that makes us feel that we are obeying the law because of the element of truth it contains and not merely because of its certitude. The problem of natural law is the problem of ascertaining where the grounds of obligations ultimately lie. D'Entrèves believes that in human nature there are certain ultimate values that determine our judgment as to whether a law is just or unjust, so determining whether we are bound in our conscience to obey it or not.

The conception of natural law as a deontology does not, for d'Entrèves, exclude the possibility of rational argumentation of these values. If ultimate values are believed, this does not imply that they cannot be rationally argued. Also, the fact that our value judgments may be historically conditioned, so that there is no principle of justice that has not been denied somewhere or at some point, does not prove that the denial was justified. Furthermore, the fear that the claim of values to absolutness might lead to fanaticism or hypocrisy can be met by a profession of humility and sincerity. He points to history to show that the recourse to natural law has indicated an earnest desire for mutual understanding.

4. *Natural Law as Related to Sociology: Philip Selznick (b. 1919)*

Selznick observes that positive law includes an arbitrary element that, though necessary, is repugnant to the ideal of legality. The proper aim of the legal order is to reduce the degree of arbitrariness. Since the basic aim of the natural law philosophy is to ground law in reason, scientific inquiry about proper ends and values is the road to a science of natural law.

As Selznick explains, the chief tenet of natural law is that abritrary will is not legally final, so that principles of legality and justice can always be appealed to. The conclusions of natural law are no more sacrosanct or eternal than any scientific generalization, but the fact that a conclusion is subject to correction does not mean that it is not firmly grounded in theory and effectively supported by evidence. Since natural law draws conclusions about nature, it presumes inquiry, that is to say, these conclusions are based upon scientific generalizations and are grounded in warranted assertions about men, groups, and effects of law. Therefore, there is no reason why the most general concepts of law, such as equality, reasonableness, fairness, etc., should not be subject to criticism on the basis of scientific investigation.

Natural law inquiry, Selznick points out, presumes a set of ideals or values, which, most broadly, is human welfare. The legal order is studied as a normative system, with a view to discovering how that system can be brought closer to its inherent ideals. Law, therefore, is tested against conclusions regarding human needs as well as against tested generalizations as to the requirements of a legal order.

Taking the functionalist viewpoint of the sociologist, he maintains that it is not necessary for natural law supporters to prove that man has any inherent duties. Rather, it is the system that has the duties. Functionalism identifies what is essential to the system and determines what is needed to sustain it at a particular level of achievement. In studying the distinctive structure of a society, its capabilities, and the forces that transform it, it is not necessary to show that all participants have a duty to uphold it.

According to Selznick, the authority of natural law depends on progress in the social sciences, so that it is limited in its authority where social knowledge is weak. While natural law pursues a quest for universals and their assertion, it presumes changing legal norms, since its basic commitment is to a governing ideal, not to a specific set of injunctions, and that ideal is realized in history. There are two ways in which these changes occur. Firstly, as inquiry proceeds, basic premises about legality and its underlying assumptions about human nature and social life are revised. Secondly, as society changes, the natural law principles are adapted to the new demands, circumstances, and opportunities by new doctrines. Thus, natural law is neither eternally stable, nor like a directly applicable code.

Selznick proposes a principle of caution in the application of natural law, since it belongs to an interdependent whole and is not to be applied in isolation from other legal materials. This interdependence creates a rebuttable presumption in favor of positive law, since the presumption helps sustain the authority of law-creation necessary to the effectiveness of the legal order and since it recognizes the merit of the funded experience of the political community and thereby contributes to the development of natural law.

5. Natural Law as Based on Anthropology: Margaret Mead (1901– 1978); and May Edel (1909–1964) and Abraham Edel (b. 1908–)

Mead defines natural law as those rules of behavior that have developed from a species-specific capacity to ethicalize and as manifested in all known societies. She maintains that there are constancies among all known cultures and suggests that their systematic observation would probably show that the kinds of cultural behavior found in all of them have been an integral part of their survival systems up to the present time. Such universal constancies include rules concerning the sacredness of life under some circumstances, rules concerning the prohibition of incest in the primary familial relationships in most circumstances, and rules concerning an individual's rights over some differentiated physical or cultural items. She realizes that the fact that such recognitions have been universal in the past does not necessarily mean their continuance in the future, but she notices that they seem to have provided ethical principles without which human societies did not exist viably.

Edel and Edel point out that anthropology has revealed an enormous range of differences in people's rules of behavior, their ideals of character, their concepts of virtue and vice, and their goals of life. These differences go far beyond matters of specific rules and regulations and relate to the structure of conscience itself. The anthropologist, therefore, does not look for common moral perceptions and instinctive moral reactions. Instead, he looks for universal moral rules and understands differences through a mode of analysis that combines psychological with biosocial and historical factors. The patterns of human social interaction represent distinct answers to essentially the same questions posed by human biology and the generalities of the human situation. Thus, these experiments in living are not simply direct instinctual expression.

However, the success of these experiments requires certain minimal standards, so that each culture must provide patterns of motor habits, social relations, knowledge, and beliefs with which it is possible for people to survive. Common needs, social tasks, and psychological processes provide some common framework for the variegated human behaviors of different cultures. This framework includes conformity in the behavior of the members of any society. Therefore, amid all the historically developed cultural diversity there is morality. Morality includes common structural patterns, common mechanisms, and, in parallel social institutions, common content. This suggests to the Edels a guide to formulating a hypothesis about morality in relation to human needs. They do not propose a simple reduction of morality to a statement of biological, psychological, or social needs but that the need-solution element be made explicit or realistic. Such a realistic morality is not made any less moral by the fact that its quality may be more rational and more open to reassessment and change. Moreover, the very idea of need-fulfillment has a value content.

In assessing the impact of their approach upon absolutes in morals, Edel and Edel argue that there is a great deal of vagueness in the general appeal to moral absolutes (whether they refer to fixed goals for all people, or fixed goals for all conditions, or unqualified rules, or completely established answers in each particular situation, and so on). Appeal to absolutes does not remove the problem of further evaluation. A clear understanding is likely only if the study of absolutes is itself conducted in context.

6. *Natural Law as Ethical Jurisprudence: Morris Raphael Cohen (1880–1947)*

Cohen argues that it is possible to reasses natural law in a new form in harmony with modern thought. From the point of view of the requirements of a scientific theory, one must ask what is the character of the principles of natural law and how are they to be established? The traditional answer has been that they are axioms whose self-evidence is revealed to us by natural reason. This, according to Cohen, is not sufficient. It must be shown that, like other scientific principles, principles of natural law yield a body or system of propositions; they are, therefore, to be tested by their certainty, accuracy, universality, and coherency. As in all normative sciences so in legal science we must ask that, if our ultimate standards are to be formulated in terms of desire, what do the people of a given time and place do desire, and what limitations does law, as an instrument of social contract, impose upon the ideal that it serves? Cohen argues that we must recognize the dependence of natural law upon ultimate ethical principles, for a doctrine of natural law cannot claim a greater degree of certainty and completeness than attaches to the basic ethical principles presupposed by it.

Cohen points out three problems that must be faced in the possibility of natural law: (a) the indeterminateness of jural ideals, (b) the intractability of the human materials with which law works, and (c) the inherent limitations of general rules. As to the indeterminateness of our jural ideals, he suggests that it is an illusion to think that our ideal of justice determines a specific answer for all questions that can possibly arise. An examination of various ideals leads him to the conclusion that no ideal is both formally necessary and materially adequate to determine definitely which of our actually conflicting interests should justly prevail. That being so, law has to be the technique for determining what would otherwise be uncertain and subject to conflict. This need for certainty enforces human inertia, which makes the law lag behind the best moral insight. As to the intractability of human materials, Cohen points out that the elaboration of legal ideals is obstructed by the inevitable imperfections in the human beings who (a) make, (b) enforce, and (c) obey the law. It is therefore wicked and stupid to insist on 'justice regardless of consequences'. Finally, as to the abstractness of legal rules, Cohen points out that legal justice has to operate with abstract general rules, but this abstract uniformity works injustice in particular cases. Thus, one cannot put an uncritical reliance on the abstract universality of legal justice.

Cohen proposes a normative or ethical legal science. While the scientific study of the social facts that law must take into account is necessary, it is not sufficient for a complete legal science. Law can be viewed as setting up rules that serve as norms, in the sense of commanding obedience and controlling conduct. These norms can be studied as legal history (what was actually decided at a given time and place), legal sociology (uniformities or abstract patterns that repeat themselves), and normative jurisprudence (questions concerning what law ought to be). The relation of technical standards to human life and welfare necessarily involves ethics. Ethics is an attempt to organize all our judgments of approval or preference into a coherent system. It, therefore, includes not only judgments concerning the traditional issues of individual morals but also questions concerning the ultimate values of all human activities. Normative jurisprudence, thus, depends upon ethics. Cohen argues that opposing the normative point of view in legal science by insisting on the study of empirical facts confuses the necessary with the sufficient conditions of a complete legal science. A normative legal science is not possible without a thorough knowledge of the actual facts of human conduct, but such a knowledge is not sufficient for all purposes.

7. Natural Law as a Relationship between Moral Truths and General Facts: Stuart M. Brown, Jr. (b. 1916–)

Brown maintains that according to the natural law theory there is a logical relationship between facts about the world and morality. The universal moral truths, which are natural laws, are logically dependent upon the world's having certain general features. This relationship connects natural law with the notion of truth. If a certain behavior is prohibited as a matter of natural law, it is prohibited by virtue of certain facts about human beings, for instance, that human beings can and do suffer. This is in contradiction with code law, since the latter need not have such logical connection with truth. It is this relationship between natural law and general facts about the world that makes, in Brown's view, the natural law theory one of the theories of ethical cognitivism.

8. *Natural law as the Inner Morality of Law: Lon L. Fuller (1902– 1978)*

Fuller maintains that in a purposive interpretation of human behavior the distinction between fact (is) and value (ought) disappears, so that understanding of activity cannot be achieved without the knowledge of the purpose of that activity. The value element, he thus claims, is intrinsic to the facts of a purposive activity. Law, in his view, is the collaborative articulation of shared purposes and, therefore, is itself a purposive activity. Therefore, according to Fuller, facts and value merge into law. Law has an inner morality that is deduced from the very nature of a legal system.

Fuller presents eight principles of this inner morality of law. These principles are not conceived as maxims of substantive natural law in the sense of ideals inspiring a society, but rather as a procedural natural law. The eight principles are: (1) generality; (2) promulgation (availability of the law to the party affected); (3) prospective legal operation (the general prohibition of retroactive laws); (4) intelligibility and clarity; (5) avoidance of contradictions; (6) avoidance of impossible demands; (7) constancy through time (avoidance of frequent changes); and (8) congruence between official action and declared rule.

Criticism

The modern theories of natural law have attempted to avoid the metaphysical trappings of the early theories. However, they have problems of their own.

Gény's belief in natural law appears to be founded upon an intuitive religious belief. His appeal to some kind of existential natural law shows the influence of Thomism upon him. The problem with this is, firstly, it makes his theory subject to the problems of knowledge and the criterion of truth discussed above. He, of course, maintains that natural law is established apart from the religious elements. However, he has failed to lay down its specific content. Secondly, there is an incongruity in his treatment of natural law. He rejects the notion of a physical, biological, economic, or sociological natural law. At the same time he urges recognition of natural law not as an ideal formulation but as a prototype of positive law that is possessed of the same kind of objectivity as positive law. Thirdly, he makes a fundamental distinction between science and technique. Science, according to him, deals with what is given and technique with what is constructed. However, the distinction lacks clarity in his work, as, for example, when he considers technique the result of arbitrary will. Fourthly, he denies the power of reason to solve the problems of the universe, emphasizing the role of intuition in grasping reality, but he does not draw detailed rules from such an approach. Fifthly, he is too unrealistic in his belief that one could arrive at solutions that will be universally accepted. Finally, his givens are changeable factors. They, thus, lose the character of being given due to their changeability.

Dabin is quite ambiguous on the relationship of natural law with positive law. While, on the one hand, he claims that many positive laws have no moral significance even though they serve society, he claims, on the other hand, that positive law is prohibited from contradicting natural law. Moreover, since positive law in his view always includes a legal sanction that natural law does not, it is not clear how positive law can logically contradict natural law. Dabin seems uncertain on the question of whether a positive law contrary to natural law is not law at all or whether it is a law but does not bind the conscience. Also, when he calls for condemnation of immoral legal rules as contrary to the public good, it is not at all clear what that condemnation means. Should they be disobeyed, repealed, or what?

Cohen's ethical jurisprudence seems inadequate without laying down its basic ethical assumptions in detail with content. Only then would a judge have a criterion for choosing one normative principle over another. Furthermore, this jurisprudence, in order to be adequate, must include the scientific method for specifying ethical content, but this becomes an impossibility if the ethical is taken, as Cohen does, as a primitive (irreducible) concept.

The naivete of d'Entrèves lies in the fact that he considers humility and sincerity as sufficient guarantees against the fanaticism that natural law makes possible.

In Fuller, it is doubtful that the is-ought distinction disappears in a purposive activity, as he claims, for several significant reasons. Firstly, the argument is predicated upon the very distinction it denies. In order to judge whether an activity possesses the value attributed to it, it is necessary to know what the value being attributed is. This value ascription made upon something otherwise valueless is possible only after identifying that thing in non-evaluative terms. Thus, the distinction remains between the value (ought) and the fact (is) to which the value is being attributed. Secondly, the interpretation of purposive behavior necessitates an inquiry into whether specific acts achieve certain goals. In such an inquiry, value judgments necessarily occur that are in addition to those intrinsic to the behavior in question. Not only are such judgments initially made on the basis of values, but, furthermore, these values are not limited by those claimed to be intrinsic to the facts of the particular behavior. Thirdly, the fact that some behavior is purposive in nature implies only that the actor has the purpose, not that he ought to have it. In other words, both are *is* statements. *Ought* is not merged with *is* merely because the purpose in fact exists.

Moreover, when law is represented as a purposive activity under this theory, the meaning of "purpose" is not clear. It may mean, for example, something of which one must be conscious, or the forces determining one's conduct, or intentional acts, or the pursuing of a specific end, or the determinant of the means-end relationship, or the proximate or ulterior considerations, or something to be discerned from observable behavior alone. Whatever meaning is ascribed, it does not follow from the fact of purpose that the purpose is an *ought*. A purpose may be as it *is* or as it *ought* to be.

Although the theory claims that *is* and *ought* merge when the activity is purposive, there at best may be a merging of purpose and *action*, from which it does not follow that *ought* and *is* have thereby merged.

Additionally, the theory seems to confuse the judgments about the purpose of an activity with judgments about its morality; the two are not the same.

Also, the knowledge of the actor's purpose, while assisting the observer in organizing the observational data in a certain manner, reveals nothing about the moral quality of that purpose. The knowledge of the actor's purpose may disclose his dispositional characteristics, his permanent possibilities of performance, or even purposive criteria for evaluating his actions. But it does not, however, reveal the oughtness of his purpose. No value is derived from the mere fact.

Finally, while it is true that the adequacy of a description can be judged only with reference to the purpose for which the descriptive account is made, the account itself does not therefore become intrinsically evaluative. What is evaluative here is not the account itself but the judgment on the adequacy of the account rendered.

Does the is-ought distinction disappear in law when viewed as a purposive activity? This claim is based upon the assertion that the eight principles of Fuller's inner morality of law constitute an intrinsic, internal morality of law. This claim is difficult to accept since these eight principles appear to be no more than the minimum components of an efficiently functioning modern legal system. Furthermore, the formula seems to omit other conditions that may very well be considered as additional minimum requirements. For example, such conditions may include establishing authoritative law-making procedures at the outset, complying with these procedures, providing institutions for the authoritative interpretation of law, and providing for the execution of a law by public official or private citizen. In any case, to assert that this formula of efficacy is a statement of moral principles in any substantial sense of the term "morality" appears to claim too much. Although infringement of any of these eight requirements may result in a less effective legal system, this consequence is hardly sufficient to arouse a sense of moral culpability. On the other hand, violations of moral principles may occur from a law-making which may have fulfilled all of these requirements. The issue of morality remains untouched by these eight principles. One could say that these requirements apply to any legal system regardless of its ideology. Moreover, a mere violation of any of these requirements does not, in itself, result in official wrongdoing; rather, such wrongdoing arises from the unjust consequences resulting from the official's action. Therefore, these eight requirements do not provide the standard for determining immorality.

Fuller, nevertheless, defends his moral claim for his eight principles on the following six grounds:

1. *Only through these principles can substantially moral laws be achieved.*[72] However, while law is admittedly a precondition to good law, it is also clear that the adoption of these eight principles can result in immoral as well as moral laws.
2. *The requirements of generality, publicity, and congruent administration tend to assure morally good laws.*[73] While this may indeed be the tendency, morally good laws do not necessarily follow from these requirements. Also, the fact that these requirements may tend to achieve moral laws in no way proves that the requirements themselves are moral.

3. *The requirement of clarity is a moral principle, since some evil purposes cannot be clearly articulated in law.*[74] However, some good purposes are as difficult to articulate as some evil ones. Conversely, some morally repugnant laws are as clearly articulated as some morally laudable ones. Moreover, a law concerning a matter upon which there is general moral agreement in society makes no great demands for clear and precise articulation.

4. *The internal morality claimed by the purposive theory is moral because it implicitly views man as a responsible agent.*[75] However, one need not conclude that because a proposition implies a view of man as responsible, the implication itself is moral. Secondly, by adopting these eight requirements, one may become responsible for the efficacy of the law but not for its morality. Thirdly, the fact that a man is responsible does not ensure that he is thereby morally good in any substantive sense.

5. *Because these eight requirements are principles of institutional or political morality, or the morality of the officials acting in that capacity, they constitute morality.*[76] No one questions that the political morality or the morality of official conduct is properly called morality; rather, the issue is whether these eight requirements are determinative of the moral character of the official act. Clearly, for reasons mentioned above, the moral question remains untouched by these requirements. Nothing morally commendable follows from adherence to these principles; nothing morally reprehensible follows from nonadherence to them. It is possible to inflict a moral wrong by laws that are general, prospective, and clear, just as it is possible to correct a moral abuse by a retroactive law, the moral character of which will not be determined by the mere fact of its retroactivity.

6. *Violation of any of these requirements undermines the integrity of the law itself.*[77] If "the integrity of the law itself" means being efficacious as a result of being (a) general, (b) promulgated, (c) prospective (d) intelligible and clear, (e) uncontradictory, (f) not impossible in the demands it makes, (g) constant through time, and (h) congruent of official action and declared rule, then the point is well taken. However,

> this concept of integrity of the law cannot determine whether
> that law itself is moral.

In an attempt to defend the claim of morality for the above eight principles, it has been argued that: (1) the requirement of consistency is a moral condition since it would be morally unsatisfactory to impose sanctions where it is impossible to comply with inconsistent directives; (2) the requirement of not making impossible demands is a moral condition since it reflects the Kantian principle that *ought* implies *can*; and (3) the requirements of promulgation, understandability, and prospectiveness are moral conditions since it would be morally unsatisfactory to be punished for directives of which one is unaware, or which cannot be understood, or which are not prospective.[78] The totality of the principles constitute the intrinsic morality of law. Since the application of these principles can achieve a morally perverse law, it can be said, consistently with the purposive theory, that although a morally bad law has been achieved, the morality of law, nevertheless, remains intact because the eight conditions have been fulfilled. This is a very curious position.

Fuller and Mullock may respond by pointing that this criticism relates to the substance of law, a matter of extrinsic morality, while they are concerned with the form of law, a matter of intrinsic morality. However, this response brings to focus my point that the morality of law cannot be apprehended by the distinctions proposed by this theory. It cannot be apprehended by including things claimed by this theory to be intrinsic while excluding things claimed by it to be extrinsic. This "inner morality of law," represented by Fuller's principles, fails to account fully for the morality of law, because a moral accounting of law must do more than limit itself to matters of form. It must take recourse to that which is of substance, to that which is external to its form. The purposive theory sets forth the conditions deemed necessary and sufficient for the existence of a legal system, but the theory by no means establishes a logically necessary connection between moral principles and law. The connection that it establishes may be necessary practically, but not logically.[79]

4

IDEALIST THEORIES
OF LAW

The idealist theories about law are based upon the idealist epistemology discussed above in Chapter I and include, most prominently,
those of Kant, Hegel, Stammler, and Del Vecchio. These theories differ
widely from each other, but they all discover their fundamental principles through an inquiry into the human mind.

A. Law as Harmonizing Voluntary Actions: Immanuel Kant (1724–1804)

As indicated in Chapter I, for Kant the rational character of life and
the world in which man lives lies in human consciousness and not in
the observation of facts and matter. The method of philosophy, according to him, is not phsychological and empirical but critical. Therefore, he makes a systematic inquiry into the functions of human reason.

Accordingly, he discovers three functions of human consciousness,
namely, thinking, volition, and feeling, which, in his works, correspond

to perception (*Critique of Pure Reason*), morality (*Critique of Practical Reason*), and aesthetics (*Critique of the Power of Judgment*). His legal philosophy rests in volition (morality). Volition is derived from principles entirely different from the principles of perception (knowledge). There is a fundamental opposition between nature and mind, for whereas nature follows necessity, the human mind has a free will whereby it can set purposes for itself. Thus, knowledge and volition are sharply distinguished in Kant. Things appear to man in a chaos and human mind brings order into that chaos, but he cannot determine their course. In contrast, he can freely set aims for himself the realization of which is a matter of belief, not knowledge.

As we have seen while examining Kant's espistemology, general principles are arrived at in the area of knowledge. The question, therefore, arises whether there likewise exist general principles that can be laid down as a basis of volition and, therefore, of ethical action. Kant maintains that such a basis must be given *a priori*. It cannot be gained from experience and laid as logical necessity. It can only be given as a postulate. The ethical postulate is possible only because man has freedom. The conception of freedom is a conception of pure reason. It is, therefore, transcendent, in that no corresponding instance can be found in any possible experience. It is not an object of any possible theoretical knowledge. Thus, there exists a pure will in us that is the source of all moral conceptions and laws.

In the practical sphere of reason, the reality of freedom may be demonstrated by certain practical principles that prove a causality of the pure reason in the process of determining the activity of the will. Certain unconditional practical laws, especially the moral laws, are founded on this conception of freedom. These moral laws appear as imperatives commanding or prohibiting certain actions and, as such, they are categorical and unconditional, according to which certain actions are allowed or disallowed as being morally possible or impossible. They are not in the form of the technical or hypothethical imperative which says if you want this do that. This gives rise to the conception of a duty, the observance or transgression of which is accompanied by a moral feeling, a pleasure or pain of a peculiar kind. However, moral feelings are only the subjective effects and not the foundation of these laws. The possibility of categorical imperatives arises from the fact that they refer to no determination of the activity of the will but to its freedom.

A categorical imperative presents the action to the mind as objectively necessary. It expresses generally what constitutes obligation. Kant renders it in this formula: act according to a maxim that can be adopted at the same time as a universal law. This he claims to be the supreme principle of the science of morals, so that a maxim not thus qualified is contrary to morality.

The science of right, Kant maintains, has for its object the principles of all the laws the promulgation of which is possible by external legislation. By applying legislation to it, it becomes a system of positive right and law. The theoretical knowledge of right and law, as distinguished from positive laws, belongs to the pure science of law, which designates the philosophical and systematic knowledge of the principles of natural right. It is from this science, he maintains, that the immutable principles of all positive legislation must be derived.

The conception of right has three characteristics. One, it relates only to the external relation of one person to another through actions. Two, it does not indicate the relation of an individual to the mere wish or desire of another. Three, in this reciprocal relation of voluntary actions it does not consider the matter of the act of will but only the form of the transaction. Right, he thus concludes, comprehends the whole of the conditions under which the voluntary actions of any one person can be harmonized in reality with the voluntary actions of every other person, according to a universal law of freedom. Accordingly, every action is right which can co-exist along with the freedom of the will of each and all in action. Ethics, as distinguished from the knowledge of positive laws, imposes upon one the obligation to make the fulfillment of right a maxim of his conduct. Kant, thus, arrives at the universal law of right, namely, that one should act externally in such a manner that the free exercise of one's will may be able to co-exist with the freedom of all others, according to a universal law. He warns that this is not to be represented as a motive-principle of action (that one ought to limit one's freedom to these conditions merely because this law of right imposes obligation upon one), for his objective is to explain what is right, not to teach virtue.

Right, according to Kant, is accompanied with an implied warrant to bring compulsion to bear upon a violator of it, for an exercise of freedom, which is a hindrance of the freedom that is according to universal laws, is wrong, and compulsion opposed to it is right. Thus, the conception of right consists in the possibility of a universal reciprocal compulsion in harmony with the freedom of all. Therefore, right and the title to compel indicate the same thing. The law of right can thus be represented as a reciprocal compulsion in accordance with the freedom of every one, under the principle of a universal freedom.

As one would expect from Kant's primary assumption of the individual's freedom, political power for him is conditioned by the need to render each man's right effective and to limit it through the right of others. Security for all can result only from the collective universal will armed with absolute power. The social contract that makes this transfer of power is not an empirical or historical fact for Kant but an idea of reason. For Kant, there is an absolute duty to obey the existing legislative power; rebellion is never justified. The state is the protector and guardian of the law. The political ideal of the state is achieved when the spirit of freedom is united with obedience to law and loyalty to the state. The citizen may critize but not resist.

B. Law as the Idea of Freedom: Georg Wilhelm Friedrich Hegel (1770–1831)

In his attempt to give one complete theory of the universe, Hegel presents a comprehensive system of thought, the starting point of which is the Idea. The Idea is Reason and Spirit. It contains everything about the universe. The Idea unfolds by means of the dialectical process that proceeds through the triad of thesis, antithesis, and synthesis. Any concept (thesis) contains its own opposite (antithesis), and the passage from one to the other occurs through a third category of synthesis. For example, the conception of being (thesis) contains its opposite nothing (antithesis) and passes through becoming (synthesis); or essence (thesis) and appearance (antithesis) find their synthesis in actuality. A synthesis, in turn, becomes the starting point of a new triad. The entire universe, in all its aspects, unfolds in this fashion. This, in Hegel's scheme, is a logical process, and each part has a necessary logical connection with any other. Any aspect of reality is, thus, based on reason. For Hegel, it is the task of philosophy to show that what is reasonable is real and what is real is reasonable. Consequently, there is no conflict for him between idea and experience or reason and reality. What matters is to perceive in the temporal and transitory appearance the immanent and external substance.

Hegel's dialectical process of unfolding of the Idea may be presented as follows:

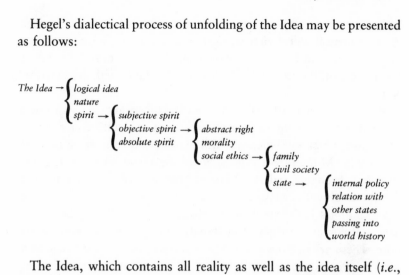

The Idea, which contains all reality as well as the idea itself (*i.e.*, the logical idea), contains as its antithesis idea outside itself (*i.e.*, nature), and the synthesis of logic and nature is the idea in and for itself (*i.e.*, spirit). Subjective spirit, *i.e.*, the categories of feeling, thinking, and consciousness, has its antithesis in the objective spirit, *i.e.*, legal and social institutions, and their synthesis is provided by the absolute spirit, *i.e.*, art, religion, and philosophy, which, as well, constitutes the full realization of the idea. Thus, absolute spirit is at the beginning as well as at the end of all things.

Law falls within the scope of the objective spirit. The triad of the objective spirit is (1) abstract right (thesis), (2) morality (antithesis), and (3) social ethics (synthesis).

Abstract right includes those rights and duties that belong to human beings not because they are citizens but simply because they are persons. These rights are of three categories, namely, property, contract, and wrong (tort and crime). Right to property results from the free will, since a thing may be appropriated by the person as a means to his satisfaction, and appropriation is manifestation of the majesty of one's will toward things by demonstrating that they have no purpose of their own. However, for Hegel, the consequence of the right to property being a result of the free will is not that property should be equally divided among persons but, rather, that it should be divided differently upon people's differing capacities and abilities. The antithesis of property is contract, whereby one can relinquish his property

111

by a voluntary act. Wrong results from the individual opposing himself to the universal will. Crime is, thus, a negation of the right, and the object of punishment is to restore right, or, that is to say, to restore the true will of the criminal, which is in accordance with the universal will.

Morality is the antithesis of abstract right. Morality, to Hegel, is a rational factor and not a subjective sentiment. It results from a wrong of the individual will when this will becomes different from the universal will. Morality consists in doing the universal when the will discovers through a dialectical process that any will opposing itself to the universal will is wicked.

Social ethics is the synthesis of abstract right and morality. It, in turn, unfolds in the triad of (a) family, (b) civil society, and (c) the state. These are institutions in which the will of the individual finds itself in concordance with the universal will. *Family* is an institution based on feelings. However, in marriage two independent personalities are given up to become one person, so that marriage is an institution based on reason, to which being-in-love is irrelevant. *Civil society* results when the members of the family acquire an independent status and no longer remain part of the family. The society, thus conceived as a society of individuals pursuing respective self-interests, is divided into estates, of which there are three: the agricultural class that depends on nature, the industrial and commercial class that depends on its work and reflection, and the universal or the governing class that depends on reason. Civil society demands an administration of justice that defines mutual relations through promulgated laws and courts, protection of the right to well-being through the police, and formation of groups of individuals into associations that promote the universal end of the society, since their aims are more universal than the aims of the individual.

The *state* is the synthesis of family and civil society. It unfolds in the triad of (i) the relation of the state to its members (internal polity or constitution), (ii) the relation of the state to other states, and (iii) passing of the state into world history. In its *internal polity*, the state is the embodiment both of the individual freedom and the universal. Therefore, it has three aspects: the universal (laws), the particular (application of laws to specific cases), and the individual (the monarch). Thus, the state is not the external authority imposed upon the individual but the realization of the individual's true universal self.

The state is conceived as freedom. The state is the manifestation of the rational will and not, therefore, the common (or the majority) will. In the *relation of the state to other states*, states have no objective sphere of universal right among them, and their perpetually shifting relations are ultimately settled by war. In the synthesis of the *passing of the state into world history*, the actual mind of a single nation that actualizes itself through the inter-relation of the particular rational minds actualizes itself as the universal mind in the process of world history. The right of the universal world-mind is supreme.

In this methodology, by right Hegel means not merely civil law but also morality, ethical life, and world history, since this concept brings thoughts together into what he calls a true system. Having examined the dialectical stages, he concludes that the right of the state stands above the preceding stages and is freedom in its most concrete shape, subordinate only to the supreme absolute truth of the world-mind.

C. Law as the Adjustment of Purposes: Rudolph Stammler (1856–1938)

According to Stammler, as with Kant, there is a fundamental distinction between perception and volition. Law belongs to volition, since it is not concerned with perceiving the world but with relating means and purposes to each other. The concept of law is the universally valid element common to all legal phenomena regardless of their content. Such an element can only be formal, a method whereby the necessarily changing material of the empirically conditioned legal rules may be so worked out, judged, and determined that they shall have the quality of objective justice. Stammler is, therefore, concerned with a universal method as such in the sense of a formal process with absolute system. He is not concerned with any specific content of particular cases that may be worked out by this method. His quest is for the process of arranging, a method of absolute validity since it is not affected by the changeable material of historical fact.

A universally valid concept of law serves two purposes for Stammler. Philosophically, it responds to the mind's desire to reduce all phenomena to a unity, which is a peculiar ultimate of ordering the contents of our consciousness. Practically, it distinguishes law from religion, morality, history, etc. Law, according to Stammler, is combining sovereign and inviolable volition. Thus, the elements of law are: (a) volition, since it is a mode of ordering acts to the relation of means and purposes; (b) volition of men in their mutual relations, which, in law, is combined; (c) sovereign volition, as distinguished from arbitrary volition of an individual, not in the sense of political sovereignty of one will over another; and (d) permanency of the bond created by law, since it is inviolable.

Thus, according to Stammler, the question of the possibility of realizing a purpose is distinct from that of the justice of its content, in that the realization of purpose considers an occurrence according to the laws of experience but the realization of justice aims at a systematic insight into the content of the volitional consciousness. A universal element of legal propositions is the idea of adjusting the individual desire to the purposes of the community. By community Stammler means the formal unity of the individual purposes, not a concrete association having certain conditioned aims. The community is thus a method of combining into an absolute unit the isolated desires of the individuals with a common and final purpose. The idea of just law means the unity of the methodical adjustment of individual purposes in accordance with the one final purpose of the community.

Therefore, Stammler's idea of law corresponds to the practical reason of Kant, mentioned above. However, in Kant pure reason (critical knowledge of things) is opposed to practical reason (purposes set by belief and volition), but in Stammler the critical knowledge of law is the analysis of purposes and not the knowledge of a physical phenomenon. The purpose of just law is to assist in the formulation of a fundamental conception of life. Just law, he claims, is the highest point in the study of social life of men, the only thing that makes it possible to think of social existence as a unitary whole, the way to unite with other fundamental endeavors aimed at right consciousness.

We, thus, have in Stammler the concept of law and the idea of law, the former providing the universal elements of law and the latter directing means and purposes to one aim. The idea, too, has to be a formal one for the reasons mentioned above and has to give expression to the idea of free will. This formal idea is the social ideal of a free-willing community of men. Thus, in Stammler there is a conjunction of the notion of community on the one hand and the notion of man being an end in himself on the other.

Derived from this analysis are the maxims concerning respect and participation. The maxims as to respect are (a) that a person's volition must not be subject to the arbitrary desire of another, and (b) that any legal demand must be of such a nature that the addressee can be his own neighbor. The maxims as to participation are: (a) that a member of a legal community cannot be excluded from the community, and (b) that a legal power may be exclusive only to the extent that the excluded person can still be his own neighbor. The adjustment of volitions in the community is made in accordance with these maxims of right law.

Finally, in addition to the concept of law and the idea of law, Stammler considers the validity of law. There he makes the admission that critical knowledge in this area needs be assisted by a psychological supplement, thereby introducing an empirical element into his purely formal theory.

D. Law as the Principle of Legal Evolution: Georgio Del Vecchio (1878–1970)

Del Vecchio is another neo-Kantian philosopher. He distinguishes between the concept of law and the ideal of law and maintains that it is an error to take an ideal for a definition. The concept of law is its logical form, which embraces that ideal as well as all other possible juridical systems. Since juridical evaluations imply an intersubjective or transubjective reference as to what a subject can juridically do with regard to another, law is the objective coordination of possible actions between several subjects according to an ethical principle that determines them and excludes the impediments thereto.

While moral evaluations are subjective and unilateral, juridical evaluations are objective and bilateral. Between these two kinds of ethical determinations (*i.e.*, subjective or moral and objective or juridical) there is a fundamental relationship in that what is a duty is always right and that what cannot be a duty is not right. Thus, if in a given system a certain action is proper, then an impediment to that action by others must not be possible, or else it would not be an ethical system.

The characteristics of law, according to Del Vecchio, are bilateralness, generality, imperativeness, and coercibility. (1) Bilateralness, according to him, is the keystone of the juridical edifice, whereunder law brings together at least two subjects and gives a norm for both, unlike morality which directs itself to the subject *per se* and imposes

115

upon him a choice between actions which he can perform. Thus, in law, what is possible for one party is not impedible by the other. (2) He concedes that generality is not absolutely necessary since it is possible, albeit in rare cases, to establish a juridical norm by a relationship that is individually determined, such as a provision in the Italian Constitution of his times that the former kings of the House of Savoy cannot enter and live in the national territory. However, he maintains that the juridical norm, according to its proper nature and as a rule, is general, since it must serve as a basis for regulating future relationships, which can only be done in a general way. (3) Law, like morals, is an imperative. (4) But law's distinction is the characteristic way in which the imperative is manifested. Law is coercible, so that it can be made to prevail by force in case of non-observance. Del Vecchio deduces this coercibility from the logical nature of law. Since in law there is always a relationship between several subjects and a limitation between them, he argues that if the limitation is not observed, as when one invades the sphere of juridical power of another, the possibility of coercion used to reject that transgression necessarily arises.

According to Del Vecchio, the confusion between the concept of law and the ideal of law has led, on the one hand, the natural law jurists to identify the metaphysical concept with the physical concept of nature and, on the other hand, the positive law jurists to consider only the existence of positive law and to deny an ideal criterion of the positive law. The former erred in thinking that to assert the validity of an ideal they needed to rely upon historical reality. The latter erred in deducing the non-existence of law as an ideal from the fact that it does not always exist as a verifiable phenomenon. As Del Vecchio sees it, the correspondence between the ideal and the empirical must be sought in more advance phases of reality. Man has a predetermined purpose toward which he must progress in experience, in order to become in appearance what he in himself already is. The ideal of law designates the goal of its historical evolution. That evolution, even though frequently interrupted, conduces to an increasing recognition of the autonomy of the human being as the fulfillment of a supreme exigency of reason in its universality. A juridical coordination of all humanity in a worldwide human law, thus, tends to be constituted positively. The principles of that universal law are predetermined in nature. Reason deduces those principles *a priori* before they are verified *a posteriori* and actualized in contingencies of fact. He finds the evidence of this evolutionary process in existing law of the more progressed states, as distinguished from the primitive juridical systems.

While justice rests in a formal idea, it also has a substantial meaning and implies a faculty of evaluation. While, on the one hand, consciousness postulates reciprocity in a formal sense, on the other hand, it produces a definite valuation. The sentiment of justice (*sentimento giuridico*) has the ability instinctively to valuate legal phenomena.

Criticism

1. Kant

One cannot doubt the exciting originality of Kant's theory. However, there are some troublesome propositions in it:

1. Kant's definition of law as the whole of conditions under which the will of each can coexist with the will of others, according a universal law of freedom, may give us an ideal but it certainly does not give us a logical definition of law that can summarize all possible juridical experience. Such a definition would exclude all those positive juridical systems that do not recognize equal liberty of all persons. That would be excluding many systems, so many that it would appear that perhaps law has never existed.

2. For Kant moral rules are absolutely imperative. His categorical imperative is the basis of his moral as well as legal philosophy. Surely there is a distinction between morals and law in his theory in that morality is a matter of internal motives of the individual and legality a matter of action in conformity with an external standard set by law, but the principle of the two is the same. Morals, for him, cannot rest on experience, history, prudence, or expediency. However, it seems that there do exist moral duties, such as not telling lies, which might be enforced by law but, instead, are left to individual conscience or social pressure for the reason that their legal enforcement would be too inconvenient or too expensive. Kant would not admit of this since this would be a matter of expediency.

3. There do exist duties that are legal but not moral, such as unintentional wrongs, but they do invite legal penalties.

4. Kant insists that justification for obedience to the legislators lies in natural or moral law. As we well know, actual laws are not always

perfectly just. However, Kant's insistence removes all possibility of disobeying laws that are contrary to nature or principles of justice and it renders the struggle for justice meaningless.

5. For Kant each rule of morality is absolute in its own right. However, people obey laws because they balance advantages and disadvantages in respect to the main body of law, and they tolerate its imperfections for lack of a feasible alternative, and not because each specific rule is absolute in its own right.

6. As is clear in Kant, his categorical imperative as the supreme principle of morals cannot yield specific moral duties, since his objective is to explain right and not to teach virtue. According to him, these duties result from dictates of conscience which, to him, are universal, clear, and absolutely certain. However, there are two difficulties with this reliance on conscience. In the first place, conscience is variable from holder to holder and very much uncertain. Secondly, that being so, the result would be a number of diverse rules dictated by the variety of conscience, but, logically, there cannot be diverse rules each of which is absolute.

7. Human existence is an empirical matter. Therefore, it seems neither possible in fact nor persuasive in thought that rules for its moral conduct can be prescribed *a priori* without empirical knowledge, merely by an exercise of some pure reason. In fact Kant's theory signifies nothing until its meaning is disclosed by empiricism.

8. The formalistic conception of justice does not yield justice. In the first place, its form cannot be satisfactory if developed by a technique uninformed by the empirical facts of living. Secondly, it cannot do justice, or breathe meaning into doing justice, without facts.

9. Right, in Kant's conception, is purely rational in origin. This means that the actual content of laws can be determined from purely logical or formal principles. But he does not show how it is possible to do so.

10. The role of the transcendental free will is suspect in matters of law. Law deals with external acts of human beings in time and place. The freedom that is at issue is empirical, not transcendental or metaphysical. The cruelty of deflecting the issue into the transcendental is well exhibited in Kant himself who, while elaborating magnificently on the transcendental free will, denies us the freedom to resist or disobey unjust laws.

11. In matters of law, necessarily a matter in the context of plurality,

it seems untenable to begin with a proposition of the absolute freedom of the individual.

12. It is not logically possible for the transcendental freedom to explain the moral life of humans, for you need the non-transcendental, or the phenomenal, in order to even know what a human being is.

13. There is an interaction between the transcendental and the temporal in that the moral determination of pure reason has practical effects in time and, conversely, temporal social arrangements are judged unjust when they conflict with the transcendental freedom. The transcendental, therefore, loses its purely rational and non-temporal character as claimed by Kant.

14. Kant's ideal of freedom, whereunder each person's freedom of will is limited only by the like freedom of will of others, is only one of the social ideals, either as a possibility in thought or as a practice in history. There have been other social ideals, such as, for example, right embodied in law, or in force, power, the supremacy of dynasties, nationalism or self-government, and so on. There is no objective truth that compels us to prefer Kant's ideal over others. It is a matter of ideological choice. As pointed out in Chapter I, here is an example of the incipience of ideology in philosophy.

15. There are problems with the proposition that law concerns only external acts. In the first place, the proposition is not entirely true to fact. There are counter examples in legal history, such as laws punishing a person for merely imagining or intending to kill the king. There is nothing inherent in the nature of law that precludes it from concerning itself with the non-external, psychic life. Also, it is not clear what is an external act. Is remaining silent an external act? Yet, remaining silent has legal consequences of liability, say, in torts, when the defendant landowner does not warn his invitee of a hidden danger.

16. Kant's justification of compulsion proceeds from the premise that in society there exist freewilling individuals and that compulsion is right since, and insofar as, it hinders the hindrance of freedom. However, it is not possible for completely freewilling individuals to live in society. If one dismisses this premise, so goes Kant's justification for compulsion or authority.

17. The test of rightness is so general in Kant that it can admit of numerous possibilities. He gives no test of choosing between them. When one observes for guidance how he himself has applied his theory, one comes out with a clear impression of utter arbitrariness. For ex-

ample, he is quite arbitrary in choosing the definition of marriage as a union of two persons of different sexes for reciprocal possession of their sexual faculties throughout their lives over any other possible definition of marriage.

18. Kant's categorical imperative is not intended to yield specific rules, but even as a general ethical guide it is unconvincing. It strikes one as an intuitive and dogmatic hunch. Moreover, one cannot be sure, in the reciprocity of relations, that the other person is proceeding in accordance with the moral maxim formulated in accordance with the categorical imperative so that one, in turn, can proceed accordingly.

19. Kant no doubt constructs the individual as a person simply, as distinguished from a person as a citizen, and makes the state bound to follow the law that results as its consequence, but he fails to show how the state must necessarily do so. The point is even further lost when he denies the individual any right to revolt against the state.

2. Hegel

1. Hegel's dialectical system is remarkable indeed. But he seems to have confused opposites with distinctions. Many of the concepts and institutions that appear in his triads, discussed above, are not opposites or antitheticals of each other but, rather, different aspects of the social life. There may even have been some progressive development among them, but not necessarily through opposition of one of another.

2. Moreover, while he purports to use his dialectical method to draw logical deductions, he has in fact used it very arbitrarily. He is so carried away by his triads that one finds in his theory such fantastic propositions as, for example, property being the antithesis of contract, wrong (tort and crime) being the synthesis of property and contract, the police being an institution of civil society rather than of the state, and so on.

3. Hegel maintains that only a rational and moral will is free, since the arbitrary will, moved only by impulses and appetites, wants incompatible things and is necessarily frustrated. He further claims that man is free only when he desires and is able to do what he ought to do. However, from the fact that man must have a rational will in order to attain freedom it does not follow that an action that is inconsistent with his own principles is not free. This action may even

frustrate or reduce his freedom, but the action may, nevertheless, be free. There seems to be a confusion in Hegel between the attributes of a free action and the requirements for attaining freedom. Conversely, a man may be entirely rational and yet not free, as when his principles are inconsistent with the established laws.

4. Hegel seems to assume that although the individual must conform to laws whatever they be in order to be fully rational, there must be a fully rational universal will, or a self-consistent moral system, in order for him to be fully rational. However, man's rationality does not depend upon a moral or legal system.

5. Hegel assumes that there is a continual development toward harmony between the individual will and the universal will in which his conception of world history represents the necessary progress of spirit toward rationality. Therefore, his system cannot admit of a plurality of legal or moral systems and universal wills, all of which could be equally rational. Denial of this plurality has the tendency to foster dogmatism.

6. Hegel maintains a close connection between the individual's rational will and the universal will, so that a man's rational will is the universal will manifest in him, all reality being universal spirit manifest. However, such an identity of the universal will with the individual's rational will does not exist. The universal will is found in laws and conventions that are not the same thing as the individual's will.

7. For Hegel it is a necessary and logical development from the concept of will that it be realized in the communities of free persons. However, it seems that will implies deliberate choice. The will is realized whenever that choice is made. This realization of the will does not have to be located only in the communities of free persons. Alternatively, if by realization of the will is meant happening of this event when people capable of making choice constitute a community of free persons, there is no logical necessity for such occurrence.

8. There seems, in Hegel, the thought, as seen in the development of will from concept to Idea, that people conceive of freedom, ascribe to it the supreme value, and attain it under certain conditions, all of this being logically deducible from the will. However, the dynamics of freedom and its attainment are not so tightly connected in logic.

9. There is also in his philosophy of right an incipience of political doctrine. That doctrine consists in maintaining that freedom and the type of community in which freedom is realized are good and, there-

fore, desirable. Man is free when he accepts the established order conscientiously and not merely from habit. In fact, it is only from this political doctrine, and not from the nature of freedom, that Hegel's condemnation of disobedience can possibly follow.

10. Hegel maintains that the state in which freedom is realized is desirable, and it is desirable to the extent freedom is realized. That he did not advocate blind obedience to an actual state is clear from his philosophy of history, where he praises Socrates and Luther who by defying authority raised humanity to a higher level. However, his theory lends itself to the danger of being used as an argument for absorption of the individual in the state. In fact, it has been used to justify such a supremacy of actual state, a responsibility which perhaps is not that of his theory if carefully understood. Nevertheless, the danger does exist.

11. Hegel equivocates in the use of his term contradiction, that which exists between his thesis and antithesis. Its several meanings in his use have been: (a) as denoting distinct but inseparable aspects of a whole, which makes his dialectical process logical; (b) as denoting a logical exclusion of one concept by another so that if one applies the other cannot, the contradiction being resolved when both can apply to the same thing; (c) as denoting contrast of one with the other, the contradiction being resolved when they are superseded by something that combines their contrasted characteristics; (d) as denoting a necessary incompatibility between them, their contradiction being resolved when they are superseded by something in which the incompatibility is removed; and (e) as denoting one implying the other in the sense either that they are inseparable aspects of a whole or that they are stages in a necessary process.

12. Examining his contradiction between abstract right and morality more closely, it appears that he means them (a) to imply each other, (b) to contrast with each other, and (c) to be necessarily incompatible with each other. Now, one cannot dispute that there can be incompatibilities between abstract right and morality, but it is not necessary that there be this conflict and its resolution.

13. Examining his contradiction between family and civil society, it appears that he is using the term "contradiction" in the sense of negation, a sense quite different from that used in connection with abstract right and morality. Civil society negates the family, since the former arises from the breakup of the latter, and this happens as of

logical necessity. Such a proposition is hard to accept. There may be certain types of family, such as the extended family or kinship group, whose breakup has given rise to civil society, but that has happened not because of a necessity internal to it but because of external, sociological, causes. It is not necessary that the family should so break up. Furthermore, in the emergence of civil society, one type of family might give way to another, instead of the family breaking up, and even that is not logically necessary. There is no necessary contradiction between the family and the civil society that is resolved in the state.

3. Stammler

1. Stammler proceeds upon the assumption that purely formal categories exist. However, the categories claimed as formal are not really formal but, rather, are categories of progressive generalization. More general categories are more formal, and the less general ones are less formal. Therefore, it is doubtful whether in social matters it is possible for purely formal categories to exist.

2. But even if we grant Stammler the existence of formal categories, there are problems in proceeding with them. Stammler, like Kant, attempts to derive specific conclusions of justice from purely formal principles. But, in logic, no particular existential propositions can be derived from pure universals. Thus, from his ideal of a community of free-willing men the particular conclusions derived by him do not necessarily follow. Other, and different, conclusions can equally be drawn from it. There is nothing in his concept to disprove the compatibility of opposing claims with the ideal. For example, he claims that most societies condemn an agreement by couples to live together without marriage, but he does not show how in logic this is contrary to the ideal of a community of free-willing men. Or, he maintains that one volition must not be arbitrarily made subject to another volition, but by use of the meaningless term arbitrary one could approve or disapprove anything. No material guidance can be provided by formal categories.

3. In his attempt to determine the external form of all just law on the basis of the Kantian distinction between form and content, Stammler rejects all material ends as empirical and sets up the pure form of the community of free-willing men as the absolute end which is valid for all times and places. However, he fails to show how a purely logical

form can determine the actual content of a law without material premises.

4. He attempts to extend knowledge through analysis of concepts, but such an analysis can yield only analytic judgments, not knowledge.

5. In his extreme logicism the noncontradiction of a concept is the only criterion of its truth. The intrinsic value of the concept is, therefore, relegated to the extraneous or the irrelevant.

6. The predominance of pure idea over reality, which is Kant's method as well, necessarily compels the follower of that method to ignore actual moral values. This is disastrous in studying such a subject as law, which is fraught with these values.

7. His conclusions of just law do not logically follow from his premises. They, rather, seem to be the product of his particular biases and social values. For one thing, there is a discomforting vagueness that leaves one unsure what are the relations of his just law to the positive law of a given place and time. He does not, for example, tell us whether the just law imposes itself on the lawmaker and becomes the basis of positive law. It is not at all clear how his ideal is to be adapted to the practical exigencies of social life. Moreover, his exclusively formalistic approach makes it logically impossible to move from concepts to realities of social life. While his formulae may possess formal virtues of unity, generality, and universal validity, they are incapable of relating to facts of life. His principles of just law, like Kant's maxims of moral law, are not proven in any way but are affirmed simply and dogmatically. Furthermore, it is hard to see how they apply to social life. Stammler's own concrete solutions seem to be independent of his formulae, rather than necessitated by them. He has not solved the relationship of just law and law, apart from propagating his own particular ideological preferences.

8. His ideal of justice is clearly a mixture of his formal proposition and his definite social ideal. Thus, his solutions depend on the very factors of ethical valuations that he meant to exclude from his formal idea.

9. Finally, there is the basic question as to whether the legal systems of the world follow any *a priori* logic. We can agree with Stammler that the notion of purpose inheres in law, but it is hard to agree that such purpose is determined by *a priori* concepts. Moreover, while logic is a valuable tool of analysis, one cannot create principles of justice from the rules of logic alone.

4. Del Vecchio

Once again, it is doubtful if an *a priori* method of arriving at the concept of law can provide the needed insights into matters of law. Such an approach dangerously separates law from the context of social life. Thus, deductions from Del Vecchio's concept of law would tell us that law deals with will-acts, but a person is in law both responsible for acts not willed by him and reaps the benefits of acts not willed by him. As an example of the former, a person is held liable in torts under the doctrine of *respondeat superior* for acts which are not willed by him but are the acts of his servants. As an example of the latter, a person inherits property under the laws of inheritance and succession as a result of acts not willed by him.

Another example of the above-mentioned dangerous divorce from reality is seen in Del Vecchio's analysis that law is always determined by some ethical principle. This is erroneous. For, in the first place, iniquitous laws are found both in the consciousness of humans as well as in the body of laws. In the second place, there are laws that do not have anything to do with ethics but are only a convenient way of doing things.

Finally, Del Vecchio's concept of juridicial sentiment (*sentimento giuridico*) as an intuitive test for valuating legal phenomena, discussed above, is so mystical that it can be used to justify anything.

In the end, therefore, looking critically at the idealist perception of law, the conclusion is inescapable that it is quite metaphysical, as natural law was in the previous chapter, and, therefore, is capable of justifying whatever ideological position its user wishes to justify.

5

POSITIVIST THEORIES
OF LAW

The positivist theories about law have as their basis the empiricist epistemology that holds that the source of knowledge lies in experience rather than reason. These include (A) the early theories, such as those of Kautilya, Shang Iang, Shuen Tao, and Han Fei Tzu, (B) the command theory of law of the utilitarians (Bentham, Mill, and Austin), (C) the normative theory of law of Kelsen, and (D) the rule theory of law of Hart. A shift from the metaphysical to the empirical is clearly evident in these theories. Moreover, they maintain a fundamental separation of law as it is from law as it ought to be. The analytical positivists regard values as irrelevant to jurisprudence. They concentrate upon the structure of the positive legal systems.

A. Early Positivist Theories of Law:

1. *Kautilya (India, Fourth Century* B.C.)

Kautilya is probably the first propounder of the positivist theory of law in history. In the traditional Indian discussions, philosophy came formally to be associated with the concern for the release of the individual soul from the cycle of reincarnation and the union of that soul with the ultimate, absolute soul (*moksha*). Values fell under the categories of *dharma* (law or virtue), *artha* (wealth), *kama* (pleasure), and *moksha* (soul). The first three, known as the *trivanga* (group of three), were generally treated as separate from the *moksha* and were usually bypassed in most metaphysical systems. Consequently, separate treatises have been devoted to *dharma*, *artha*, and *kama*. *Artha*, viewed as political and not merely economic power, is treated most elaborately in Kautilya's *Arthasastra*, who was the minister of the Emperor Chardragupta in the fourth century B.C. Kautilya believes that monarchy has advantages over other forms of government, and he identifies the welfare of the people with the welfare of the monarch.

According to Kautilya, therefore, the Rod of the king is the means for ensuring the pursuit of philosophy, the duties established by the Vedas, and economics. The purposes of wielding the Rod are: (a) the acquisition of things not possessed, (b) the preservation of things possessed, (c) the augmentation of things possessed, and (d) the bestowal of things augmented on a worthy recipient. The orderly maintenance of worldly life depends upon the wielding of the king's Rod. In order to maintain order of worldly life, the king should always hold the Rod up to strike, since there is no better means for the subjugation of human beings than the Rod. A king without the Rod is a source of terror to human beings, a king mild with the Rod is despised, and a king just with the Rod is honored. When used after full consideration, the Rod endows the subjects with spiritual good, material well-being, and pleasures of the senses. When used unjustly—that is, in passion, anger, or contempt—it enrages people. If not used at all, it gives rise to the law of the fish wherein the stronger swallows the weak. Administration of the Rod brings security and well-being to people when it is rooted in discipline. Discipline is both inborn and acquired, since training gives discipline only to one suited for it.

2. Shang Iang (China, ?–338 B.C.)

Legalism in China was a product of the Chinese politics of the fourth and third centuries B.C., which were marked by the tendency for consolidation of power through absorption of small states by larger ones, elimination of the authority of the nobles over their peasants, administration of justice directly by the officials of the central government, and centralization of tax collection. While the earlier Confucianism dealt with ethical norms, legalism analyzed the realities of power. It was, therefore, an expression of the positivist view of law. It emphasized state power rather than popular welfare. In fact, it was not so much concerned with law as with increase in the power of the state governments both at home and in inter-state relations.

The contention between the Confucianists and the Legalists related to the scope of official judgment as against fixed and impersonal laws. The former contended that laws must be enforced by men, so that, if the ruler and his officials were upright, a permanent body of laws would be unnecessary. The latter contended that a uniform set of standards ought to apply to the entire population, so that law ought not to be subject to the discretion of magistrates. Moreover, they conceived of law as self-operative in the sense that the ruler publishes his decrees and a fixed penalty is imposed for each offense, without any exceptions for rank or extenuating circumstances.

The notable propounders of Chinese Legalism include Shang Iang, Shuen Tao, and Han Fei Tzu, the last one being the leading exponent of this theory of law.

Kung-sun Iang, the later Lord Shang, or Shang Iang, is ranked among the most prominent statesmen of ancient China. He speaks of the supremacy of law and maintains that a country is governed through three instrumentalities: (a) laws, (b) the certainty that the laws will be enforced, and (c) the power to carry the laws in effect. The king alone is the custodian of power. The administration of law rests jointly with him and his ministers. In order to establish the supremacy of law, it is their joint duty to apply it strictly.

Laws are fixed standards of justice. The ever-changing minds cannot be trusted as guides. Thus, he argues, we cannot do away with laws. Although once in a rare while a generation may produce a perfectly wise and unselfish ruler, it is better to be content with a government by fixed laws, in spite of its defects, than wait for a wise governor and meanwhile suffer the evils of a commonplace ruler who is neither wise nor restrained by laws. Therefore, he maintains that laws are necessary in the community as it exists. Consequently, those who behave within legal bounds must be protected and rewarded by the government, and those who defy the laws must be punished without mercy. He believes that people will find an unfailing guide of legality in the system of rewards and punishments when that system is well settled and promulgated, in which case they will have have no occasion for disputes.

The ruler, he maintains, has no right to treat his power as a personal monopoly, so that he must exercize it for the national welfare. Maintaining the supremacy of law results in justice and avoids mischiefs of personal judgment. The former is achieved since justice is the consummation of unselfishness and laws are the very means for bringing it about, so that an unselfish ruler necessarily maintains the supremacy of law. The latter is achieved since placing transitory opinions before laws would give rise to deceptive and oppressive practices of the magistrates.

3. *Shuen Tao (China, Contemporary of Shang Iang)*

Shuen Tao defines law as a body of uniform and impartial rules of civil conduct designed to regulate the activities of a nation. He argues that within the definite limits of law there is no room for the cunning and the wicked. Therefore, law should never be violated. Laws tend to unify the minds of the people. Therefore, even a legal system that is not perfect is better than lawlessness. Statutes and sanctioned customs are intended to work out justice and equity, just as the standard weight is designed to establish fair dealing.

4. *Han Fei Tzu (China 280?–233 B.C.)*

Han Fei Tzu partly opposes Confucianism and partly reinterprets it in accordance with his way of thinking. Like his teacher Hsün Tzu, he regards human nature as fundamentally evil. But unlike Hsün Tzu, he does not believe that education and culture are capable of redeeming it. As noted above, the Confucianists argue that government ministers should be selected on the basis of their upright character, but Han Fei Tzu believes that all officials are potentially dishonest so that each should be made to act as a check upon the others. The masses, in his opinion, are ignorant and incapable of seeing beyond their own immediate interests and government should direct itself to them. Proceeding from these premises, he concludes that a strict set of laws and penalties, impartially enforced, is indispensable to public order. The sovereign, like the helmsman of a ship, makes slight movements with the two handles of reward and punishment and the whole state follows his dictates. While statecraft keeps the sovereign in power, the laws are to be obeyed by the people. The intelligent ruler ensures that his subjects do not let their minds wander beyond the scope of the law. Once laws have been established, everyone should obey them. In fact, he maintains that in the state of the intelligent ruler only the laws serve as teachings. There are no other books and records. This, incidentally, led the first emperor of the Chin Empire to burn the books.

5. Criticism

In Kautilya, there is a naive belief that the Rod of the king has the power of ensuring the pursuit of philosophy, the duties established by the Vedas, and economics. He ignores the role of the intrinsic worth of these particular matters as an account for their realization.

Chinese Legalism avoids the naive idealism of some of the Confucianists, but its own ethical deficiencies issue from its emphasis on the state power almost to the exclusion of popular welfare, its condemnation of the people as necessarily possessed of evil nature, and its almost blind trust in the government. Also, its trust in the self-operativeness of law is mistaken inasmuch as it views that operation of law is strictly a matter of promulgating decrees and imposing penalties for their violation without any exception or any regard to extenuating circumstances. Moreover, its explanation for obedience of law as exclusively a matter of rewards and punishment ignores the fact that laws are obeyed in a general sense because values are achieved thereby. Furthermore, to regard laws posited by the ruler as the only source of wisdom to the exclusion of all other sources, as Han Fei Tzu does, is clearly mistaken. Finally, the Legalist theory ignores the fact that at least a minimal tacit consent of the populace is required for any government to function.

B. Later Positivist Theories of Law

1. Command Theory of Law of the Utilitarians:
Jeremy Bentham (1748–1832), John Stuart Mill (1806–1873),
John Austin (1790–1859)

The command theory of law takes utility as the foundation of morals. The concept of utility is primarily propounded by Jeremy Bentham and John Stuart Mill.

Bentham maintains that the public good ought to be the object of the legislator and general utility ought to be the foundation of his reasoning. Thus, the science of legislation consists in knowing the true good of the community, and its art lies in finding the means to realize that good.

As Bentham sees it, nature has placed man under the empire of pleasure and pain, to which we refer all life's determinations and judgments. Utility is the attribute of a thing to prevent some evil or procure some good. That which conforms to the utility for an individual is that which tends to augment the total sum of his happiness. That which conforms to the utility for a community is that which tends to augment the total sum of the happiness of the individuals that compose that community. Good is pleasure, evil is pain. The purpose of law is to attain good and to avoid evil, or in other words, to serve utility. Bentham uses pain and pleasure in their ordinary signification and excludes metaphysics from his consideration of them. Moral good or moral evil are so because of their tendency to produce physical good or evil, respectively, although the physical includes the senses as well as the soul.

Thus, Bentham's utilitarianism is clearly individualistic and egalitarian. However, this leads him not to anarchism but to law, which must serve the totality of individuals in a community. Consequently, he conceives of the end of legislation as the greatest happiness of the greatest number. The logical result of this is the subordination of the individual's right to the need of the community, hence Bentham's opposition to any theory of inalienable rights.

He believes that any particular legal or political philosophy is a matter of faith. Its premises in themselves are not capable of deduction. For his own utilitarianism he claims no more. He freely concedes that its rectitude cannot be either formally tested or directly proved, since that which is used to prove everything else cannot itself be proved.

The problem arises of reconciling the happiness of the greatest number with the sum of the pleasures of each individual. Bentham uses sympathy as the means to provide this reconciliation or identity between the two, since amidst unhappiness no one would be happy. It is pain, therefore evil, therefore not in conformity with utility, to be among unhappy people. Unrestrained behavior of one would justify unrestained behavior of others and thereby reduce everyone's happiness. This, incidentally, is reminiscent of Kant's definition of law, discussed in the previous chapter, except that while Kant derived this result from his categorical imperative, Bentham derives it from his principle of pleasure.

John Stuart Mill, who was Bentham's disciple as well as critic, recognizes the naiveté of Bentham's belief in the non-existence of conflict between individual and general utility and attempts to relate justice to utility. He points out that the meaning of justice is exceedingly unstable and controversial and that the eternal notions of justice are incompatible with the changing notions of utility and interest. He, therefore, provides the notion of the sentiment of justice as the means for reconciling justice with utility. The sentiment of justice is the feeling of right within an individual that would in itself lead him to resent anything disagreeable to him, which feeling is tempered by the social feeling. He conceives of just persons resenting a hurt to society even though that is not a hurt to themselves and, conversely, not resenting a hurt to themselves unless it is such that the society has a common interest in repressing it. The sentiment of justice therefore combines individual self-assertion with consciousness of the general good. This, too, is reminiscent of Kant's categorical imperative, discussed in the previous chapter. Through the individual's will and his sentiment for justice, Mill, like Hegel, has resolved the individual with the social interest to the point of eliminating any dualism between the two.

Law, to Bentham, is a collection of signs declaring the sovereign will of the state concerning the conduct to be observed by its subjects, which observance is achieved by means of expectation of certain events to occur with the intent of making the possibility of such occurrence a motive for that conduct. Thus it can be considered in eight respects: source (person whose will it expresses), subjects (persons or things whereupon it applies), objects (acts and circumstances to which it applies), extent (the generality of its application), aspects (various manners in which it applies to its object acts and circumstances), force (motives it relies on to bring the desired effect and means, or corroborative appendages upon which it relies to bring those motives into play), expression (nature of the signs by which the sovereign's will is declared), and its remedial appendages, which may occasionally be used to obviate mischief.

John Austin's theory of law is considered the most comprehensive formulation of a modern system of analytical positivism, although his definition of law, as we shall see below, is substantially similar to that of Bentham's.

Law, for Austin, is a rule laid down for the guidance of an intelligent being by an intelligent being having power over him. Thus, law is defined as completely apart from justice. There are laws properly so-called and improperly so-called, all of which are of four kinds: (1) divine laws or laws of God, (2) positive laws, (3) positive morality, and (4) laws merely metaphorical or figurative. Broadly, therefore, there are laws of God and human laws. Laws of God have no juristic significance and are comprised of the principle of utility. Human laws are divided into positive laws, which are laws properly so-called, and positive morality, which are laws improperly so-called. Laws properly so-called, or positive laws, are either set by political superiors to political subordinates or are set by subjects in pursuance of legal rights given to them. Laws improperly so-called, or positive morality or moral laws, are not set by a political superior to a political subordinate and include such rules as rules of club, laws of fashion, international law, and the like.

Law, therefore, is a command. It is a signification of a desire, and what distinguishes it from other significations of desire is the fact that the party to whom it is addressed is liable to evil from the party issuing it in case of non-compliance. Being liable to evil means to be bound or obliged or to be under a duty to obey the command. The evil that will probably be incurred for its disobedience is sanction or enforcement of obedience. Reward is not a sanction, since it does not oblige one to render service called for by the command. Thus command, duty, and sanction are inseparably connected. Law is distinguished by Austin from a command that is occasional or particular. Law is a command that obliges a person or persons generally to acts or forbearance of a class. Furthermore, laws, as well as other commands, proceed from a superior to a subordinate, since one who can oblige another to comply with his wishes is the superior and the one who is obnoxious to the impending evil is the subordinate. Positive law is set by a sovereign, who would be either a person or a body of persons, to the members of the independent political society wherein that person or body is sovereign. Customs, when turned into legal rules by judicial decisions, are tacit commands of the sovereign. The sovereign is a determinate human superior who is not in a habit of obedience to a superior and who receives habitual obedience from the bulk of the political and independent society. An independent political society or an independent and sovereign nation is a political society that consists of a sovereign and subjects and not, therefore, a body that consists entirely of subjects. Law, thus, is characterized by command, sanction, duty, and sovereignty.

2. Normative Theory of Law: Hans Kelsen (1881–1973)

Although there is a noticeable affinity between thoughts of Kelsen and Austin, the two issue from very different philosophical bases. While the philosophical basis of Austin is utilitaranism, the philosophical basis of Kelsen and the Vienna School is Neo-Kantianism.

Kelsen, unlike the Neo-Kantian Stammler, makes a complete break, with his pure theory of law, from any theory of justice. The objective of his pure theory is knowledge of that which is essential to law; therefore, it has nothing to do with that which is changing and accidental, such as ideals of justice. Kelsen completely rejects the legal idealism of Neo-Kantians such as Stammler and Del Vecchio, both of whom, as seen in the previous chapter, attempted to combine the Kantian distinction of content and form with an ideal of law (Stammler) or an intuitive idea of justice (Del Vecchio). Kelsen insists on the theory of law being purely formal in its entirety.

Kelson's pure theory of law proceeds from the Kantian distinction between the realms of cognition and volition, or *is* and *ought*. Science is knowledge, not volition. Legal theory is a science, and therefore not volition; it is the knowledge of what law *is*, not what it *ought* to be. All sciences are divided into causal sciences and normative sciences. The former deal with reality, *i.e.*, the *is* of actual events. The latter deal with ideality, *i.e.*, the ethical, legal, esthetic, or other *oughts*. Law is a normative science, the normative here meaning knowing the norm and not constructing it. Being normative, law deals not with the actual world of events (is) but with norms (ought). The realms of *is* and *ought* being logically separate, the inquiry into the sanction of an ought can lead only to another ought. The content of the *is* may or may not coincide with the content of the *ought*, but a coincidence of content does not affect the logical separation of the two spheres of knowledge.

Being a formal and universal theory, the pure theory of law is concerned with essentials of law of any kind, at any time, and under any conditions, without being mixed with the alien elements of morality and ethics. The legal relation contains the threat of a sanction from an authority in response to a certain act. The legal norm is a relation of condition and sequence, in the sense that if a certain act is done, a certain consequence ought to follow, and only in this sense is law an ought.

A legal system is composed of a hierarchy of norms, each being derived from its superior. The ultimate norm from which every legal norm deduces its validity is a highest basic norm, the *Grundnorm*. The *Grundnorm* is not deduced from anything else but is assumed as an initial hypothesis. By validity of a norm is meant its existence and not its efficacy. A norm is a valid legal norm only by virtue of the fact that it has been created according to a definite rule, with the basic norm of the legal order being the postulated ultimate rule from which the legal norms are created or annulled.

Law, therefore, is created or annulled by acts of human beings. Therefore, it is positive. It is independent of morality, so that it is for legal theory only to clarify the relations between the basic norm and other legal norms and not to evaluate the goodness or badness of the basic norm. It does not matter for Kelsen's theory which particular basic norm is adopted by a legal order. All that matters is that such basic norm has a minimum of effectiveness, that is, it commands a certain amount of obedience, since the efficacy of the total legal order is necessary for the validity of its norms. State and legal order are identical for Kelsen, since the compulsive order of the state is the same as the legal order and only one compulsive order can be valid at a time within one community.

3. The Rule Theory of Law: H. L. A. Hart (b. 1907)

Hart performs the feat of combining, within his analytical positivist theory of law, the matters of recognition and social obedience pointed out by the historical (Savigny)[1] and sociological (Ehrlich)[2] theories as the essential element of law with the matters of authority, command, and sanction pointed out by other analytical positivist theories (Austin and Kelsen, above) as such elements.

Hart posits a society, corresponding to primitive communities, whose structure is one of primary rules of obligation. These rules contain restrictions on the free use of violence, theft, and deception. While in such a society there are tensions between those who accept the rules and those who reject them, the latter must be a minority in order for the society to endure. According to Hart, such a simple form of social control suffers from three defects, namely, uncertainty of the social structure, the static character of the rules, and the inefficiency of the diffuse social pressure by which the rules are maintained. He argues that the remedy for these defects lies in supplementing the primary rules with three secondary rules: the rule of recognition, the rule of change, and the rule of adjudication. The defect of uncertainty of structure is remedied by the rule of recognition whereby the rules of behavior are acknowledged as authoritative. This rule, therefore, provides a proper way of disposing doubts as to the existence of the rule. The defect of the static character of rules is remedied by the rule of change, which empowers a person or a group of persons to introduce new primary rules for the conduct of the life of the community. The defect of inefficiency of diffuse social pressure is remedied by the rules of adjudication which empower individuals to make authoritative determination of the breach of a primary rule in a particular situation. Thus, the primary rules impose duties and the secondary rules confer powers. The heart of a legal system lies in the combination of primary rules of obligation with secondary rules of recognition, change, and adjudication.

4. Criticism

The basic question that the non-positivists raise against the positivists is whether there is any value to the purely formal conclusions delivered by legal positivism. By divorcing itself from the content of the law, analytical positivism loses its usefulness in promoting peace and order.

Below, we shall present some specific criticisms.

a. Bentham

1. Bentham, in equating good with pleasure and right with conduciveness to pleasure, has subverted the moral content of the terms good and right. If an act is good because it gives pleasure to the actor,

then that excludes all possibility of its moral evaluation. To say that it is right because it pleases the actor is to eliminate the very moral question we raise when we ask if the conduct is right even though it gives pleasure. The morality of an act consists not in its tendency to promote pleasure but in a moral judgment of it.

2. Bentham is not merely describing what is good or right but also prescribing that we should attain it. The purpose of law, for him, is to serve utility. In doing so he really is proposing the acceptance of the ethics of the greatest happiness principle. This ethics or ideology is neither universally accepted nor derived as a logical necessity from his definitions. Or, more precisely, it derives only from the falsity of his definitional propositions, mentioned above, so that once those premises are accepted the syllogistic conclusion, of course, follows in the syllogistic maneuver.

3. He exaggerates the role of rationality in moral matters. In order to persuade someone to a particular moral viewpoint, he believes that all you need is to show that it promotes happiness.

4. He is suggesting that the greatest happiness principle is the only absolute or universal rule, being the only rule that promotes happiness, therefore it ought to be followed. In doing so, he commits the logical fallacy of deriving *ought* from *is*, discussed above in Chapter III, for he suggests that from something that is universally desired it follows that we ought to aim at it. That is not so.

5. Although it is true that a feeling of pleasure accompanies a person's success in achieving what he desires, it seems that he is satisfied when he attains the object of his desire. Therefore, his object is not pleasure but the attainment of something. A person does not desire pleasure for its own sake.

6. Bentham assumed it to be a clearly understandable proposition that we desire only pleasure for its own sake. However it is not clear, either in Bentham or in Mill, who analyzed the matter in greater detail than Bentham, whether pleasure is a feeling about the experiences called pleasant, or a quality inherent in the experiences, or something inherent in pleasant sensations, or a quality that varies in intensity and not in kind, or merely a desire to continue having the pleasantness of a sensation, or a separate feeling annexed to the experiences called pleasant in the sense that the experience comes first and then comes a feeling of pleasure. With so many unclarified distinctions, Bentham's

proposition cannot be validly assumed to be understandable by all, as claimed by him.

7. Bentham and Mill do admit that we can quite possibly desire the means of something as much as the thing itself and that we can even continue to desire the means when we have forgotten the end. If that is so, then it is not the case, as claimed, that the only thing that we desire is pleasure for its own sake.

8. Bentham's felicific calculus is too fanciful as well as quite impossible. It is too fanciful in that the properties of pleasure—its amount, its intensity, its duration, its likelihood of being enjoyed, and so on—are not capable of being put to a single standard of measurement and put together in some quantity of happiness. It is impossible in that we cannot get this kind of information for our calculations.

9. In his account of what people want, Bentham entirely excludes ideals. However, it seems that ideals go a long way in determining what people want, which in large measure depends upon what they think is worth having. There is more to a man than merely the satisfaction of his one desire after another. The complexity of man is alarmingly missing in Bentham.

10. When it comes to balancing the interests of the individual with the interests of the community, Bentham seems to be a total conceptual failure. He merely believes that the interests of the individuals composing a community automatically promote the interests of the community. He fails to explain why this should be so.

11. Finally, one detects in Bentham a concept of a society that necessarily develops to a certain goal. This, however, is an illusion. Such neat development of society to a certain neat goal is nowhere to be found, either in history or in contemporary times.

b. Austin

1. Analytical positivism has been criticized for taking ideals out of consideration of law. It is said that the positivists do not think that matters of ideals are of any concern to the lawyer. However, this is not quite true. Austin himself instructs magistrates to apply utility in deciding cases. It is not his position that ideals are of no concern to the lawyer's entire task. However, it is true that his theory of law, inasmuch as it identifies the essential elements of law, does exclude the matter of ideals altogether.

2. As has been pointed out by Maine, Austin unduly generalized from the particular. His identification of law with the product of legislation, along with a coherent explanation for custom, is a characteristic of only the western societies of his times. From this he constructs a universal explanation of law itself. Moreover, as Bryce has shown, Austin's confusion between the notions of unlimited power and final authority obscures the essential features of even the legal order that was his prototype, namely, the United Kingdom.

3. Austin's focus on command and sanction as the essentials of law is criticized by the proponents of the historical and sociological theories of law who maintain that law exists independently of authoritative commands. However, it is possible to argue that the two viewpoints are talking about two different things. While Austin is talking about the nature of authority in law, the historical and sociological jurists are talking about the source of such authority in society, which could very well be done without dismissing Austin's position on authority of the command.

4. Austin describes legal relations (*e.g.*, legal powers, rights, privileges) as commands of the sovereign. However, it does not seem quite congruous to characterize the private rights, administrative acts, and declaratory laws as commands made by one having superiority over the addressee.

5. The place of the sovereign in Austin's theory of law has given rise to many problems, some of which have been pointed out by other analytical jurists themselves. Thus, Gray believes that the real rulers of a political society cannot be discovered. Moreover, while the state must be accepted as fundamental in law to which the machinery of government attaches, the interposition of another entity, namely the sovereign, is quite irrelevant. Hart thinks that the notion of sovereign oversimplifies the character of a political society, for, according to him, it is the notion of rule that is the ultimate test for identifying laws. Being set by a sovereign is not the defining characteristic of law. Moreover, as Hart points out, the habit of obedience to a sovereign with unlimited power, which is a defining characteristic of Austin's sovereign, does not account for the continuity of the lawmaking authority possessed by a succession of different legislators. Nor does it account for the persistence of laws long after their maker and those who accorded him habitual obedience have disap-

peared. Nor, again, does it account for legal limitations on legislative power.

6. Austin is not clear about the meaning of the sovereign in his theory. It could be a real or actual thing, as when he says that it is a determinate person or group of persons, or it could be a juristic construction arising out of his interpretation of facts.

7. Austin's view of law as a command has been the source of a lot of intellectual anxiety. Even other analytical jurists have found it a sore point. Thus, Kelsen considers that the analytical purity of a theory of law is compromised by introducing into it this psychological element. Or, Hart points out that laws are to be defined in terms of the notion of rule, and he claims that it is dogmatic to insist that the status of a law as law is derived from a prescription, whether express or tacit.

8. Defining law in terms of the state, as Austin does, has the merit of distinguishing the legal order from other orders, but the historical jurists have argued that, far from being the distinguishing characteristic of all law, the state is only an incident of mature systems of law. Anthropologists have argued that we should look for the essence of law in its function and not in its form, so that law should be defined by what it does in society rather than by the fact that it is commanded by a sovereign.[3]

9. Austin maintains that one of the essential elements of law is sanction, since it naturally follows from the notion of command that there be a fear of evil. However, this does not account for the bulk of law that is enabling rather than restrictive, such as the powers given to a testator over the distribution of his estate after his death. Moreover, sanction is not a satisfactory explanation for obedience to law. It seems that while sanction has its own role to play for those who do not wish to obey the law, there are other factors, such as respect for law as such or the desire to have the advantage of a system of legal protection of acts, that significantly explain the phenomenon of obedience to law.

10. The basic question is whether the source of validity of law lies in the command of the sovereign. This view of validity is in sharp contrast with the view, seen in the preceding chapters, that law is valid because it is the expression of natural justice or some other ideal, or the view, discussed in the next chapter, that law is valid because it is the embodiment of the spirit of a people.

c. Kelsen

Apart from the criticisms made of the analytical positivism in law through the preceding pages, Kelsen's pure theory of law suffers from certain particular difficulties.[4]

1. Based upon the methodological dichotomy between natural (casual) sciences, which operate by the method of causality, and social (normative) sciences, which employ the volitional method, Kelsen posits that law is a normative science concerned with *ought* rather than a natural science concerned with *is*. However, the truth seems to be neither that the method of natural sciences is purely causal and rigidly deterministic, nor that the method of social sciences is rigidly volitional. In natural sciences, the choice between alternative hypotheses is often one of convenience, wherein identical conclusions may even be derived from different premises.[5] Experiments cannot possibly be made without preconceived ideas; conversely, each experiment yields generalizations that serve as predictions for other experiments. For example, in physics, this interaction between speculative assumptions and experiment is well demonstrated by the persistent inquiries and continually changing theories concerning the structure of the atom, the theory of relativity, and the interchangeability of matter and energy.[6] Likewise, the method used in the social sciences is not exclusively volitional; instead, an increasing emphasis is being placed on certainty and measurability. Even in law, the American realist movement has emphasized fact research and analysis in the legal decision-making process and, in more recent times, behavioral research, which employs quantitative techniques in the analysis of factual data, has been put to significant use.[7] Therefore, a closer examination of the methods of science disallows the methodological dichotomy claimed by the pure theory of law.

2. Another difficulty lies in the descriptive function of this theory. It holds that the rules of law formulated by the science of law are descriptive, while the legal norms enacted by the law-creating authorities are prescriptive, and it maintains that, as a general theory, its task is not to describe a particular legal system but merely to show how a particular legal system should be described, *i.e.*, which concepts should and should not be used in making this description. The resulting description must take the form of rules (or ought statements) in a descriptive sense. This conclusion is puzzling because, at this point of

141

inquiry, the description would not be a set of rules or ought statements, but instead, a set of statements explaining the meaning of the rules.[8] Indeed, it may be a mistaken belief that law, a science of norms, can be explored using norms as tools, for then law becomes a science with conclusions of law, not a science with norms or legal rules as its objects of inquiry.[9] Perhaps Kelsen simply meant that his purely scientific statements explaining the meaning of a law mention certain rules or ought statements as the equivalent in meaning of that law.[10] This interpretation of Kelsen's theory appears to be overly generous. Nevertheless, it has been ingeniously argued in Kelsen's defense[11] that the use of words differs from the mention of them, the latter being descriptive. Thus, although the law-creating authority within a particular legal system may employ certain words to enact a law, the formulation of the meaning of the law by the science of law merely mentions these words in conjunction with other words that explain the meaning of the law.

3. The pure theory makes a division between reality (causal sciences) and ideality (normative sciences), with law and morality pertaining to the latter. Positive law is viewed as a system of valid norms. Thus, according to the theory, morality cannot also be a system of valid norms. Consequently, a valid rule of law cannot be contradicted by a valid moral rule, since "[n] either the jurist nor the moralist asserts that both normative systems are valid. The jurist ignores morality as a system of valid norms, just as the moralist ignores positive law as such a system. Neither from the one nor from the other point of view do there exist two duties simultaneously that contradict one another. And there is no third point of view."[12] This theory describes the collision of moral and legal duty in the mind of an individual as the psychological result of his being under the influence of two ideas that pull him in different directions, not the simultaneous validity of two contradictory norms.[13] Consequently, the pure theory of law regards this collision as one of "factuality" rather than "normativity."[14] This position would seemingly apply both to the case of the individual involved in the conflict and, *mutatis mutandis*, to the case of an observer who considers the law in question to be valid but in conflict with morality.[15]

The difficulty with the pure theory's conclusion lies in the fact that when an individual experiences this conflict he believes not only in the existence of the conflict but also in the impossibility of discharging both the duties. Thus, the requirements of a valid law conflict with the requirements of a moral principle. This finding is clearly one of normativity, not of factuality. Moreover, even if one accepts Kelsen's claim that neither the jurist nor the moralist asserts the validity of both normative systems, it does not follow that such assertions of conflict between law and morality cannot be made meaningfully.[16]

4. The is-ought dichotomy in the pure theory of law results in separate, unconnected worlds of nature and validity. This result is unsatisfactory, for if the purpose of the system of norms is to interpret the social reality by revealing its consonance with the normative system, then the two systems must have something in common. Only the synthetic association of reality and validity makes the normative system a meaningful referent of social reality to the category of validity.[17]

5. The theory fails to maintain the purity of the is-ought dichotomy that it claims. Under the pure theory of law, the legal norms derive their validity from the basic norm,[18] but the validity of the basic norm is presupposed. If this means that there are basic procedures accepted in a particular society for identifying authoritative rules,[19] then they are not presupposed, but experienced,[20] and thus are found in the realm of factuality, not normativity. Moreover, under this theory, the determination of the valid basic norm is founded upon its "principle of effectiveness,"[21] the conformity of man's actual behavior to the legal order. The proof of the minimum of effectiveness necessary for the legal order obviously requires an inquiry into political and social facts; therefore, the proof is a matter of *is*, not *ought*.

6. There are at least six admissions within the theory that infuse factuality (is) into a structure of normativity (ought) and, consequently, fail to support the claimed dichotomy of *is* and *ought*. These admissions are: (1) the admission that the efficacy of the legal order taken as a whole is a condition of the validity of individual norms; (2) the recognition that legal norms may be created by a revolution; (3) the acceptance of the fact that an individual norm may lose its validity due to the inefficacy of the legal order; (4) the assertion that the basic norm is not an arbitrary creation, since its content is determined by facts; (5) the view that the basic norm effects the transformation of power into law; and (6) the suggestion that law is a specific technique of social organization. Moreover, the very hierarchy of legal norms involves ranking various manifestations of legal will, such as statutory enactments and judicial decisions, and thus implies a certain evaluation

of state activity.[22] This ranking cannot be achieved by separating the realm of facts from the realm of norms. Thus, contrary to its pretensions, the theory does not imply a minimum of rationality in the structure of law, and the law is bound to include in its structure certain ontological elements, giving content to the concepts that formalize it.[23]

7. One might also raise doubts as to the claimed universality of this theory. The hierarchy of the pure theory purports to express the pure and universal form of law. In order for that claim to be valid, no possible legal system could fall outside it; but that is not the case.

8. Finally, one cannot help but raise the question whether a true picture of law can be had merely through observing the formal hierarchy of norms and ignoring the social forces, including ethics, that create law.

d. Hart

1. Hart defines law as the union of primary rules of obligation and secondary rules of recognition, change, and adjudication. However, this does not assist us in distinguishing the legal order from any other order, such as a social club or a religious order. The latter systems may very well have primary and secondary rules of those sorts.

2. Hart's exclusion of morality from his rule of recognition has led some critics, such as Dias, to say that Hart cannot possibly exclude morality from this rule of recognition since social and moral considerations go into the making of law and prevent it from validating abuse of power. However, it seems that this criticism of Hart's theory is not warranted. An assertion that the rule of recognition is an analytic element of law does not mean that it cannot have a content that is determined by social and moral considerations. Morality is excluded only from the analytic elements of law.

3. Hart makes a rather sharp distinction between his primary rules that create duties and his secondary rules that create powers. However, it seem that the same rule can possibly do both. Its interpretation as to whether it is creating a duty or creating a power depends not on the rule but on the circumstances to which it is applied.

4. Hart does not clarify what he means by rules, that is to say, he does not distinguish rules from principles, standards, and policies that possess the quality of law. If he means to exclude these, then he is excluding too much of the legal phenomena in his definition of law.

If he means to include these, then he is eliminating the distinctions that do exist between rules and principles, standards, and policies without giving reasons why these distinctions either do not or should not exist.

5. In Hart's theory the primary rules create duties and the secondary rules confer public and private powers. Hart, thus, applies the term power to comprehend everything that is regulated by law that is not a duty. However, in doing so, he uses the term to signify things that cannot in ordinary legal usage properly be called power, such as, for example, capacity or competence.

6. In Hart's theory the transition from the primitive or prelegal societies to legal societies is made by addition of the secondary rules. However, it seems that the former societies do have the secondary or power-conferring rules, as seen in their institutions of marriage, promise, and so on. If it is argued in defense of Hart that the secondary rules of recognition, change, and adjudication are meant to denote not such things as marriage, promise, and so on, but such things as rules of legislation, administration, and jurisdiction, then it appears that these are hardly the most important factors, as claimed by Hart, in the transition of a prelegal society to a legal society.

6

HISTORICAL THEORIES OF LAW

The most prominent historical theories about law include the theory that views law as a manifestation of the spirit of the people in history (Savigny), the theory that views law as the development in history of personal conditions from status to contract (Maine), and the theory that views law as an auxiliary in a stage of economic determinism (Marx and Engels). These theories arose in revolt, firstly, against the rationalism of the eighteenth century, which paid no attention to the historicity of social conditions and propagated its belief in natural law, first principles, and power of reason to deduce the theory of law reform, and, secondly, against the premises of the French Revolution, which believed in the power of human will over traditions and circumstances.

A. Law as a Manifestation of the Spirit of the People in History: Friedrich Karl von Savigny (1719-1861)

History, for Savigny, is not merely a collection of examples but the only way to acquire true knowledge of the human condition. Therefore, in history he gains his knowledge about law.

He likens law to a people's language, manner, and constitution, so that, in his view, the law of a people has already attained a fixed character peculiar to that people in the earliest times of history. These phenomena, instead of existing separately from each other, are united in nature and represent the particular tendencies and faculties of a people. The common conviction of the people binds them into one whole. Law, therefore, excludes all notions of an accidental and arbitrary origin. It is located in the consciousness of an inward necessity. It grows with a people and dies when a nation loses its nationality. It is developed first by custom and popular faith and next by jurisprudence. It is, thus, developed not by the arbitrary will of a law giver but by internal, silently operating powers.

Therefore, according to Savigny, law is not made but found. Its growth is essentially an unconscious and organic process. The organic connection of law with the being and character of the people is manifested in the progress of the times. The spirit of the people (*Volksgeist*) manifests itself in the law of the people. In primitive communities, law is a matter of a few easily grasped legal relations. In modern societies, it grows to a greater complexity in which the *Volksgeist* can no longer manifest itself directly. Instead, it is represented by lawyers who formulate the technical legal principles. The task of the lawyers is not to create law but to bring into legal shape that which exists in the *Volksgeist*. In this process, legislation is merely a last stage.

Since law under this theory is the manifestation of the peculiar character of a people, it is not of universal validity. Like the language of a people, it cannot apply to other peoples. Legal institutions must, therefore, be studied with reference to their particular time and place and not with reference to general or abstract principles.

B. Law as the Development in History of Personal Conditions from Status to Contract: Sir Henry Sumner Maine (1822–1888)

Maine makes a study of legal evolution in different societies in history and concludes therefrom that there are two kinds of societies, static and progressive. The static societies include the greatest part of mankind, including India and China, whose social and legal development stops at a certain stage, outlined below, and which show not a particle of desire to improve beyond that point. In contrast, the progressive societies include an extremely few societies of Europe, which represent a rare achievement of civilization in the history of the world and are propelled by a desire to improve and develop.

There are three successive stages of legal evolution in static societies. The first stage is that of law making by personal command of the rulers who are believed to be acting under a divine inspiration. This is succeeded by the epoch of customary law, which is marked by a gradual crystallization of habits into customs. An aristocratic minority replaces the original law makers of the theocratic power and formulates the legal customs. The third stage in the evolution is the era of codes. According to Maine, the evolution of the static societies is arrested at this stage and is characterized by a fixed legal condition dominated by family dependency. He calls this condition status. In the condition of status, the member of a household is tied to the family dominated by its head. Laws still have an extremely limited application and are binding not on individuals but on families. Legislation and adjudication reach only to the heads of the families. The rule of conduct for the individual remains the law of his home, as distinguished from civil law, and his legislator is his parent.

Only the progressive societies, represented by the few societies of Europe, are characterized according to Maine by a desire to improve and develop. Therefore, they move beyond the stage where the static societies stop. The sphere of civil law tends to enlarge itself. The agents of legal change become active, and at every point of the progress a greater number of personal and property rights are removed from the domestic forum to the public tribunal. These agents of change or development are, in historical order, (a) legal fiction, (b) equity, and (c) legislation. Legal fictions change the law in accordance with the changing needs and signify assumptions that conceal the fact of alteration of a law by keeping its letter unchanged but modifying its operation. Equality exists alongside the original civil law due to a superior sanctity inherent in its principles. Legislation represents an increased law-making power of the state and its obligatory force is independent of its principles.

According to Maine, the distinguishing feature in the movement of the progressive societies through these instrumentalities of change has been the gradual dissolution of family dependency and its replacement by individual obligation. The civil law increasingly applies to the individual. The movement has been from personal conditions to agreement, or, in other words, from status to contract.

C. Law as an Auxiliary in a Stage of Economic Determinism: Karl Marx (1818–1883) and Friedrich Engels (1820–1895)

According to Marx and Engels, the history of all human society has been the history of class struggle, in which the oppressor and the oppressed stood in sharp opposition to each other. Political power is the organized use of force by one class in order to subjugate another class. Social evolution moves toward the disappearance of class distinctions.

People enter into definite relations in the social production that they carry on. These relations are independent of their will and correspond to a definite stage of development of their material powers of production. These relations of production in their totality constitute the society's economic structure. Definite forms of social consciousness correspond to this economic structure. People's social existence determines their consciousness, not *vice versa*. It is the mode of production in material life that determines the general character of the social, political, and spiritual processes of life. When material forces of production conflict with the existing relations of production, as they do at a certain stage of their development, social revolution follows and changes the economic foundation, thereby transforming the entire superstructure.

Broadly speaking, the epochs in the progress of the economic formation of society are the Asiatic, the ancient, the feudal, and the modern bourgeois methods of production. The bourgeois relations of production are the last antagonistic form of the social process of production. The material conditions for the solution of that antagonism are created by the productive forces developing in the bourgeois society.

Thus, the starting point of the materialist conception of history is the principle that production and exchange of its products are the basis of every social order, so that the distribution of the products and the division of society into classes are determined by the features of production (*i.e.* what is produced, how it is produced, who produced it, and how the product is exchanged). Therefore, the causes of social changes and political revolutions are to be found not in the minds of men (philosophy) but in the mode of production and exchange (economics).

The realization of injustice in social institutions indicates that the social order has not kept up with the changes that have been quietly taking place in the methods of production and forms of exchange. Likewise, the means to get rid of the abuses are also present in the altered conditions of production or, that is, in the existing material facts of production. The capitalist means of production transform the great majority of population into proletarians and thereby bring forth the force that carries out the revolution. The process proceeds in the following manner. The proletariat seizes state power and transforms the means of production into state property, but in doing so it puts an end to itself as the proletariat. Class differences and antagonisms are ended, as is the state. The state, being an organization of the exploitative class, was needed to forcibly hold down the exploited class in the oppressive conditions determined by the existing mode of production, and it is rendered unnecessary when there is no longer any class of society to be subjugated. State interference becomes superfluous in social relations and the state withers away (it is not abolished) with the replacement of the government of persons by the administration of things and the common direction of the processes of production.

In this scheme of things, law has little to contribute except to exist, like the state, as a means whereby those controlling the production maintain their control over those who are oppressed. With the withering away of the state, law too would wither away.

D. Criticism

1. *Savigny*

1. History belies some of the suppositions of the historical theory pioneered by Savigny. The theory takes an organic view of law and maintains that there is an organic connection of all social institutions in the spirit of a people (*Volksgeist*). Law is an expression of this *Volksgeist*. This would mean that one people cannot borrow the law of another. Such, however, has not been the case in legal history. Law or custom of another has been imported by conquest, invasion, or peaceful penetration. Examples abound.

2. The theory maintains that history determines the present, so that law is not a matter of conscious human effort. However, acceptance of such a view deprives the historical knowledge about law of all its practical importance.

3. This theory, by taking the deterministic view of law, discourages all efforts at consciously improving the legal condition.

4. Since law in Savigny is an expression of the conviction of righteousness of a people, an evaluation of its justness is made impossible. Savigny does grant the possibility of a bad law being opposed to the spirit of the people, but he cannot do so consistently with the positivistic or empirical claim made of the *Volksgeist*.

5. A historical study may tell us how a particular proposition of law fared in its own circumstances, how it was interpreted and applied then. However, it cannot help us evaluate present laws under present conditions.

6. Although this approach denies the abstract methods of evaluation, it becomes unconsciously metaphysical when it attempts to govern modern life by ancient texts. Moreover, in doing so, it presupposes the values of conservation as opposed to the values of change. These processes are far from being empirical and their method far from being historical.

7. Custom is regarded by this theory as a manifestation of the *Volksgeist*, but it is difficult to say that all customs carry with them the general conviction of rightness as suggested by a notion of *Volksgeist*. Such is the case with the custom of slavery in domestic laws or the custom of war in international law. Moreover, there are customs that are so local in their origin that they cannot be said to have arisen

from any widespread conviction, as illustrated by the cosmopolitanism of many commercial customs. Furthermore, many customs arise from convenience or imitation rather than a conviction of their righteousness. Finally, custom is a combination of the inner manifestation of social tendencies (feelings, desires, consciousness) and their external manifestation in conduct. It is not sufficient to concentrate, as Savigny does, only on the inner aspect.

8. The role of the jurist under Savigny's theory is only to make an exposition of the existing law from the characteristic customs of the community, not to add anything creative to it. However, this account of juristic activity fails on several grounds. In the first place, judicial decision making is not such a non-creative, mechanical process as conceived by the historical theory. It seems very much in the nature of laws that they are not apprehended by all men in a like manner. They need be expertly interpreted. This is a creative activity and is much influenced by the judge's own values, as brought to our attention by the American realists, discussed below. Secondly, great advances have been made in law by the great expositors of laws who have projected in it their personal genius, which is not the same thing as mechanically relating the customs of the society or as representing the *Volksgeist*.

9. Savigny was probably correct in detecting an idea of the spirit of the people in the Germany of his times, which was characterized by a growing feeling of nationhood. However, he extended the idea to all societies. He thereby used an *a priori* conception in claiming the universal validity for his idea, no longer remaining true to his own historical method.

10. The creative role assigned to the *Volksgeist* is considerably exaggerated in this theory. There is no doubt that there is some interaction between traditions and legislation. However, traditions are not all-controlling of the emergent law. Sometimes they are even deliberately changed by new law. Far from reflecting the *Volksgeist*, law sometimes changes it.

11. Savigny has not provided us the means for discovering the *Volksgeist* or proving it. As a matter of fact, it is impossible to ascertain the existence of a national mind. The concept, therefore, is not unlike that of natural law, quite mystical and quite capable of supporting any ideology.

2. *Maine*

1. Maine's claim of cultural superiority of the European societies over the rest of the mankind, is too chauvinistic and is not sustained by the history of non European societies. As demonstrated in Chapter I above, the role played by law in the social organization of European societies is the result of the particular historicity of European cultural experience, which is not shared by other cultures. Maine is mistaken in reading this as an evidence of the inferiority of other cultures to the culture of Europe.

2. Likewise, his generalizations about primitive law and primitive societies are dubious in many respects. For example, he maintains that law and religion are indistinguishable in these societies. However, anthropologists are divided over this issue; while some believe that such is the case, others point out that the association of law with religion is only a late development among primitive societies.

The primitive societies do in fact possess a phenomenon which can be called law, if by law is meant the function performed by it and the attitude of people toward it. It can be said, as it is by many anthropologists,[1] that law is found in such features, evident in primitive societies, as rules of behavior regulating relations of individuals and groups, reciprocity of services characterized by their obligatory character, obedience, machinery for dispute resolution, such as reconciliation, compensation, sanctioned vengeance on part of the person wronged, and so on.

Maine believes that early development of societies took place through the successive stages of personal judgments, oligarchic monopoly, and code. However, primitive societies have been more complex than the simple, single pattern conceived by Maine. They exhibit a wide range of institutions, on the basis of which some anthropologists have classified them as First Hunters, Second Hunters, First Agriculturalists, First Pastorals, and Second Pastorals. Other classifications exist as well. In any case, it is not possible to accept the simple model of Maine for all primitive societies.

Nor has the later development in Maine's progressive societies been in the sequence of legal fiction, equity, and legislation, as claimed by him. Legislation came first in these societies, whereafter fiction and equity played their own part.

Primitive law is not as rigid and inflexible as Maine supposes it to be. Primitive societies are not characterized by a blind obedience to law, without regard to the dynamics of human behavior in its interaction with the purposes that people pursue and with the social structure within which they pursue them.

It is often said in defense of Maine that the above knowledge about primitive societies was yielded by the anthropological investigations undertaken only since his times and, therefore, criticizing him on the above grounds may not be fair. That may be so but, at best, this is a tribute to the genius of the man that, nevertheless, does not augment the validity of his theory.

3. Maine's most important conclusion, namely, that the movement in progressive societies has been from status to contract, is not borne out by a close observation of these societies. Maine's own examples of this movement are faulty. For example, he observes that the status of the slave had been superseded by the contractual relation of the servant to his master. However, if one is not deluded by the seduction of the contractual form, one can see that what had happened was not that the fetters of status were superseded by the freedom released by contract but that the old slavery was replaced by a new slavery which, as Friedmann points out, was founded not on legal incapacity but on the economic helplessness of the worker.

The correction to this type of status came about by two factors that have nothing to do with contract, namely, the association of workers in trade unions and state interference against horrible injustices of the freedom of contract. The case, therefore, is not that there has been a movement from status to contract, as claimed by Maine, but, rather, that there has been a reform from contract to status.

Further erosion of the freedom of contract is seen in social legislation that compulsorily provides for such things as workmen's compensation, minimum wages, safety in the workplace, worker amenities in the workplace, social security, and so on.

Both the worker and the industrialist have sought advantages through giving up individual freedom of contract by joining the trade union and the business association or cartel, respectively, and taking recourse to long-term collective agreements.

Maine's freedom of bargaining contemplated in his contract has been increasingly replaced by the status-like conditions in many areas of economic life resulting from the standardized contracts prevalent in these areas, which range from government contracts to transportation, insurance, leases, mortgages, and so on.

The rise of totalitarian governments, even in Maine's progressive societies of Europe, demonstrates a movement away from, and not toward, contract.

Finally, it is too simplistic to classify all legal relations into the categories of status and contract and, furthermore, to put them on a progressive scale wherein status is left behind and contract is approached. Legal relations in modern society are complex, some of which may be in the nature of status, some in the nature of contract, and some quite indifferent to the concerns of either status or contract. And all of these converge upon the individual or corporate legal entity contemporaneously, instead of exhibiting a movement from one to the other.

3. Marx and Engels

1. The Marxist theory gives a scientific form to social development. Moreover, it claims that since that development is scientific, it is inevitable. Thus, it discovers the method of production as the single cause of all cultural phenomena. However, in spite of its claim, this approach does not equate with the method of science. It is not necessity but probability that characterizes the scientific method, and it is not a single all-comprehensive law but pluralism that characterizes its quest. At least, it is not so in modern science, although a search for an all-comprehensive law of causal necessity may have been the case when science was still seeking its method. As Dewey has remarked, science is not a competitor with theology for a single ultimate explanation. Economic factors no doubt influence matters of social organization, but they are not the sole cause of all developments in culture.

2. According to the Marxist theory, class conflict is a method of social progress. One would conclude, therefore, that if you aim at social progress, you must intensify the class conflict. However, it is quite possible to regard these conflicts as deleterious to progress, since they tend to waste or destroy resources, human and other, needed for progress.

3. Marx and Engels may have been accurate in observing the social conditions of a particular place in a particular time. However, it is fallacious to claim from this anecdote a scientific, universal principle,

since their conclusions are not based upon data that would represent the conditions of all societies.

4. The deterministic view of social progress denies its process, the creative element of which seems crucial to an idea of progress. It engenders a fatalistic belief in recurrent cycles of history. This is both erroneous, in that history does not repeat like that, and dangerous, in that it puts a damper on other elements of culture that play their role in improving the human condition.

5. Marx and Engels regard ideology as false consciousness or illusion. The implication is that it is to be condemned. However, this view is mistaken both historically and as a principle of action. Historically, ideologies have actually played their part in mobilizing people to certain goals. That is no illusion. As a principle of action, they represent commitments that move peoples to achieving that in which they believe. This, too, is not an illusion. It may very well be that the values that peoples attempt to realize through their ideologies are not necessarily materialistic and not controlled by the method of production, but that does not make them illusory. As pointed out in Chapter I, what is objectionable is not the existence of ideologies but the confusion of ideology with philosophy, or, in other words, the passing off of a value preference as objective truth. We have seen this incipience in many philosophies examined here, including that of Marx and Engels. Values do exist, they do conflict, and a choice has to be made from among them. Acknowledging the choice as such, rather than disguising it as philosophy, places the responsibility of making that choice on those who make it. Dismissing the whole issue as illusion is misleading.

6. There are many problems with the political theory of Marx and Engels that we shall not analyze within the scope of our inquiry here. Therefore, we shall not examine here such questions as whether in their classless society administration can possibly consist only of business management and adjudication of disputes, or whether group conflicts would not arise in such a society, and so on. We shall only point out that by conceiving law merely as an instrument of suppression, their theory prevents any inquiry into the useful roles that law might possibly have in society.

7

SOCIOLOGICAL THEORIES OF LAW

The sociological theories about law fall in three categories: (A) law viewed in sociological aspects, (B) the jurisprudence of interests, and (C) the free law.

A. Law in Sociological Aspects

The significant theories that view law in sociological aspects include those of Ihering (law in the social purpose), Ehrlich (law in the inner order of human associations), and Duguit (law in the objective conditions of social solidarity).

1. Law in the Social Purpose: Rudolf von Ihering (1818–1892)

Ihering defines law as the sum of the conditions of social life in the widest sense of the term, as secured by the power of the state through the means of external compulsion.

He points out three elements that are crucial to law, namely, its dependence upon coercion, its norm, and its purpose (or the conditions of social life).

a. Coercion:

According to Ihering, law consists of those rules laid down by society that have coercion. Since the state is the sole possessor of coercion in society, it is the only source of law. The other associations that have the right to make their own laws, such as the Church, have that right either by the express grant or tacit toleration of the state. The criterion that distinguishes law from ethics and morality is the recognition and realization of it by the force of the state. Ihering reconciles his insistence on coercion in law with the concept of international law and the concept of that part of public law that concerns the duties of the monarch by maintaining that both of these are laws with coercion as an essential element, but that the organization of coercion in these cases meets with insurmountable obstructions.

b. Norm

While coercion is the outer side of law, the element of norm is its inner side. Norm is an abstract imperative for human conduct. Thus, it is a proposition of a practical kind inasmuch as it is a direction for human conduct. It is thus a rule, but it is distinguished from all other rules by virtue of its concern with conduct. It is distinguished from maxims by virtue of its binding or imperative character. Abstract imperatives in the ethical world order are social imperatives, since the subject of their purpose is society. These imperatives are of law, morality, and ethics. In law, they are regularly laid down by the state and realized exclusively by the state authorities. The legal imperatives are directed to the organs of the state that are entrusted with the management of coercion. Thus, norm, like coercion, is a purely formal element.

c. Purpose

Norm and coercion being formal elements, they do not inform us of the content of law. It is through the content of law that we learn of the purpose served by law in society. This content is infinitely various. There is nothing universal about it. Law cannot make the same regulations for all the time and for all the people. It must adapt them to the conditions of the people, to their degree of civilization, and to the needs of the time. The standard of law is not truth, which is absolute, but purpose, which is relative. Certain legal principles found among all peoples have a resemblance to truth but to call them truths would be like calling the fundamental arrangements of human civilization (houses, streets, clothing, use of fire and light, etc.) truths. They are results of experience assuring attainment of certain purposes. Science may separate those institutions that have endured the test of history from those that have had only a temporary usefulness, but the former is nothing other than the useful placed beyond doubt.

Law exists to realize some purpose. It is to secure the conditions of social life. Conditions of life include the conditions of physical existence as well as those goods and pleasures that give one's life its true value in his judgment. All legal principles of any kind and wherever found can be reduced to the security of conditions of social life. The conditions of social life or the requirements for the existence of society, as related to the attitude of the law toward them, are of three types: (i) extra-legal, (ii) mixed legal, and (iii) purely legal. (i) The extra-legal conditions of life belong to nature and are offered to man with or without requiring his effort. Law has nothing to do with them. (ii) The mixed legal conditions belong exclusively to man and include preservation of life, reproduction, labor, and trade, corresponding to his instincts of self-preservation, sex, and acquisition. Their security does not depend upon law, but upon nature, and law comes to assist these three instincts only in the exceptional cases when they fail. (iii) The purely legal conditions are those that depend entirely on legal command, *e.g.*, the command to pay debts or taxes.

The realization of the law by the state enables the individual to desire the common interest as well his own individual interest. Thus, Ihering makes the individual interest part of a social purpose by connecting one's purpose with the interests of others. The reconciliation between the interests of the individual and those of the society is achieved through the levers of social motion. Society acts upon individuals through the two basic motives of egoism and altruism. Consequently, there are two kinds of levers of social motion: egoistic and altruistic. The egoistic levers are composed of reward and coercion. The altruistic levers are made of the feelings of duty and love.

2. Law in the Inner Order of Human Associations: Eugen Ehrlich (1862–1922)

Ehrlich finds the center of gravity of legal development not in legislation, not in juristic science, not in judicial decision, but in society itself. He believes that it is the inner order of associations, not legal propositions, that determines the fate of man. He points out that the explanation for social phenomena comes not from their juristic construction but by inferring the underlying modes of thought from facts. Accordingly, people regard their rights as issuing from the relations of one person to another and not from legal propositions about those relations. Thus, the state precedes the constitution, the family precedes the order of the family, possession precedes ownership, contracts precede the law of contracts, the testament precedes the law of wills, and so on. The inner order of human associations not only comes temporally before legal propositions but is also the basic form of law from which legal propositions are derived.

As Ehrlich sees it, in a social association human beings come together and recognize certain rules of conduct as binding. Generally speaking, they regulate their conduct in accordance with these rules, which are social facts produced by the forces operating in society. These rules are of various kinds. Examples include rules of law, work, religion, ethics, decorum, tact, etiquette, fashion, etc. Ehrlich maintains that the legal norm is of the same nature as all other rules of conduct. The essential compulsion behind the legal norm, just as behind other norms of conduct, is social compulsion, not state authority.

The state is merely one legal association among numerous others, such as family, church, or corporate bodies. Consequently, there are many legal norms that have not been expressed in legal provisions of the state. Also the state norms of compulsion have the function of protecting norms formed in society, their other function being the protection of the various institutions of the state.

According to Ehrlich, there are social facts of law that exist in the conviction of an association of people. These facts are usage, domination, possession, and declaration of will. Norms of law are derived from these facts. State compulsion is not necessary to this process. These facts of law affect legal relations in three ways: (a) they give enforcement to these relations; (b) they control, hinder, or invalidate these relations; and (c) they impute legal consequences to their relations that are not derived directly from them. Only one type of legal norms, namely, the norms of decision, is state-made. The transformation of state norms into a fundamental legal norm takes place, if at all, when the norms become part of the living law. The living law, or the law as it actually exists in society, is always in a state of evolution and always ahead of the state law. Jurisprudence has the task of solving this tension between the two and is thus a product of social development, as well as a stimulus to them.

The norms of law regulate the relationship between the state law and the facts of law. That relationship exists in three modes: (a) there may be legal norms purely based on facts of law (*e.g.*, contracts, bylaws of corporate associations, etc.) or directly derived from them (*e.g.*, remedies for damage, unjust enrichment, etc.); (b) there may be state commands that create or deny social facts, *e.g.*, expropriation or nullification of contracts; and (c) there may be norms that are unconnected with social facts, *e.g.*, taxation, trade concessions, etc. The task of the jurist is fairly technical where the social facts of the law are quite clear, but where they are not so clear, Ehrlich instructs the jurist to seek guidance in the principles of justice. The static justice of the ideal forms, which tends to consolidate existing conditions, is mitigated by dynamic justice, which is characterized by the competitive forces of the individualistic and the collective ideals.

3. Law in the Objective Conditions of Social Solidarity: Leon Duguit (1859–1928)

Duguit's theory is inspired by Auguste Comte's scientific positivism and Durkheim's distinction between collective and individual consciousness. Durkheim himself was much influenced by Comte. Comte opposes the empirical method to the metaphysical method and believes that all reflections must be derived not from preconceived ideas but from experience and observation. He applies this method to the evolution of mankind and discovers that human history has gone through three phases: (a) the theological phase wherein forces of nature are explained through personified dieties; (b) the metaphysical phase wherein those personified forces are explained through causal relations; and (c) the scientific or the positivist phase wherein personification is expunged from nature so that nature is viewed experimentally and objectively.

Corresponding to these phases of human history are the branches of human knowledge. Sociology, according to Comte, builds a real science of human society based on facts and not ideology. Durkheim followed this approach and discovered two kinds of needs and aptitudes of people that hold them together in societies, namely, common needs that are satisfied by mutual assistance and by bringing together of similar aptitudes, and diverse needs that are satisfied by an exchange of services wherein one utilizes his aptitudes to satisfy the needs of others. Social cohesion is thus attained by this division of labor and, Durkheim argues, social solidarity will increase with energetic and free development of individual activities.

Duguit seizes upon social solidarity as a fact of social life, which to him is indisputable, non-ideological, and non-metaphysical. Contrary to Durkheim, who believed in the existence of objective ideals that are immanent in the experience of the society and that manifest themselves in objective realities, Duguit believes that social norms, like biological laws of organism, are based on the fact that is society. Solidarity is the law of the social body according to which that body is maintained. Law, too, is a fact, since it is an aspect of social solidarity. Law exists by virtue of facts, and not because of any higher principle of good, interest, or happiness, and these facts are that people do live and can only live in society. The duty to maintain social solidarity is also, for Duguit, an indisputable fact. Acceptance of this as a fact prompts him to establish a rule of objective law that is free from the arbitrariness of human will. State sovereignty, therefore, is assailed as a myth. The state is not a person distinct from individuals but only the individual will of those who govern. Those who govern are just the individuals who exercise preponderant force. Correspondingly, they have a duty of performing a social function, namely, organizing certain services, assuring the continuity of these services, and controlling their operation. The government and the state are, thus, a part of the social organism and have their own task to perform in the division of labor whereby social solidarity is attained.

As a consequence, Duguit advocates strict principles of state responsibility to control abuse of state power, recommends decentralization and group government, rejects state intervention in transforming a social norm into a legal norm, denies any division between public and private law since both are parts of the social body with certain functions to fulfill, and rejects the necessity of individual rights since everyone cooperates for a common end and fulfills a certain function. He, thus, manages to demolish both state sovereignty and individual rights.

B. Jurisprudence of Interests: Philip Heck (1858–1943) and Roscoe Pound (1870–1964):

The jurisprudence of interests was originally conceived by certain German jurists, most prominently Philip Heck, and elaborated, with striking similarity, by certain American jurists, most prominently Roscoe Pound.

The jurisprudence of interests focuses on the problem of legal interpretation. As Heck points out, it is a method designed to serve the practical ends of law and it aims at discovering principles that judges should follow in deciding cases. It attempts to replace the conceptualizations of the traditional jurisprudence with a maxim of analysis of interests or a theory of conflicts. As Heck sees it, each command of law originates from a struggle between opposing interests, and the law determines this conflict of interests. Law, therefore, is the result of these opposing forces. The degree in which its purpose is achieved depends upon the weight of those interests that are superseded by it. The conflict of interests that underlie each rule of law, Heck argues, must be analyzed. The judge has to adjust interests and decide their conflicts in the same way as the legislator does, although the legislative evaluation of interests has precedence over the judge's individual evaluation.

However, since the wealth and variety of the actual problems of daily life make laws inadequate, incomplete, and sometimes contradictory, it becomes the judge's task not only to apply a particular command but to protect the totality of interests as well. For this purpose, it is necessary to adopt a method of systematic inquiry into the interests involved. According to Heck, this method must distinguish the function of framing rules from that of arranging them. The jurisprudence of interests grounds itself in the study of reality and the needs of practical life, and it frames rules with a view to the competing interests. It, thus, explains given rules of law as the outcome of these competing interests.

Pound sets up social engineering as the crucial task of all thought about law. Toward that task, he formulates and classifies social interests. Legal progress is achieved, he believes, by balancing these interests. Legally protected interests are classified by him as follows: (a) public interests, (b) individual interests, and (c) social interests. (a) Public interests include the interests of the state (i) in subsisting as a state and (ii) in acting as a guardian of social interests. (b) Individual interests consist of (i) interests of personality, such as protection of physical integrity, freedom of will, reputation, privacy, and freedom of belief and opinion; (ii) interests of domestic relations, such as protection of marriage, maintenance claims, and legal relations between parents and children; and (iii) interests of substance, such as protection of property, freedom of testation, freedom of industry, and contract. (c) Social interests are composed of interests in (i) general security, (ii) security of social institutions, (iii) general morals, (iv) protection of social resources from waste, (v) general progress, and (vi) individual human life.

C. Free Law: Eugen Ehrlich (1862–1922) and Hermann U. Kantorowicz (1877–1940)

The free law theories do not merely analyze the legal process as a matter of social reality but also bid the judge to alter the statute law in accordance with the demands of justice.

According to Ehrlich, the basis of free decision lies in the fact that no rule is just for all times, so that a great bulk of rules of decision are determined by the changing social conditions to which they are applied. However, he maintains that free decision is not arbitrary, for it grows out of the principles of judicial tradition. It is a characteristic of the judicial office that the judge's decision represents not his personal opinion but the law found primarily in past legal records, statutes, judicial decisions, and legal literature. The administration of justice has always contained the personal element of the judge. This is a welcome fact for Ehrlich, since the judge's personality must be great enough to be entrusted with the judicial function. Consequently, the concern of the free decision is not with the substance of the law but with the proper selection of judges.

According to Kantorowicz, there are two forms of law: formal, being that which has completed a definite process of formation or interpretation, and free, being that which has not completed these processes. Formal law is explicit or implicit. In its explicit form, it issues either from the original legislative authority (statutes), or from delegated legislative authority (orders-in-council, rules of court, bylaws, ordinances, regulations, etc.), or from customary authority (judge-made law). In its implicit form, it is customary law. Free law is either nascent, in the sense that it would be formal had it completed the process of formation after entering that process, or desired, in the sense that those who apply it desire it to become formal law. Both the nascent and the desired free law may be either explicit or implicit. Free law is not only required by the incompleteness of the formal law but has to be accepted as existent, since judges create new formal law, and it cannot be the case that, prior to that, there was no law at all governing the matter. Sociological studies and concepts assist in the formation of the nascent law by providing the necessary knowledge of recent history of law and present social conditions. The formation of desired law proceeds through juristic relations, which means applying that particular interpretation of the statute among several possible interpretations that allows the realization of the purpose of the statute, but if that purpose cannot be ascertained, then it means applying the judicial ideal of the interpreter.

D. Criticism

1. Ihering

1. Ihering locates law in the social purpose. But when one proceeds with the idea of purpose in law, one faces the crucial question of deciding between conflicting purposes. Ihering is of no help in making this crucial determination as to purpose.

2. Nor has he resolved the conflict between individual and collective interests. He attempts the reconciliation between the two through his levers of social motion, which consist of reward and coercion in the egoistic mode and feelings of duty and love in the altruistic mode. However, reward and coercion can subjugate individual interests, not reconcile them. And to say that deeply abiding conflicts of interests can be eliminated simply by feelings of duty and love is nothing other

than wishful thinking and not a method of reconciliation of the interests in conflict.

3. Some of his conclusions do not flow from his fundamental assumptions and seem to contradict them. For example, he assumes conscious egoism as the motivating factor of human life so that its levers of reward and coercion build social institutions of commerce and law, but he ends up condemning legal egoism. Or, he makes his distinction between the point of view of sacrifice of the individual's purpose and the point of view of identifying the individual's purpose with social purpose, but such a distinction is inconsistent with conscious egoism.

4. Ihering posits his law of causality as the principle of sufficient reason according to which everything that happens is the consequence of another antecedent change, and he maintains that this law is postulated by our thinking as well as confirmed by our experience. This law, thus, asserts the unity of man and nature and regards man as a coherent part of nature. He then applies this law to human action and discovers that matter is different from life so that the type of causality that exists in physical nature (matter) is quite different from that which exists in the human will (life). The former is characterized by mechanical or efficient causes and reacts to the past, he observes, whereas the latter is characterized by psychological or final causes and reaches for the future. Life, he concludes, is the application, through purpose, of the external world to one's existence, and purpose is the idea of a future event that the will attempts to realize. However, in so arguing he has lost the coherence and unity of man and nature that he earlier asserted, for human situation is now treated as unique, and human behavior is referred to a distinct principle. This conclusion has, thus, lost its congruity with the principle that was fundamental in his scheme.

5. The thrust of Ihering's theory is to consider those conditions of man and society that are independent of law, that are prior to it, and that define law's functions and goals. One, therefore, would expect that this calls for an inquiry into extralegal sources of law. However, his own subsequent inquiry confines itself to analyzing concepts and techniques that law develops and uses in dealing with the issues of problems dealt by law, its purposes, and its values, instead of clarifying the objective conditions and purposes that call for the application of law and define its functions.

2. Ehrlich

1. One basic difficulty with Ehrlich's theory is that it fails to distinguish law from customs and morals. This is all the more disappointing for the fact that he himself warns us that the lines between morals and law are shifting, from which one would expect that the investigator has to be very clear about the distinctive features of the law in order to observe the shifting lines.

2. Ehrlich points to the basic elements governing human communities that underlie law and are expressed in fact before becoming precepts of law. However, the basic problem of resolving conflicts, which is law's calling, remains untouched. His sociological investigations do not give us any assistance in dealing with the problem of conflicting interests.

3. His conception of living law does not take adequate account of the differences in social institutions that exist in different societies. For example, the meaning of marriage is quite different in India from that in the United States.

4. He treats the distinction between law and custom too simply, in that he fails to observe how law and custom influence each other. There is a reciprocal relationship between the two, which he has ignored. For example, as Patterson has pointed out, the ritual and sanctity of the marriage ceremony was brought about by the fact that the law of property denied the right of inheritance to an illegitimate child.

5. Ehrlich maintains that the social institutions arise spontaneously, so that there is an automatic ordering of various social relations, such as marriage, family associations, possessions, contracts, succession, and so on. However, such complex and far reaching forms of social relations do not sprout spontaneously. It seems more likely that these social institutions have emerged as a result of interplay between values cherished and modes of life pursued in society, not spontaneously.

6. The interplay of custom and law is not as pervasive as suggested by Ehrlich and his followers. There are important aspects of law that are in no way expressions of usage and custom of a people. A common example of such type of law is tax. Other examples include the law of social insurance or social security, workmen's compensation law, etc.

7. Nor is the relationship between custom and law such that it could be said that the law is always an expression of the customs of those

whom it governs; such is the case with infants, incompetent adults, and the unborn, for example.

8. Law is often a deliberate and conscious act to alter certain practices found in customs and usages, which puts law far from being an expression of these customs and, in fact, makes it quite in contravention thereof.

9. Ehrlich fails to distinguish the two aspects of custom, namely, custom as a source of law and custom as a type of law—a distinction that is quite familiar in international law and primitive law. The more formalistically tight legal systems, as modern societies are, are characterized by a great amount of specific law produced by the legislative process that may have usages, customs, and mores of the people as its source but validity of which is in no way derived from them.

10. Ehrlich makes a distinction between legal norms created by the state for specific state purposes, such as those needed to protect its constitution, finances, administrative structure, etc., and legal norms whereby the state contributes only its sanction to social facts. However, contrary to Ehrlich's conclusions regarding the importance of custom, it seems that deliberately created state law for specific state purposes has been greatly expanding in response to modern social conditions that have called for greater state control, increasingly pushing custom to its place of innocent irrelevance.

3. Duguit

1. Duguit claims scientific positivism to be his method so that his theory is grounded in the premises of facts, not ideology. Through this method he discovers social solidarity as a fact. As his conclusion, he derives three rules of conduct from his facts: one, that one ought not to prevent the accomplishment of the end of social solidarity and one ought to cooperate toward achieving that end; two, one ought to abstain from an act contrary to the end of social solidarity; and, three, one ought to do everything to increase social solidarity. He thus claims to derive his values (ought) from facts (is). This is a fallacy. As demonstrated in Chapter III, above, in connection with natural law, one cannot derive an *ought* conclusion from an *is* premise. He commits this fallacy again when he argues that courts should nullify statutes that do not promote the public service.

2. As a result of the above fallacy, Duguit's conclusions amount not

to logical derivations but dogmative expressions. Instead of respecting facts, as professed by scientific positivism, he has replaced the dogmas of some of the earlier theories of law with the dogmas purported by his own theory. More specifically, he has replaced the dogmas of individualism, subjectivism, and moralism with the dogmas of collectivism, objectivism, and realism. In doing so, he has marshalled the assistance of the least discernible of all facts, namely, history, in which facts can be found to support either of these dogmatic sets.

3. Duguit asserts that laws are dictated by the objective conditions of social cooperation. However, while congruence of laws with such objective conditions may be a desirable goal to strive for, laws are in fact made by humans in accordance with their perceptions, proclivities, and prejudices, often either in ignorance of or disregard for the objective conditions for good.

4. As mentioned above, Duguit gives judges the power to nullify statutes that contravene social solidarity. This is dangerous. Giving such broad power to the court, with no restrictions other than the injunction to apply social solidarity, can easily lead to judicial despotism and thwart progress intended by reform legislation. In fact this has many times been the case even in systems that have worked more under an idea of checks and balances than under an unbridled principle of social solidarity.

5. Duguit is quite correct in pointing out the fact that social tasks and needs increase as the society grows in its complexity. However, it seems that he underestimates the growth in governmental authority as being the instrumentality that has the requisite capability for meeting these needs. He may not be entirely oblivious of this rise in the strength of central authority, for he does suggest that a proof of the existence of a legal norm would be found in the rising of an active group against someone attacking social solidarity. However, such rising is no antidote to the miscarriage of social solidarity by the central authority.

6. By expunging ethics from law and infusing service in its place, Duguit believes that he has avoided idealism and metaphysics. These he abhors. However, in postulating his own law of social solidarity he has set up yet another idealist concept, the metaphysics of which are quite comparable to those of Kant's idealism of freedom or the precepts of the natural law philosophers.

7. Finally, Duguit's social solidarity, too, like the idealist and natural

law precepts, is capable of being filled with whatever content one wishes of it, ranging all the way from liberty to suppression thereof, from social progress to social reaction, and so on. As Friedmann has pointed out, Duguit's notion of function and duty has been used in Soviet jurisprudence to exclude individual rights, eliminate private law, and assimilate all law to administration, and his anti-revolutionary syndicalism has been used by the Fascist jurisprudence to combat Marxist conceptions, to thwart organization of workers in trade unions, and to impose an all-powerful state.

4. Jurisprudence of Interests:

1. In addition to the problems from which the sociological jurisprudence generally suffers, the jurisprudence of interests points to the balancing of interests but does not give much assistance to the crucial question of how that balancing is to be done.

2. The classification and enumeration of interests with which Pound has filled his volumes cannot give us a reliable guide to identifying conflicting interests in society, since these change from time to time and from society to society. Moreover, the classification scheme itself manifests the particular evaluation judgment of the classifier.

5. Free Law:

1. The free law argument gives too much power to the judges with practically no restraints. Thereby, it paves an easy path to judicial despotism. To say, as Ehrlich does, that judicial decision is not arbitrary because it is characterized by the principles of judicial tradition that heeds to the past legal records, statutes, judicial decisions, and legal literature, is to ignore the fact that all of these have to be interpreted and applied as the judge sees fit.

2. To shift the concern altogether from the substance of law to the proper selection of judges unduly minimizes the role that law plays in expressing the collective and dominant values of the society.

8

PSYCHOLOGICAL
THEORY OF LAW

A. Leon Petrazycki (1867–1931)

Leon Petrazycki is the most prominent exponent of the psychological theory of law.[1]

Petrazycki maintains that realities consist only of physical objects and living organisms, on the one hand, and psychic phenomena, on the other. Imaginary, abstract, and verbal objects do not exist as independent realities. According to Petrazycki, observation is the fundamental method of studying all phenomena, whether physical or spiritual. Legal phenomena occur in the consciousness of one who is experiencing rights and duties at a particular point of time. Self-observation or introspection of the phenomena are necessary for one to have any cognition of them. We acquire knowledge of only those psychic phenomena that we have ourselves experienced. However, our inward, psychic acts may be observed externally in the bodily movements produced to communicate them, such as gesture, speech, and so on. By observing the same actions on the part of others, we suppose that they are based on the same psychic experiences. Consequently, as Petrazycki sees it, the scientific method of cognition is a joint method of inward and outward observation. Accordingly, the study of law is the study of different classes of external manifestations of legal experiences and of the differences between these experiences and the manifestation of related psychic processes. This method can be simple or experimental. The experimental method is just as applicable to this study as to the study of any field of psychic experiences of others.

These positivistic and empirical foundations lead Petrazycki not to see legal rules and abstract legal principles as crucial to the understanding of the legal phenomena but to see the actual workings of the human mind, experiencing the sense of duty and the rightfulness of a claim. Law and morality are to be observed in our experiences of obligation. They are psychological human experiences containing negative or positive valuation and a dynamic consciousness of duty. The negative valuation occurs when, in contemplating or observing certain action, we experience a restraint not to perform it or a repulsion against it issuing from a mystical authoritative pressure as if from some superior source. The positive valuation occurs when, in such contemplation or observation, we experience a feeling of approval and attraction accompanied by a prodding, impulse, or stimulation to perform the action in question, which feeling, too, issues from a mystical authoritative pressure from above.

Therefore, law or morality is a projection of our legal or moral emotional experience. The meaning of the term emotions in Petrazycki's theory is not limited to the feeling of pleasure and pain but extends to motoric drives or impulsive urges to action. These drives or impulses are distinguished from decisions based on will in that the latter are deliberate choices made between alternative ways of action. Emotions are of two kinds: one, emotions that have specific well defined objects, such as the appetitive emotions wherein the objects attract us (e.g., hunger, thirst, sex) and the repulsive emotions wherein the objects repel us (fear); and two, abstract or blank emotions that can be connected with a variety of actions as their stimuli and objects. Legal, moral, and aesthetic emotions are of the latter kind.

Thus, in Petrazycki's theory, both law and morality exist in the psychic realm. They are distinguished by difference in the kinds of emotion. In moral experience, there is only the awareness of duty, that is to say, an authoritative restraint impeding a certain action but unaccompanied by the conviction that someone else has the right to its non-performance, or an authoritative impulse to perform a certain act but unaccompanied by the conviction that someone else has the right to its performance. An example would be giving alms to a beggar. In legal experience, the sense of one's own or someone else's duty is accompanied by the conviction that another person has a right to it. Thus, legal emotions are imperative-attributive, that is to say, they are both imperative of duty and attributive of claim or right at the same time. While, therefore, moral obligations remain general, legal obligations tend toward concretness of what is due. Consequently, Petrazycki concludes that there are no moral rights. The entire field of justice (intuitive laws) belongs to law, since justice is a process that occurs within the realm of legal psychology. The case is not that moral sentiments influence and modify legal rules, as claimed by traditional theories, but that intuitive law emotions produce changes in positive and official law.

The consequence of regarding the attributive-imperative character as the distinguishing feature of law is that the realm of law is extended to a much broader area than traditionally understood. As Petrazycki points out, it includes games, sports, domestic behavior of children, parents, and maids, behavior of teachers, behavior in social hospitality and etiquette, religious law, relations among members of criminal gangs, relations of lovers, friends, and relatives, and so on.

Law, on the basis of imperative-attributive experience, is divided by Petrazycki into the categories of (1) intuitive and positive law, and (2) official and unofficial law. The division of law into intuitive and positive comprises imperative-attributive experiences that are completely independent of the idea of any authoritatively normative facts, such as statutes, customs, etc.

Intuitive law is distinguished from positive law not in the sense of the former being the desired or ideal law and the latter the existing law but in the sense of whether or not the imperative-attributive experiences refer to normative facts. The content of intuitive law is intellectual and is characterized by the absence of ideas of normative facts. Four consequences follow from this. (1) The content of intuitive law is individually diverse, since that content is defined by each person's individual conditions, although it may very well be that these conditions are common to a number of individuals, which fact results in a congruity of their intuitive law. Positive law, however, has a uniform pattern of rules for larger or smaller masses of people, since its content is defined by perceptions of external facts. (2) The directives of intuitive law conform with the individual circumstances of a given life situation, whereas the directives of positive law are constrained by a preordained pattern of precepts, customs, or decisions that ignore individual peculiarities. (3) Intuitive law develops gradually and symmetrically, with free variability and adaptability, whereas positive law lags behind the present spiritual and economic life due to the fixation of its content by normative facts, which are facts of the past.

It is important to note here that, as Petrazycki clearly points out, it does not follow from the above that intuitive law is necessarily better in content or more perfect or ideal than positive law. In fact, the contrary is quite possible. Its content can be poorer than that of the corresponding positive law because it depends upon the conditions of individual development that may be lacking in the family's legal education, or because the intuitive law worked by mutual psychic communion in groups of persons whose respective common interests are opposed to each other would prefer its own interests to the prejudice of others, or because that part of society that directs legislation may be more enlightened than the intuitive law of the backward strata of the society.

And (4) the propositions of intuitive legal consciousness are infinite in scope and unlimited in applicability, whereas the rules of conduct are based on authoritative-normative facts and are, therefore, limited to the time subsequent to the publication of the command and prior to its abrogation, to the place (state, city, or house) to which they relate, and to the persons to whom they are related.

While, therefore, rights and obligations of positive law are temporary and local, those of the intuitive law are universal and exist always and everywhere. Moreover, since in intuitive law impulsions are connected to the ideas of certain conduct as such, regardless of anyone's commands or customs, intuitive norms are true and valid *per se*, whereas the significance of positive norms is conditional. In the legal mentality, therefore, they have a higher ranking.

Intuitive law is an essential factor of individual conduct and social phenomena. It operates exclusively in many areas of our relations, such as relations with neighbors, family members, lovers, friends, and so on. In those areas where problems of conduct are foreseen and decided by positive law, people are guided not by legal injunctions but by their intuitive law. Therefore, according to Petrazycki, it is not positive law but intuitive law that is the basis of legal order and the power that actuates the social life.

There are certain causal tendencies that, according to Petrazycki, are found in the functioning of legal psychology but not in the functioning of moral psychology, namely, (1) the tendency to reach the implementation of law regardless of the obligor's wishes; (2) the tendency toward hate and repression in law because of its attributive character, as distinguished from the peaceful character of morality; (3) the tendency to construct a unitary, positive, and heteronomous pattern of general rules to prevent disputes and determine rights and duties, as distinguished from morality, which lacks such a unifying tendency; (4) the tendency toward concreteness of content and scope of legal duties and rights, as distinguished from moral duties, which remain mostly vague and general and indicate only a direction of an action but not its specific limits; (5) the tendency to anchor rights and duties in verifiable facts and not in facts that cannot be publicly scrutinized; and (6) the tendency for submitting legal conflicts to third-party judgment, state courts being one such means. These tendencies result in the establishment of a durable, well defined, and coordinated system of social behavior that we recognize as the legal order.

Law, according to Petrazycki, performs two social functions, namely, the distributive function, which consists in the distribution of goods of economic value mainly through the concept of ownership, and the organizational function, which consists in attributing to certain persons the right to issue orders and in attributing to other persons the duty to obey.

According to Petrazycki, the long-range history of law exhibits three evolutionary tendencies, (1) a decrease in the motivational pressure (sanction and award) of the law; (2) a shift from crude stimuli (fear) to subtler incentives (profit motive), from egoistic to the mixed to the altruistic motives; and (3) a steady increase in the demands of law.

B. Criticism

1. Petrazycki distrusts the linguistic usage of words in ordinary language. Ordinary language, he maintains, is often misleading. Freed from it, he makes his inquiry into law and, as a result, expands the realm of law to such areas as games, sports, etiquettes, relations of

lovers, relations of criminal gangs, and so on. However, it is one thing not to let ordinary language restrict the scientific inquiry but quite another, and not very satisfactory, to use the term law for matters so far afield as relations between lovers or gangsters. There may very well be a common psychological element in all of the above relations and law as commonly understood in ordinary language, but is law of jurisprudence the correct notion to designate that element?

2. There is no scientific criterion in Petrazycki's theory for judging whether intuitive law is good or bad. Consequently, what is left of it is merely a formal system. In that respect, it is not unlike the purely legal positivism of Austin or Kelsen, discussed in Chapter V, which Petrazycki criticizes. His own theory, inasmuch as it fails to provide a scientific method of distinguishing between the good content of legal impulsions from the bad, remains formal like the positivist theories and, to that extent, unsatisfactory. This is especially so for a theory that professes, as Petrazycki's theory does, to provide a scientific theory of legal reform.

9

REALIST
THEORIES OF
LAW

There are two distinct types of realist theories about law, the American realist theories and the Scandinavian realist theories. The two are related only by the word realism; otherwise, there is no similarity between the two. American realism is a pragmatic and behavioral approach to social institutions. Scandinavian realism is a philosophical critique of the metaphysical foundations of law, a psychological approach to law, and sometimes a combination of the behavioral and psychological approaches.

A. American Realism

John Chipman Gray (1839–1915) and Oliver Wendell Holmes, Jr. (1841–1935) were the founders of the American realist movement in law. The movement found its philosophical support in the logic of John Dewey (1859–1952) and the pragmatism of William James (1842–1910). It was furthered by other exponents, prominent among them being Karl N. Llewellyn (1893–1962), Joseph W. Bingham (b. 1878–), and Jerome Frank (1889–1957).

First we shall make a note of the philosophical underpinnings of American realism that were provided by Dewey's logic and James' pragmatism, although these appeared about the same time as the theories of Gray and Holmes. Thereafter, we shall examine the propositions of American realism.

1. Philosophical Framework of American Realism: John Dewey (1859–1952) and William James (1842–1910)

Dewey developed an instrumental or experimental logic as a theory of inquiry, the function of which is to study the methods used most successfully to gain and warrant our knowledge. There are three stages in this process of inquiry, an antecedent condition of which is the indeterminateness or internal conflict of a situation wherein the inquirer experiences a 'felt difficulty.' The first stage is the formulation of problems to be solved. This may be successively refined in the course of the inquiry. The second stage is the suggestion of a hypothesis relevant for solving the problem. The hypothetico-deductive reasoning may have to be resorted to in some complex inquiries in order to refine the hypotheses and ascertain their logical consequences. The final stage is experimental testing wherein the suggested hypotheses are confirmed or disconfirmed. If the inquiry is successful, the original indeterminate situation is transformed into a unified whole. The objective of inquiry is knowledge. Knowledge gained in a specific inquiry serves as the background for further inquiry.

This is a general schema for all inquiry, and its specific procedures will vary with different types of inquiry and different kinds of subject matter. Moreover, a specific inquiry cannot be completely isolated from the context of other inquiries, since its rules, procedures, and evidentiary requirements are derived from other successful inquiries. Furthermore, all inquiry presupposes a social or public context that is the medium for funding the warranted conclusions and norms for further inquiry. Finally, inquiry is essentially a self-corrective process, so that a knowledge claim, norm, or rule may be criticized, revised, or abandoned in light of subsequent inquiry. For Dewey, therefore, there are no absolute first truths that are given or known with certainty.

The rationality of inquiry and of its object, knowledge, arises from the fact that inquiry is a self-corrective process whereby we gradually become clearer about the epistemological status of both our starting points and conclusions.

The method of American legal realism follows this logic of inquiry. It is also governed by pragmatism, the principal exponent of which is William James, although its origin must be ascribed to to C.S. Peirce. James himself acknowledges that origin.

According to James, the pragmatic method is a method of settling otherwise interminable metaphysical disputes. It interprets each notion by tracing its respective practical consequences. If no practical difference can be traced from holding one notion or another true, then all dispute with respect thereto is idle, since the alternatives mean practically the same thing. In a serious dispute, we must be able to show some practical difference from the fact of one side or the other being right.

Our whole conception of an object consists of our conception of the effects of a practical kind that the object may involve. Thus, pragmatism takes the empiricist attitude, rejecting *a priori* reasoning and turning to facts. It is claimed only as a method, and, therefore, does not stand for any special results. It consists in the attitude of orientation that looks away from first things, principles, categories, and supposed necessities and that looks toward last things, fruits, consequences, and facts.

American realism developed within the philosophical framework of experimental logic and pragmatism.

2. Expressions of American Realism

a. Law as Rules of Conduct Laid Down by Judges: John Chipman Gray (1839–1915)

Gray maintains that the state exists to protect and promote human interests. It does so primarily through the means of rights and duties. However, there is no universal knowledge of these rights and duties, so that no one knows perfectly his own rights and duties and those of others. The state needs and establishes judicial organs in order to determine the rights and duties of the state and its citizens in actual life. The judges determine these rights and duties by settling what facts exist and by laying down rules according to which they deduce legal consequences from facts. These rules, according to Gray, are the law. Therefore, he defines the law of the state or of any organized body of men as the rules that the judicial organs of that body lay down for the determination of legal rights and duties. As he sees it, the courts, with the consent of the state, have been constantly applying rules that were not in existence and were, therefore, not knowable by the parties when the causes of the controversy between them occurred. The courts are not willing to face this fact because they do not wish to call attention to the fact that they are making *ex post facto* law. However, the main function of a judge is not to declare the law but to maintain peace by deciding controversies. In a question that has never been decided, he must decide the case somehow and he lays down some rule that meets acceptance with the courts. That rule is the law, which was not known or knowable by the parties to the controversy.

b. Law as Prophecy of What the Courts Will Do: Oliver Wendell Holmes, Jr. (1841–1935)

Holmes approaches the understanding about the nature of law from the point of view of results. Therefore, he takes the viewpoint of a bad man, who cares nothing about good or evil or about praise or blame of his fellow men and is deterred only by tangible penalties. Holmes maintains that this bad man does not care for the axioms or deductions, and he only wants to know what the courts are likely to do in fact. Accordingly, Holmes defines law as the prophecies of what the courts will do in fact. This prediction, then, is all that we are interested in knowing in matters of law.

According to Holmes, it is only in the broadest sense of logic that law is a logical development, like everything else, wherein every part of the universe is effect and cause. However, it is not the case that a system of law can be worked out from some general axioms of conduct. Any conclusion can be given a logical form, but behind this form lies a judgment as to the relative importance of competing legislative grounds. Such judgments of relative importance vary with time and place.

c. Law as What Certain Officials Do About Disputes: Karl N. Llewellyn (1893–1962)

Llewellyn, too, concentrates on disputes in identifying the field of law. He observes that actual disputes call for somebody to do something about them so that there may be peace for the disputants and others disturbed by the dispute and a solution may be reached. It is the task of law to do something reasonable about disputes. The persons who perform this function are officials of law, such as judges, sheriffs, clerks, jailors, or lawyers. Accordingly, he defines law as what the officials of law do about disputes.

Llewellyn modifies this definition by pointing out that the main thing is what the officials are going to do, whether their actions relate to disputes or anything else. He admits that this definition is only a partial statement of the whole truth in that it fails to give an adequate account of law as a shaped instrument that is changing or questing for the ideal.

However, the essential feature of the realist jurisprudence, he points out, is a movement in thought and work about law. He enumerates nine features of this movement: (1) the conception of law as a judicial creation and as being constantly in flux; (2) the conception of law as a means to social ends so that it needs be continually examined for its purpose and effects; (3) the conception of society changing faster than the law so that the law has to be reexamined for society's needs; (4) the temporary divorce of *is* (observation, description, and establishment of relations between the things described) and *ought* (value judgments) for purposes of study; (5) distrust of traditional rules and concepts to describe what courts or people are actually doing, and emphasis on rules as generalized predictions of what courts will do; (6) distrust of the theory that traditional presecriptive rule-formulations are the exclusive factors in judicial decisions; (7) the belief in grouping cases and legal situations into narrower categories than in the past; (8) the insistence on evaluating any part of law in terms of its effects; and (9) the insistence on sustained and programmatic attack on the problems of law along any of these lines.

Consequently, the movement follows the following lines of approach: (1) a rationalization that views opinions not as reflecting the process of deciding cases but as arguments made after the decision has been reached, in order to make the decision seem plausible;

(2) a discrimination among rules as to their relative significance; (3) a replacement of general categories by specific correlations of fact-situations; and (4) a study of personal (personality of judges) as well as quantitative (statistical inquiries into available remedies) factors in the law.

d. Law as Generalization of Potential Legal Effect and Considerations Weighed by Courts in the Decision of Cases: Joseph W. Bingham (b. 1878)

According to Bingham, law is the field of a practical science and of a practical art, in that lawyers try to forecast potential legal consequences of particular causal facts as well as influence the actual trend of concrete legal consequences.

Judicial generalizations have three aspects. Firstly, they often make historical summaries of past decisions. These summaries are not important in solving a present legal problem and have no logical authoritative force upon future decisions. Secondly, they often predict legal consequences, thereby dictating or promising decisions. Thirdly, they may be considered as elements that cause decision, so that they must be weighed and analyzed with other facts to determine their causal efficiency in inducing the decision. Past judicial generalizations do not possess any intrinsic authoritative force for future decisions.

Thus, Bingham says, it is superstitious to believe that law necessarily preexists, that it is general and authoritative, and that judges do not have power to make the law but only to interpret and apply it. The judicial function consists in the orderly settlement of disputes between the parties, not in legislation, and adjudication concerns only concrete cases. It would be illogical to settle most questions by generalizations that are broader than the concrete case. To dictate decisions in future cases not yet before the court is to legislate, and courts do not legislate. A generalization may be a material step in the court's reasoning toward a decision, but it does not thereby become a rule of law. Moreover, judicial generalizations have defects that are inherent in most reasoning, such as determinations by instinctive processes, lack of experiments to cover the entire field of generalizing in detail, and misapprehension and misinterpretation of controlling ideas and impulses. Due to these defects, judicial generalizations cannot be relied upon without thorough scrutiny, analysis, and corroboration.

Therefore, there is nothing authoritative in the existence of a rule or principle. A rule or principle is an abstract comprehension of considerations that would weigh with courts in deciding a concrete question. These generalizations are valid rules or principles of law only if they accurately indicate potential legal effect. It is the courts that produce these effects.

e. Law from a Psychoanalytical Point of View:
Jerome Frank (1889–1957)

Frank observes that law is uncertain, indefinite, and subject to incalculable changes. But he maintains that this uncertainty, far from being an unfortunate accident, is of immense social value, for otherwise the society would be straitjacketed and unable to adapt to the realities of the ever changing social, industrial, and political conditions.

Law, from the point of view of the average man, is a decision of a court with respect to a particular set of facts affecting a particular person. No law exists for those facts until a court has decided on them. Until then, there is only the opinion of lawyers, which is none other than a guess as to what a court will decide. As to a given situation, therefore, law is either actual as to a specific past situation or probable as to a specific future decision.

Frank analyzes the psychology of the process of judging and concludes that this process seldom begins with a premise from which a conclusion is subsequently worked out. Instead, judgments, including judicial judgments, are worked out backward from tentatively formulated conclusions. Decisions are based on the judge's hunches. These hunch-producers, or the stimuli that prompt a judge to try to justify one conclusion rather than another, include rules and principles. But there are other hunch-producers as well. These are the hidden factors in the inferences and opinions of ordinary men, the judges being ordinary men. These factors depend upon the peculiarly individual traits of the persons whose inferences and opinions are to be explained. The peculiar traits, disposition, biases, and habits of the judge determine what he decides to be the law. Therefore, in order to know the hunch-producers that make the law we must know the personality of the judge. Law may vary with the personality of the judge who happens to decide a given case. This variation from judge to judge is not discoverable, or at least not so at the time when Frank wrote, due to the method of reporting cases and the verbal tricks used by judges to conceal disharmony among them. Rules and principles do not constitute law, although they are among the causative factors of the conduct of judges. Personality of the judge is the pivotal factor in that conduct.

Law, therefore, is not certain. The desire for certainty in law is a childish emotion seeking a father-figure. Modern mind, Frank argues, must grow out of this father complex, become pragmatic, and eliminate the childish dread of paternal omnipotence and respect therefor, which dread and respect are strongholds of resistance to change. Frank's ideal is the 'completely adult lawyer' who needs no external authority and who is possessed of a constructive doubt that enables him to develop law in accord with advancing civilization.

3. Criticism

1. The American realist approach suffers from the limitation that it can only be applied where the judiciary is not intimidated by the legislative forces and where the interaction of social forces is sufficiently free so as to enable their scientific weighing. It, therefore, fails for those who seek a universal definition of law.

2. Moreover, it can apply only to a legal system the method of which is case law. Only in such a system can one find judicial decisions as a body of facts.

3. The American realists identify the field of law as exclusively judicial. In doing so they expunge rules and principles. This, however, is an exaggeration of the unimportance of rules and principles. As pointed out below, they do have a role to play.

4. There are four types of problems with American realism as related to the question of ideals. One, it does not adequately deal with the question of ideals of law. The fact that these ideals do exist cannot be doubted, or is it doubted by the realists. But by separating *is* from *ought* and concentrating only on *is*, they have ignored the problem of ideals. Two, as a result of this procedure, realism, too, becomes only a formalistic approach, incapable of the reform that its advocates seem to desire. Three, it allows a framework in which any preferred ideology can be promoted. Even at that, the range of ideologues permitted is limited to those who become judges. Four, it provides no means for distinguishing good law from bad law.

5. By reducing law to the fact of judicial behavior, American realism has eliminated any distinction between facts and law. However, such a distinction does exist both in the legal profession and in the ordinary usage of language. The distinction needs be clarified, not eliminated.

6. The method of legal rules, as distinguished from the realist method, consists both of formal rules and judicially formulated rules filling gaps in the former. The realists' criticism of that regime as totally mechanistic does not reflect that process accurately or completely.

7. The American realists focus upon the wording of the law, and then they criticize the law as being an inadequate statement of legal phenomena and therefore inappropriate for defining that phenomena. However, this way of regarding law misses the fact that it is not the wording or the text of a law but its meaning that is operative in the decision.

8. In maintaining that law would stand still if rules decided cases, the American realists ignore the fact that law adapts itself to the constantly changing conditions by asking what the legislator in a stat-ute or the judge in an opinion would have meant, or, in other words, by discovering the objective meaning of the statute or the opinion.

9. When the realists point to the uniqueness of the concrete case and hold that the legislator could not have intended the inclusion of that which has not yet occurred, they overlook the fact that the statute refers to classes of things and not to individual objects.

10. The realists hold that an institution exists in the fact that people behave in certain patterns. However, a social institution cannot be studied without recourse to the rules that govern it.

11. A great number of jural relations never make it to the court. The realist approach, by looking at the courts as the exclusive field of law, would simply have to ignore them.

12. The realists cast legal science in the model of natural science and claim that it is empirical and its purpose is prediction, instead of it being a rational and normative science that attempts to transform the given law into a generally consistent system of rules. As Kanto-rowicz has pointed out, such an approach is marred by six confusions. Firstly, it confuses natural science and cultural science. Natural science deals with laws of nature that remain inviolable, whereas cultural sciences deal with human actions, governed by human laws, which actions can be lawful or unlawful. Secondly, it confuses explanation with justification. The method of natural science is explanation

through cause and effect, whereas the method of a rational and normative science is justification through reason and consequence. The judicial decision is not an explanation but a justification. Thirdly, it confuses law and ethics. It confuses legal with moral norms, since the former demand external behavior but the latter always take into account the motive. Fourthly, it confuses realities with their meaning. Law is concerned with the meaning of observable realities, but meanings are not empirically observable. Fifthly, it confuses the concept with a constituent element of that concept. The case is not that law is what the courts administer but that courts are the institutions that administer the law. Finally, it confuses cases and case law. It is not the cases but the case law that is binding by reason of the fact that only the *rationes decidendi* are binding. *Rationes decidendi* are not facts that could be put to empirical research but, rather, are constructions of purposive interpretation.

13. It does not seem correct to call a decision the behavior of the judge, as the American realists do. Behavior connotes those physical acts that are connected with the judge's organism. However, the legal effect of his decision is quite different from the physical effects of his behavior. A legal decision relates remote situations through a purely logical connection, whereas a judge's behavior relates to the physical world and operates continuously in time and space.

14. Nor does a legal decision follow the pattern of physical causation. Thus, obedience to the decision by one on whom it is legally binding depends on an independent judgment and will.

15. Holmes' bad man is not a very convincing character, for Holmes makes him worry about judicial scorn but be totally indifferent to extralegal penalties. It is hard to conceive of a temperament that would be so worried about judicial penalty but not at all worried about other penalties. Be that as it may, it seems that his calculus of whether it is worth risking the judicial penalty for his action would involve a moral evaluation of his act, and that is not a matter of fact.

16. Holmes maintains that rights and duties resolve themselves into nothing other than a prediction of what the courts will do about them. However, an inquiry into what the courts are going to do involves an investigation into the reasons underlying the institution that gives rise to these rights and duties, for only by such an inquiry is it possible to predict what the courts will do.

17. Bingham has substituted the behavior of the judge for the be-

havior of the people as the substance of the law. Rules, according to him, are not part of the law but are merely subjective ideas in the minds of those who think about the law. His dualistic metaphysics posit a mind and a world external to it. While the external expression of principles and rules exists outside of the mind, the principles and rules themselves cannot exist outside of the mind. Thus, according to him, meaning exists only in the mind of the speaker or writer. However, that is not true. It seems that the meaning of things follows from the nature of the things considered, whereas its apprehension depends on the objective existence of such meaning and on our ability to apprehend it. Therefore, it is not correct to say that the meaning of things depends on the mind of the speaker or writer. Meanings are genuine parts of the objective world that we apprehend. As Morris Cohen points out, the nominalist (denial of rules) thinking in which Bingham engages confuses the existence of particular images in individual minds with the objective meaning of principles or rules in the world that is common to us. Therefore, rules and principles exist in objective reality and not, as claimed by Bingham, in the minds of those who think about the law. Even Bingham himself admits that courts are and should be governed by constitutional provisions and legislative enactments, which are clearly formulated in general rules.

18. Frank has ridiculed the craving for certainty as childish. However, denial of it would be "complete madness. If I actually doubt that stones will continue to lie on the ground if undistributed, that my body is material, and that my fellow beings continue to exist, the last-named will for their and my protection have to lock me up in some asylum."[1] Frank's aim in his theory is to deny certainty of the law. However, his crucial mistake lies in not being able to see that the problem in law is not the eradication of certainty but finding the precise relation between the certain and uncertain elements in the law.

B. Scandinavian Realism

The most prominent exponent of the Scandinavian realism is Axel Hägerstrom (1869–1939). It is further developed by his disciples, namely, Karl Olivecrona (b. 1897–), A. Vilhelm Lundstedt (1882–1955), and Alf Ross (b. 1899–). They all reject natural law as well as analytical positivism and introduce their own concepts of law as below.

187

WHAT IS LAW?

1. Law as Conative Impulse: Axel Hägerstrom (1869–1939)

Hägerstrom examines the psychological implications of a command. He maintains that the content of a command is different from the content of a threat accompanying that command. The imperative in a command is meant categorically and is not intended to arouse the idea that something ought to happen merely in the realization of a positive value or the avoidance of a negative value on the part of the person commanded. Consequently, threat is only an appendix to the command. Its use consists in inducing the addressee to act in a certain way by means of additional motives. Command does not refer to any value for the recipient. The issuer of the command influences its receiver by his mere utterance of it, not because the utterance is intended to arouse in the recipient the idea that a certain wish or volition exists in the issuer, or because it is a direct expression of a personal wish or volition of the issuer, or because it arouses in the recipient a wish to act in a certain way, for that can be done by advice, promises, or threats, but because it directly creates in the recipient an intention to act in a certain way, without referring to the recipient's scheme of values. Without arousing wishes as motives, it effects an association between a feeling of conative impulse and the idea of a certain action. This mode of influence has the character of a practical suggestion, since it does not use the motives of the person influenced, and has, as its condition, the existence of special relations between the active and the passive party, such as a superiority of power that makes the recipient susceptible to the issuer's influence.

The imperative form is explained by Hägerstrom as something that functions merely as an auxiliary to the power accruing to the mention of an action when that mention makes the idea of that action predominant. Its function is to break down the resistance to the command arising from opposing impulses, doing so by arousing a direct intention to act in the way commanded. When that is not necessary, all it does is to keep in check possible opposing conative impulses.

The imperative form is concerned with the state of consciousness that is intention. There are two factors in consciousness of intention, namely, a feeling of conative impulse and the idea of a certain action. The imperative form ('Thou shalt') represents the former. 'I will' represents the latter. An imperative does not express an already existing feeling of conative impulse in the issuer of the command. Rather, it arouses such a feeling in the recipient. Therefore, the question arises of how someone can have a consciousness of intention that refers to someone else's action. Hägerstrom resolves this question by arguing that one's consciousness of intention regarding someone else's action can be conceived as involving an idea in the former person of a certain intention in the latter person. Thus, in an imperative the issuer of the command has a feeling of conative impulse associated with the idea of a certain action on the recipient's part. The state of consciousness that the imperative aims at producing exists in this way also in the issuer.

Therefore, Hägerstrom maintains that the suggestion in a command does not appeal to the recipient's system of values. Consequently, the consciousness of intention that it aims at producing does not attach any valuations to the feeling of conative impulse. It follows, then, that the command, in order to be effective without the assistance of threats, must cause in the recipient an intention that is devoid of valuation. This impulse is determined not by values that are significant for himself but by the imperative form. This explains why being influenced by a command is accompanied by a feeling of inward constraint.

Duty is connected with the imperative and consists in a feeling of inner compulsion toward a certain action. This feeling of duty, as Hägerstrom sees it, is also not a matter of valuation. Ascribing an inner value to a person who fulfills his duty is secondary to the feeling of duty itself. The feeling of duty is not determined either by valuation of the action as necessary to avoid unpleasantness or by reference to objective values. Rather, it is an impulse toward a certain action, and its compulsive feeling is determined by something external to the individual, regardless of his evaluatory attitude as to that action. The feeling of duty, thus, is a conative feeling, a feeling of being driven to act in a certain way.

Law is, thus, viewed as a conative impulse.

2. *Law as Independent Imperatives: Karl Olivecrona (1897–)*

According to Olivecrona, a rule of law is concerned with people's conduct. Its purpose is to influence their actions. Its content is an idea of an imaginary action by a judge in an imaginary situation. Its form is imperative, not narrative. However, this imperative is neither a command nor a creation of the state.

It is confused thinking, he says, to say that law is the will of the state and that it consists of the commands of the state. A command is not a declaration of the will, for command is an act through which one person seeks to influence the will of another, whereas a declaration of will is an assertion or a statement of fact intended to convey knowledge. Consequently, if rules were declarations of the will of the state they could not possibly be commands. Furthermore, a rule of law is not a command, since a command presupposes one person who commands and another to whom the command is addressed; that cannot be said of an organization called the state, whose machinery is run by an ever changing multitude of persons, such as heads of the government, members of the government, and members of the legislative body. These persons find rules of law in existence and enforced on the whole. No one of them could think that the law consists of his commands, and each can only cause change in some part of the law. Nor, according to Olivecrona, is law a creation of the state. The state is not an entity existing independently of law and, therefore, law cannot emanate from it. Olivecrona explains that the misconception about the state being the creator of law is due to the fact that the state organization provides a machinery for making rules psychologically effective through legislation.

Therefore, according to Olivecrona, rules of law are given in the imperative form, but they are not commands, since a command in the proper sense implies a personal relationship. They are independent imperatives. They are nobody's commands, although the form of language used to express them is characteristic of a command. They are imperative statements that function, independently of any person commanding, as guides for people's conduct and cause people to act in certain ways. Moreover, the imperative is connected with an idea for an action, or an idea of entering into certain relationships, or the establishment of a right or duty, and not with directing a person. The law of a country consists of ideas about human behavior accumulated over centuries through the contributions of innumerable collaborators, expressed in the imperative form by their originators (especially through formal legislation), preserved in the books of law, and continually revived in human minds. There is no fundamental difference between moral and legal rules. Their distinction lies not in the objective character of the rule but in the response it evokes in the mind.

For Olivecrona, law chiefly consists of rules about force. The case is not that law is guaranteed or protected by force, but that it consists chiefly of rules about force that contain patterns of conduct for the exercise of organized force. It is true, Olivecrona admits, that rules contain patterns of conduct for the private citizens but, he points out, these patterns are only another aspect of the rules about the use of force.

3. Law Determined by Social Welfare: Vilhelm Lundstedt (1882–1955)

Lundstedt believes that the only possible approach to coping empirically with questions of law is his method of social welfare, which, rejecting the method of justice of the traditional jurisprudence, is based on historic facts, logical criticism of legal ideology, and psychological experience. For him, legal activities are indispensable for the existence of society. Preservation of society forms the incentive for the continued pursuit of legal activities. Therefore, the shaping of these activities by lawmakers and courts must be determined by the social organization, social organization being the most frictionless and undisturbed functioning of the legal machinery.

Law, for Lundstedt, is the very life of mankind in organized groups. It is the conditions that make it possible for individuals and social groups to coexist and to cooperate for ends other than mere existence and propagation. As mentioned above, he rejects the method of justice. Instead, he points to the importance of the feelings of justice in legal machinery. The feelings of justice are guided and directed by the laws as enforced (maintained). The common sense of justice would lose its ability to play its role in the legal machinery without the rules of law actually maintained. If the legal machinery stopped working, the feelings of justice would lose all bearing and control.

Law, according to Lundstedt, is determined by social welfare. Social welfare in his scheme has nothing to do with any absolute values. Instead, it involves actual evaluations of what is best for the society. It is something that is actually considered (evaluated) as useful to men in society at a certain time. Social welfare means the encouragement of that which people in society generally strive to attain. This includes all conceivable material comfort and spiritual interests. Lundstedt

191

takes notice of the treatment of interests by the proponents of the jurisprudence of interests, discussed in Chapter VII, and denounces their categories as another legal ideology. As for himself, he claims that he wishes to establish as a fact what can be observed in general, namely, that the overwhelming majority of people wish to live and develop their lives' possibilities. The area of social welfare comprises the general spirit of enterprise and a general sense of security. From this he derives such postulates as the common production and exchange of commodities, the reliability of promises, the sense of safety to life, limb, and so on.

4. Law as a Scheme of Interpretation for a Set of Social Facts that Constitute the Counterpart of Legal Norms: Alf Ross (1899–)

Ross presents a concept of the validity of law that combines behavioristic and psychological aspects. According to him, the concept of validity involves (a) the outward observable and regular compliance with the pattern of action, and (b) the experience of this pattern of action as being a socially binding norm.

According to Ross, legal norms serve as a scheme of interpretation for a corresponding set of social acts in such a way as to make possible (a) the comprehension of those actions as a coherent whole of meaning and motivation, and (b) their prediction within certain limits. The capacity of legal norms to serve as above is based on the fact that these norms are effectively complied with because they are felt to be socially binding. The body of norms known as a national legal system is distinguished from other bodies of norms by the fact that a national law system is the system of rules for the establishment and functioning of the state machinery of force. The validity of a system of norms means that the system, because of its effectiveness, can serve as a scheme of interpretation. As applied to legal norms, this means a synthesis of psychological and behavioristic realisms. Psychological realism finds the reality of law in psychological facts, so that a norm is valid if accepted by popular legal consciousness. Behavioristic realism finds the reality of law in the actions of the courts. A tenable interpretation of the validity of the law lies, according to Ross, in a synthesis of the psychological and the behavioristic views. Law, therefore, is a process of reality, that has stabilized itself in an idea of validity as understood in this fashion.

5. Criticism

1. The conception of law as the expression of a sociological probability, as argued by Lundstedt, is very difficult for the common man on whom the law operates to accept, for he conceives of law as a binding norm. More so with the judge, who cannot perform the task of law, which is his calling, by merely calculating the probable social reactions from his actions. The questions in law are not how people have decided and acted in the past or how they will probably act in the future, but how one ought or ought not act.

2. It is difficult to see how the Scandinavian realists can use such propositions as social welfare and claim to get away from the normative. The conception of social welfare is claimed by Lundstedt to be based on observation of facts. But how do you merely observe facts and categorize them as welfare or its opposite? This necessarily involves a role for the normative. Welfare is not a category of fact but of evaluation.

3. Essential to the realm of law is the question of rightness or wrongness, of goodness or badness, or, in other words, the moral evaluation of posited laws. Scandinavian realism fails to approach this problem. Even Lundstedt's concept of social welfare is fixed by its own premises of evaluation and does not admit of principles of *ought* other than what *is*. The Scandinavian realists might dismiss these questions of rightness or wrongness as metaphysical, but that only avoids the issue.

10

PHENOMENOLOGICAL
THEORIES OF LAW

The German philosopher Johann Heinrich Lambert (1728–1777) was the first philosopher to mention phenomenology as a discipline. He viewed it as the theory of illusion, since phenomenon, to him, denoted the illusory features of human experience. Immanuel Kant (1724–1804) gave it a broader meaning by classifying objects and events into noumena and phenomena. Noumena are things-in-themselves, or those objects and events that are as in themselves, independently of the cognitive forms that we discussed in Chapter I. Phenomena are objects and events as they appear in our experience. Consequently, Kant believed that only phenomena can possibly be known.

Hegel (1770–1831) disagreed with Kant and believed that the spirit (or mind) develops through various stages, from where it apprehends itself as phenomenon until, at the height of its full development, it is aware of itself as it is itself, or as noumenon.

Phenomenology attempts to know mind as it is in itself, through studying the ways in which it makes its appearance to us. In the mid-nineteenth century, phenomenon came to denote whatever is observed to be the case. Consequently, phenomenology became a purely descriptive study of a subject matter. Thus, William Hamilton (1788–1856) spoke of it as a purely descriptive study of mind, and Eduard von Hartmann (1842–1906) thought its objective was to render a complete description of moral consciousness. Charles Sanders Peirce (1839–1914) believed it to include not only a descriptive study of the observable but also of whatever is before the mind, real or illusionary. It was to address itself to whatever is 'to be' in the widest possible meaning of the term. The meaning of phenomena has thus grown from the middle of the eighteenth century when Lambert wrote (1764) to the early twentieth century when Peirce wrote (1902).

Although the meaning of phenomena thus changed, phenomenology itself remained one field of study related to philosophy, such as logic, ethics, or aesthetics. However, with Edmund Husserl (1859–1938), who wrote in the early twentieth century, phenomenology became a way of doing philosophy, a method. Husserl believed that the phenomenological descriptions of intentional acts are distinguished from the descriptions of ordinary psychology by the transcendental-phenomenological reduction. This reduction is a methodological device, and it consists in the transition from an ordinary attitude toward events and objects to a reflective attitude. By performing this reduction we discover the transcendental ego or pure consciousness, and we discover that whatever is in the world is so only as object for our pure consciousness. By this method phenomenology explores and describes a realm of being that is not accessible to empirical observation. It is accessible only to what Husserl called the eidetic intuition.

The concept of transcendental ego evolved and changed as Husserl's work progressed from 1907 to 1936. The transcendental ego at first had an absolute character, so that everything else existed relative to it. Eventually, in his work, it lost its absolute status and became correlative to the world. Moreover, while the world earlier used to be what it is for any transcendental individual, it is now an intersubjective community of individuals. Phenomenology, thus, changed from description of a separate realm of being to reflection upon (i) the ways in which our communal experience comes to be, (ii) the criteria for the coherence of different types of experiences, and (iii) the adequacy of these experiences. Of course, there have been other phenomenologists since Hussel, such as Moritz Geiger, Alexander Pfänder, Max Scheler, Oscar Becker, Adolf Reinach, Hedwig Conrad–Martins, and perhaps even Martin Heidegger, Jean–Paul Sartre, and Maurice Merleau–Ponty.

Observing the overall phenomenological tendencies, it can be said that phenomenology indicates two things: one, a way of doing philosophy by using the phenomenological method as primarily outlined by Husserl; and, two, certain doctrinal themes developed by different phenomenologists, or the ontological, metaphysical, and anthropological consequences drawn by them by using the phenomenological method. Thus, phenomenology appears as a variety of things, for example, as an objective inquiry into the logic of essences and meanings, or as a theory of abstraction, or as a psychological description of consciousness, or as a speculation on the transcendental ego, or as a method of approaching concretely lived existence, or as existentialism itself. There are several kinds of phenomenology in the work of Husserl alone.

What gives a conceptual unity to this philosophical movement is its method. This method consists of a series of three reductions: (a) the philosophical reduction, which is achieved by bypassing all theories and explanatory concepts about things and thereby returning to things themselves; (b) the eidetic reduction, which is achieved by eliminating the factual elements of the object under investigation so as to perceive its essence (*eidos*) through discerning in it its typical structure; and (c) the transcendental reduction, which is achieved by bypassing other objects of consciousness so as to disclose the thing consciousness, or intentionality, thereby enabling the consciousness to perceive itself in pure transcendental ego. The seven steps of the phenomenological method, according to one observer,[1] are: (i) investigating particular phenomena; (ii) investigating general essences; (iii) apprehending essential relationships among essences; (iv) watching modes of appearing; (v) watching the constitution of phenomena in consciousness; (vi) suspending belief in the existence of the phenomena; and (vii) interpreting the meaning of phenomena.

Various attempts have been made to apply the phenomenological method to the description of law. This has resulted in various phenomenological theories of law. These theories display three main approaches: (a) an approach that proceeds from the key concept of *Natur der Sache* (nature of the thing) and is seen in the works of certain German philosophers; (b) an approach that derives from the German phenomenological value philosophy (*Wertphilosophie*) and is adopted by certain Latin American philosophers; and (c) an approach that takes the positivist and existentialist viewpoint and is found in the works of certain French philosophers.

A. Nature of the Thing Approach

The *Natur der Sache* (nature of the thing) approach takes as its key concept the translation of the reality of phenomena, which have certain immanent values, into the world of legal institutions, as seen in the philosophies of Gustav Radbruch, Helmut Coing, Gustav Fechner, and Werner Maihofer. According to Radbruch, *Natur der Sache* is the moving force that transforms legal institutions in response to social change. It is a dynamic concept whereby law, being an instrument of change, responds to the changing social relationships. Thus, for example, the growth of trade unions and employer associations demanded the new institution of collective contracts to represent the new type of social relationship. Radbruch insists on the separation of the *Natur der Sache* from natural law thinking.

Coing, however, attempts to combine *Natur der Sache* with natural law and derives certain highest principles of law from basic values and institutions. There are, according to him, basic values (*e.g.*, elementary feeling of justice) as well as institutional values (*e.g.*, the values represented by the state, the economic institutions, and so on). Legal institutions have immanent values.

Fechner points to the physical factors of the *Natur der Sache* that determine legal rules, *e.g.*, gestation, paternity, and so on. Maihofer regards *Natur der Sache* as a source of law and a measure of justice that brings the abstract imperatives of the law in accord with the norms of conduct prescribed by the social situation of a concrete legal condition, as, for example, seen in the concept of good faith or reasonableness applied to statutory provisions.

B. Value Philosophy Approach

This approach is derived from the phenomenological value philosophies (*Wertphilosophie*) of the German philosophers Max Scheller and Nicolai Hartmann and is seen in the works of certain Latin-American philosophers, such as the Spanish-Mexican Luis Recasens–Siches, the Mexican Eduardo Garcia–Meynez, the Uruguayan Juan

Lambias de Asevedo, and the Argentinian Carlos Cossio. According to the value philosophy, values are real, objective, and autonomous essences. They can be experienced and apprehended intuitively. Experience is not a reaction to physical experience, but something that permeates our practical conscience immediately, intuitively, and emotionally. It is an *a priori* consciousness of values. Since values can be intuitively apprehended, they are a source of obligations.

According to Scheller, values exist in a scale. Their hierarchy or ranking is determined by five criteria. One, the degree of detachment of the values from a temporal situation determines their durability, so that spiritual values are higher than material values. Two, the higher the values the less do they increase by extension and decrease by division. Three, lower values are founded in higher values. Four, the rank of a value is determined by the depth of satisfaction yielded by its realization. Five, the rank is determined by its relation to a specific experience, so that moral values have a more general quality than the sensual ones. Hartmann clarifies that the hierarchy of values is not an invariable and absolutely valid good. Everybody has a choice between good and evil, and there is a range of actions between the two from which he has to choose.

With the above value philosophy as the basis, certain Latin-American philosophers have developed their phenomenological philosophies. Thus, Recasens–Siches seeks to reconcile the objectivity of juridical values with the historicity of juridical ideals. According to him, there are five sources of this historicity: (a) the diversity and changeability of social reality; (b) the diversity of obstacles in the way of materializing a value; (c) the adequacy of the means to materialize it; (d) the priorities as determined by the social needs; and (e) the multiplicity of values that engender particular norms for a particular community in a particular situation. He argues that since individual consciousness is the center of all reality and human life the starting point of all philosophy, the values of humanism or personalism that regard the state and the law as subservient to the individual are higher than the values of transpersonalism, which regard the individual subservient to the state.

Garcia–Meynez points out that while juridical values are objectively valid, they are not absolute. They are characterized by various forms of relativity. This relativity arises (a) as to persons, (b) as to concrete situations, and (c) as to space and time. Asevedo sees positive law as a mediation between the values of the community and human conduct. Cossio presents his egological theory of law that regards law as an egological object, that is to say, as human conduct in its intersubjective interference. The judicial decision consists of (a) the logical structure given by a framework such as a constitution, (b) the contingent contents of a situation supplied by the circumstances of the case, and (c) the juridical evaluation imposed by the judge. Judges are obliged to make decisions in accordance with a conception of justice.

C. Positivist and Existentialist Approaches

Certain French philosophers have taken a positivist and existentialist approach to the phenomenological explanation of law; most important of these is Paul Amselek. He reminds us that in order to return to law itself and to see it in its objectal purity, the phenomenological method calls for the method of reduction in both its philosophical and eidetic senses. He finds that there are three series of irreducible elements in the *eidos* or the typical structure of the object law: (1) generic eidetic elements, wherein law presents itself as a set of norms and, therefore, belongs to the eidetic genus of the normative; (2) specific eidetic elements, wherein the norms that constitute law present themselves as ethical norms with the function of command; and (3) particular eidetic elements, wherein these commands that constitute law are part of the function of the public direction of human behavior. These three elements constitute the *eidos* of law. Amselek's aim is to establish a phenomenological positivism. His theory, therefore, is anti-metaphysical. The juridical phenomenon consists in the application of a norm to an object. The structure of the norm model rejects any order of values as an external model to which the norm must conform. There exist objectively observable juridicial norms that are obligatory instruments of judgment. Since norms are models of occurrence in the course of things, they are models as existential content. They are, thus, opposed to concepts that are mental modes of structural content.

D. Criticism

1. The phenomenological assertion is that facts constitute legal values *per se*. Thus, the theory claims a fusion of fact and value. Human existence, by its very ontological structure, is deemed a value, such

that man cannot exist or act without values. Therefore, these values are created because man must exist. The process of comprehension of juridical values must be perceived through the practical activity of man at a given place and moment of history. Values are, thus, objectively realized in the factual activity of man. *Ought* does not represent an autonomous sphere of phenomena, but only an essential particularity of the structure of certain phenomena (such as law) that express a thing to be realized. Instead of a dualism between fact and value, there is an immanent sense of the real, the totality of which is comprised of both fact and value. In law, the identification of fact and value is exhibited by the existence of certain factual relationships that have "immanent" legal value. For example, the courts have been able to attribute legal consequences to certain relationships that fall outside the forms prescribed by the relevant statutes, thereby demonstrating a direct and immediate transposition of the practical situation into the juridical universe. However, it is difficult to accept this surfacing of the immanent as either a fusion of fact and value or as the abolition of the distinction. This may be one explanation of the interrelationship of law and social change, and there are others. The mere adjustment of legal values to new social facts does not indicate fusion of the two.

2. If fact and value merged in the nature of things, certain inevitable values would surface. This is an axiological fatalism. Such merging would eliminate the crucial question of choice between different values or ideologies and would dismiss the conflict between them as non-existent. This is clearly not the case. The very issue of morality is predicated upon the existence of these choices. If one did not have these choices, there would be no need for moral judgment of such human acts as laws.

3. The phenonmenological thesis provides a convenient disguise for any particular ideology. Thus, this thesis has led some of its adherents to believe in the development of human freedom as an existential role (Poulantzas), or in the progress toward human freedom and the classless society as essential realities of our time (Maihofer). To believe that human freedom or the classless society, or even progress toward these ends, are realities of our time is certainly too fanciful to accept. Even apart from the incredulity of this account of contemporary reality, the theoretical point remains that such a characterization is merely a disguise for a preferred ideology.

11

CRITICAL LEGAL STUDIES

The Critical Legal Studies (CLS) movement does not compare in originality with the theories discussed in the preceding chapters, nor has it as yet presented a coherent theory. Nevertheless, it is of sufficient importance in contemporary jurisprudential thought to warrant us taking note of it. The movement grew in the United States in the 1970s, primarily with the Conference on Critical Legal Studies, first held in 1977, and it has found a sympathetic chord in the *Critique du Droit* in France and the Critical Legal Conference of Britain. It grew in the period of disenchantment of the post-Vietnam era for the purpose of denouncing the established notions about law and legal institutions and creating an alternative view of law and society that would promote a substantive vision of human personality.

We shall observe the philosophical moorings of the CLS movement, examine major aspects of its thesis, and present its criticisms. We shall do so with an awareness that its scholarship is diverse (more than 150 scholars identify themselves with it in the United States alone) and that its positions have been shifting and even mellowing.

WHAT IS LAW?

A. Philosophical Moorings

The philosophical moorings of the movement are found in the Critical Theory of the Frankfurt School, the Relativist Epistemology, and the American Legal Realism.

1. Critical Theory of the Frankfurt School

The Frankfurt School was a group of German intellectuals in the 1930s (primarily Georg Lukacs, Max Horkheimer, Theodor Adorno, Herbert Marcuse, and Jürgen Habermas) who, at the *Institut für Sozialforschung* (Institute for Social Research), reinterpreted Hegel and Marx and proposed a critical theory. According to this School, it is a mistake to interpret Marx as a scientific social analyst giving an account of history. The appearance of being scientific arose from the idea that Marx's theory would confirm itself in social life along the scientific model. However, according to the Frankfurt School, Hegel and Marx must be understood as critics whose central claim consisted not in denouncing the naturalist philosophy and adopting the positivist philosophy but in putting the necessary distance between philosophy and critique.

To the extent Marx claimed to have delivered an objective and predictive analysis of social life, the critical theorists consider him wrong. They maintain that it is wrong to think that social theory can deliver scientific axioms. They posit two opposing tendencies: cognition and liberation. Cognition is established by dialectics of self-reflective criticism examining the resolution of theoretical conflict. Liberation is achieved by a series of assumptions about the consciousness of the agents who are being considered by the critical theory. The self-reflective nature of the theory induces the agents to liberation.

Thus, the critical theory is presented as a form of knowledge (cognition) that is inherently liberating. However, this claim in itself is not unique to the critical theory. What is unique to it is the claim that the critical theory simultaneously achieves cognition and liberation by avoiding what it considers the mistaken paths followed by positivism and naturalism. As the critical theory sees it, positivism achieves a liberating methodology by expunging the cognitive content from it but, at the same time, defining liberation in terms of a subjective empirical world. Naturalism achieves cognition by sacrificing a methodology that would confirm itself in social life. Consequently, the critical theory proposes a dialectic-of-criticism between its claims about the social world and its claims about the value of self-reflection.

Methodologically, the critical theory distinguishes itself from the empiricist method of science, from the method of theoretical consciousness (e.g., Marx), and from the method of hermeneutic inquiry or interpretation. Although it accepts the usefulness of these methods to the extent they contribute to a total method of the critical theory, it is conscious of the fact that the empirical method objectifies aspects of social life through theory or evidence, that the theoretical consciousness method attempts a similar control of social life through theory or analysis, and that the hermeneutic method of providing the best possible interpretation of the texts of theory and practice does not consider the separation of theory and action as fundamental. None of these, therefore, is considered by the critical theory as either liberating or cognitive to the full extent. The critical theory is suspicious of external control or external cognition. It adopts self-reflection.

The critical theory claims to be liberating, on the one hand, by existing in the world of action and, on the other hand, by acting as a theory for social change. To that end it seeks a critical distance from facts, a necessary distance that empiricism violated. It restricts the role of empiricism to that of elaborating the facts from which the critical distance must be kept. It considers liberal reform tendencies as wrong because they are grounded in social life, and therefore cannot possibly comprehend the structure that contains and limits them. The critical theory claims to be liberating not in the sense of either providing a strategy for achieving notions of freedom held by actors or persuading a set of reforms to the agents; rather, it aims at the description of assumptions about social conditions, which assumptions could be altered by a process of theoretical and political enlightenment. When the theory produces those results, the claim is substantiated. Thus, the liberating claim becomes cognitive as well.

2. Relativist Epistemology

The CLS movement attempts to use for its purposes the relativist epistemology of the twentieth century, the tenets of which are the rejection of traditional certainties and the denial of objective truths.

Traditionally, truth was sought by relating to some permanent neutral framework, such as connecting, as in Plato, the mutable world of appearances with the immutable realm of forms. Understanding is reached when language comprehends the form, or the essence, of an object. Objective reality exists and is mirrored by language. In medieval thought, the realm of forms became the work of the Christian God. By the eighteenth century, the Enlightenment resulted in a shift from theistic metaphysics. Thus, Descartes located the idea of certainty in the individual mind. Kant moved it from the individual mind to the transcendental realm of *a priori* universal mental structures. In the twentieth century, a new epistemology has emerged that rejects transcendence of any sort and confronts the absence of absolutes.

This relativist epistemology was brought forth by developments in mathematics and physics. Traditionally, mathematics and physics were thought to correspond to an objective reality. However, the mathematicians of the 1820s produced geometrics based on postulates that were fundamentally different from those of Euclidean geometry. Geometries, by the late nineteenth century, became formal systems that were not necessarily connected with empirical reality. In the twentieth century, Einstein demonstrated a similar truth in physics, namely, that Euclidean geometry did not necessarily describe the physical universe. His relativity theory disproved that the universe is capable of a single objective description. It did so by rejecting the Newtonian concepts of absolute space and time and by claiming that both space and time constitute a four-dimensional continuum so that each must be measured against another. Quantum mechanics further separated science from transcendental reality by challenging the Newtonian physics that atoms are solid bodies moving in empty space. The quantum theory held that atomic events do not occur but only show tendencies to occur and the subatomic matter does not exist with certainty at definite places but only shows tendencies to occur. Consequently, instead of the epistemological case being that objective reality exists and is mirrored by language, the inadequacy of everyday language was exposed because quantum theory had now to redefine atoms. While traditionally atoms were viewed as particles, they now had to be redifined as both waves and particles. Moreover, Heisenberg's uncertainty principle, according to which any increase in the accuracy of the measurement of an electron's position in space decreases the probable accuracy of the measurement of its velocity, established that observers affect the phenomena observed. Furthermore, the mathematician Gödel's incompleteness theorem proved that consistency in arithmetic cannot be shown by the formal deductions of arithmetic. This demonstrated the fact that the language of mathematics is necessarily an incomplete description of reality, a learning that was transferred to all languages.

The relativist epistemology resulted in two major critiques of the metaphysical or the transcendental. Firstly, the American pragmatists held that no objective *a priori* rationality existed that corresponded to experience. Secondly, the logical positivists, originating in the Vienna Circle, held that only those propositions are true that can be observationally or experimentally verified, so that all metaphysical, transcendental, and *a priori* concepts are meaningless.

One consequence of the rejection of absolutes was the embracing of ethical relativism. Sociologists argued that value systems could only be products of social, economic, and psychological pressures. Anthropologists demonstrated a range of human values. However, most American thinkers restrained relativism only to creating a dichotomy between fact and theory. They denied abstract logic as having a necessary connection with reality and they maintained that facts, not theories, describe objective reality. Facts, thus, became the source of certainty, despite Einstein's relativity theory and Heisenberg's uncertainty principle. In jurisprudence, the American Legal Realists rejected absolutes and trusted science to make objective reality accessible. They called for empirical studies of law, which they believed would yield the design for reform.

However, the objectivity of facts came to be challenged by developments in linguistics and visual arts. These developments demonstrated that facts and their perception are shaped by the preconceived categories of the observer. Linguists, such as Ferdinand de Sassure, Edward Sapir, and Banjamin Whorf, demonstrated the contingency of human categories, displacing the notion that language is governed by objective referents. Objective facts were shown to be inaccessible to human beings. Even perceptions were shown to be subject to the contingent categories of language. Artists and art historians, too, demonstrated that facts are dependent on the observer's interpretation.

The experience of certainty came to be reexamined, especially through the examination of language by the linguists and the examination of culture by the anthropologists. Thus, among the linguists, Sapir contended that no two languages are sufficiently similar to be regarded as representing the same social reality. Whorf maintained that linguistic pattern determined perception as well as thought. Saussure argued that the meaning of signs issued from their relationship to other signs within a sign system and not from some actual relationship to referents in the world. For Sausure, therefore, knowledge depended on human beings alone, not upon fixed referents. This approach was applied to the study of culture. Thus, historians, such as Lucien Febvre, moved the historiographical focus from the history of ideas to the history of mental structures. Philosophers, such as Ludwig Wittgenstein, argued that no single reality existed independently of the observer's interpretations. According to him, the basis of cognition is human agreement and not a transcendent reality. He thus moved the relativist epistemology beyond ethical relativism by proposing the standard of human agreements.

In the 1970s, thinkers began to examine the relative status of science and literature and argued that all disciplines, whether scientific or nonscientific, provided only interpretations of texts and not access to objective truth. Science had no superior status to that of mere subjectivity. Thus, historians of science, such as Thomas Kuhn and Paul Feyeraband, contended that scientific models did not describe outside reality objectively. Scientific models were interpretations dependent on the observer's perspective. Anthropologists, such as Clifford Geertz, substituted an interpretive theory of culture for the objective observations of behavioral facts. Any interpretation, Geertz maintained, is partial. The French post-structuralists, such as Roland Barthes, argued that a text could have meaning only in terms of the interpretative framework chosen, so that no interpretation could be objective. Literature, according to them, institutionalized subjectivity. They also pointed to the pervasiveness of ideology in interpretation, so that no interpretation is innocent. Post-structuralist thought, thus, went beyond the classical structuralism developed by the French anthropologist Claude Lévi-Strauss after World War II, who had argued that culture generates meaning because of the relationships among its elements and not because these elements are inherently meaningful. The post-structuralists shifted their eyes to interpretation.

The post-structuralist discovery that no objective texts exist led to two interpretations in the 1970s and 1980s. On the one hand, critics such as Stanley Fish maintained that everything in the text is the product of interpretation. Therefore, a description of what the text does to the reader is a description of what the reader does to the text. However, this does not result in interpretive anarchy because there exist interpretive communities made up of those who share interpretive strategies not for reading but for writing texts. On the other hand, the deconstrutionists, pioneered by the French philosopher Jacques Derrida, posit that all texts reflect the belief in objective truth. Therefore, he argued, the critic's role is to deconstruct this metaphysics by exposing how the text undermines its own claims to truth and how its meaning is in fact contingent.

3. American Legal Realism

The CLS scholars claim their ancestry in the American Legal Realists of the 1920s and 1930s, discussed in Chapter IX. They connect themselves to the critical tradition of the Realists, but they reject the Realist program. Thus, they accept the indeterminacy contention of the Realists that legal reasoning can rarely require, in any objective sense, a particular result. They accept the debunking of formalism in legal reasoning. However, they reject the social policy analysis of the Realists, whereunder decision-makers must identify social interests at issue in a particular controversy, balance them, and understand the consequences of legal decisions through studying the operation of the legal system with the help of concepts drawn from sociology and political science. They charge that the legal-policy arguments are similar in nature to the discredited formal-doctrinal arguments and result only in defending the *status quo*, since the policy choice under this methodology is not based on a vision of good and just life.

The CLS movement abhors liberalism and individualism, extols community, criticizes the legal order, challenges the social hierarchy, and calls for a fundamental change in human relations. It is reminiscent therefore, of late eighteenth and early nineteenth century utopian socialism, particularly of Fourier and Owen, and the revolt of romanticism of the early nineteenth century in literature, religion, and philosophy against the rationalism of the eighteenth century.

B. Major Aspects

We shall note below the major aspects of the CLS thesis.

1. Rejection of Liberalism

Liberalism is a tradition of political philosophy grounded in the social contract theories of Hobbes, Locke, and Hume, that believes that society consists of autonomous individuals entertaining values based on subjective desires, that society has common values, and that these values can be accommodated through social, economic, political, and legal institutions. Liberalism, thus, accommodated these values, rather than transforming them. CLS rejects this tradition. In the first place, as CLS sees it, liberalism creates a false vision of human sociability. Its view of society as composed of right-bearing citizens engenders a rights-consciousness that isolates individuals and forces them to juxtapose their existence with that of others. Secondly, liberalism envisions the world into dualities, such as, for example, individual and altruism, subjectivity and objectivity, freedom and necessity, which, lacking a consistent normative theory, enables decision makers to rationalize any result. Thirdly, liberalism offers legitimacy to capitalism and disguises exploitation with pretensions to freedom and individual rights. This disguise misleads the masses into supporting the system that oppresses them. The capitalist welfare state is, thus, a capitalist maneuver to deceive the oppressed.

2. Exposing the Fundamental Contradiction

CLS points to the fundamental contradiction of the liberal theory, which lies in the liberalist demand that the individual be free to pursue his self-interest whereas this pursuit requires restraint of other individuals. It exposes liberalism's curious position that freedom is possible through its negation. That contradiction, it argues, is institutionalized in creating a political state to limit freedom.

3. Other Contradictions

The liberal tradition's fundamental contradiction of advanced capitalism denotes for CLS conflicting social forces in a Marxian dialectic, whereunder concentration of economic power in the dominant class results in exploitation of the proletariat, which conflict engenders revolution for destroying capitalism. The contradiction between procedure and justice means that in the liberal system a failure to follow the right procedures defeats a just cause. There are contradictions between individual and community, between subjectivity of personal values and the hope for an objective moral truth, between rules and standards, between free will and determinism, between active rights of liberty and passive rights of security, and between democracy and the antidemocratic practice of judicial review.

4. Trashing or Delegitimation

Liberalism must be trashed, delegitimized, demystified, and unmasked because simply tinkering with the system to improve it only reinforces the prevailing economic realities. Thereby, liberalism distorts reality, provides false hopes for a more humane society, and fails to change the fundamental structure of society. As CLS sees it, social institutions are socially created, contingent, and unjust while they appear natural, necessary, and just. Law legitimates the *status quo* by perpetuating the mass delusion about the naturalness of social institutions. This realization enables one to create a new society.

5. Deconstruction

As mentioned above, the intellectual source of CLS' deconstruction is Jacques Derrida's post-structuralist technique of interpretation of texts in which texts have no objective meaning. Meaning found in text is the result of an act of interpretation by the reader and not of an inherent objective quality of the text. Derrida's method would reveal in texts those points that are at odds with their ostensible thesis and, consequently, reveal meaningful, but not otherwise evident, tensions within them. This method, thus, dislodges ordinarily understood meanings and demonstrates the perpetually elusive nature of the essence of meaning, since intelligence is frustrated or distorted by the mediation of concepts-in-words between pure meaning and the subject. CLS applies this deconstructionist technique to legal doctrine, which enables it to point to the value-bearing character of legal language and to conclude that an interpretation of a text or a social action is a function of power, not proof. The CLS deconstructionism exposes the indeterminacy of the text and delegitimizes liberal legalism's claim about the existence of a knowable, objective, and value-neutral law.

6. Hermeneutics

The idealized notion of judicial activity perceives the judge as a neutral facilitator interpreting objectively the intent of the law or the intention of the parties in dispute. CLS maintains that since objective meaning is an impossibility, law cannot be value-free. Interpretation is not a neutral or apolitical task. The interpreter's value judgments, his thought process, and his social context are inextricably woven into the interpretation.

7. Ideological Unmasking

To CLS, what appears as natural forms of human association are nothing but unexamined social conventions or constructs. Law reinforces these constructs. CLS debunks legal reasoning as a subterfuge for ideologies. The ideological unmasking of law is executed by showing that a system of legal rules and practices is applied differentially by favoring some interests over others. Much of the CLS work in labor law has concentrated on this unmasking.

8. Exposing Indeterminacy

The essential claim of CLS is not so much that the systems are biased as that they are indeterminate. They are erected upon contradictory assumptions. Therefore, their failure to produce a necessary outcome results not from the insincerity of the decision maker but from the indeterminacy produced by the contradictory nature of the system's assumptions. The appearance of law's ability to provide that outcome derives from the privileged position given unconsciously to one element of the contradiction over the other.

9. Rejection of Formalism

CLS understands legal formalism as the notion that law is a self-contained deductive system, so that decisions result from applying principles, precedents, and procedures without reference to the political, economic, and social context, social goals, and values. CLS rejects the notion that society can resolve disputes through a value-neutral system of rules and doctrine. It maintains that all decision making is contingent on the beliefs of the decision maker. It argues for the rejection of formalism for the purpose of enabling individuals to recognize injustices and inequalities perpetuated by liberal legalism. According to it, there can be no plausible legal theory without a social theory.

10. Rejection of Positivism

CLS adopts the anti-positivist approach of the Frankfurt School and rejects the notion that empirical or scientific knowledge is possible in law.

11. Rejection of Reification within Law

The notion of reification of concepts is borrowed from Marxist theory, whereunder the concept is endowed with qualities additional to the qualities of the particular human beings who either created it or use it. The concept thus acquires an independence from its social context. CLS points in this reification of legal concepts the fallacy of confusing "human nature" with historically contingent social experience.

12. Rejection of Rationality in Law

Liberalism claims that it is rationality that distinguishes legal discourse from other kinds of social force, that in law there is a rational foundation for doctrine and development. CLS rejects this notions as a myth. Passion or will, it claims, is not expunged from law.

13. Exposing the Contextuality of Law

CLS claims that the individual's institutional or imaginative assumptions are shaped by his context, which is determined by his political, social, and economic surroundings. It debunks liberalism for ignoring this type of contextuality. The significance of understanding

211

contextuality in law and society lies in the realization that any context can be broken or changed. One context-breaking creates another context, so that there is no ultimate context-breaking. However, individuals achieve self-assertion by experimenting with new relationships through context-breaking.

14. Establishing Unity of Law and Politics

For CLS, law is nothing but an expression of politics. The Marxists viewed law as an instrument of the ruling class for coercion. However, the neo-Marxists, which the CLS scholars tend to be, see it as an instrument of political propaganda that legitimates the class structure by masking exploitation with apparent fairness, with the consequence that the exploited are co-opted into supporting the system that exploits them. Thus, for example, theft is viewed as a departure from a normatively justified system of property rights rather than as a part of the struggle for control over resources, or limiting victim's consent at the time of the criminal act is viewed as the vindication of an economy characterized by unrestrained market and contractual deals.

15. Rejection of Reform and Call for Transformation

The CLS program is not interested in reforming the existing legal system. Instead, it aims at transforming social, political, and legal institutions.

16. On the Possibility of a General Theory

The CLS scholars are divided on the issue whether it is either possible or desirable for them to construct a general theory. While some argue for elaborating an alternative general theory, others, influenced by modern pragmatist philosophy, deconstruction, and poststructuralism, argue that constructing a general theory is senseless.

17. On the Epistemological Explanation

The above assertions of the CLS are generally not subject to proof or refutation in empirical terms. CLS, therefore, claims that the validity of their propositions is a matter not of empirical proof but of evaluating the appropriateness of their questions about the legal rules. It argues that since the purpose of explanation of a legal rule is to assist in making a normative judgment about it, it follows that the explanation must be in terms that reveal the normative structures of the rule.

C. Criticism

AS TO REALIST ANCESTRY.—The claimed connection of CLS with American Legal Realism, especially the claim that CLS is a matured version of Realism, is not well taken. Even though there are common points of methodology between the two, namely, the debunking of formalism, the demystifying of the law, and the exposing of the indeterminacy and non-objectivity of law, the essential difference lies in the fact that while Realism's objective was to aim its critique toward making law an effective instrument of sound public policy, the aim of CLS critique is to delegitimize law. The differences is fundamental, both methodologically and substantively.

Methodologically, the Realist approach derives from the scientific rationalism of the Enlightenment and finds its roots in an empirical search for common principles in law, as pioneered by Blackstone's systematizing of categories of precedents and developed by Langdell's case method of tracing the growth of doctrines through a series of cases. The CLS methodology, on the contrary, is grounded in the critical theory of the Frankfurt School and is directed against the rationalist position.

Substantively, Realism proceeded from the fundamentally positivist position that law and morals are separable, and it believed that just decisions would result if the decision makers used scientific procedures of inquiry. It, consequently, proposed behavioral research in the judicial process. Realism's attack was not so much on the formalist tradition's claim to neutrality of legal reasoning as on its choice of the first principles that constituted the premises for arriving at the legal conclusions, which choice was made by the formalists on the basis of their personal ethical choice. That is why it became fundamental to the Realists that fact (is) be consciously distinguished from value (ought). The Realists' pursuit was to prevent formalism from distorting law at its abstract level by insisting on moral neutrality during legal investigation. CLS, on the contrary, rejects the very proposition, believed in by the Realists, that an objective decision is possible at all.

For CLS, there is a basic indeterminacy of legal doctrine that makes a value-free jurisprudence impossible.

AS TO REPUDIATION OF LIBERALISM.—The CLS' repudiation of liberalism is worrisome.

There are various schools of liberal political thought in Europe, where it originated, and in the United States. Thus, while some liberals think that freedom means being able to do what one wants to do, others think it means being able to do what one ought to do. Or, while some see freedom as something that belongs to the individual and to be protected from the encroachment of the state, others see it as belonging to the society and the state can be made to enlarge and improve it. In modern jurisprudential thought, there are several traditions of liberalism. For example, one tradition considers political autonomy of law as essential to democratic pluralism (Otto Kirchheimer and Franz Neumann). Another maintains the primacy of freedom of citizens and their freely-formed associations against the state (F. W. Maitland and J. N. Figgis). Another propounds a legal order that its citizens accept as legitimate (H.L.A. Hart). Yet another emphasizes the need to recognize friend-enemy relations and the state of exception in the formulation of the rule of law (Carl Schmitt).

Liberal pluralism believes that the freedom of citizens and their associations is of primary value, that public power itself must be rule-governed, and that freedom exists because of the conflict of interests when regulated by law. It maintains that a legal order depends on the existence of the state. It maintains that a pluralistic civil society has law and a political system wherein distinct political forces compete to influence the public power, wherein their competition is based on a broad associational pluralism, wherein no body of citizens is excluded from participation in this competition, and wherein no body is subordinated to another. It does not tolerate informal justice. It regards law not merely as a constraint but as a guide to action. It assigns to the public power a limited set of functions for regulating the interaction of agents and associations. It implies acceptance of ethical pluralism.

CLS rejects this liberalism. However, in order to persuade people to throw away these propositions, CLS must provide not only an alternative but a better one. It has been lacking in that. The CLS critique of liberalism lacks persuasiveness when it concentrates on ideology but ignores social experience. Thereby it fails to show how the ideological content is incorporated into institutions. CLS indulges in an excessive reductionism when it uses its dualisms of contradictions, mentioned above. Further, its occupation with delegitimation, deconstruction, and so on has deflected its attention away from proving that liberalism has been inadequate in meeting people's needs, fulfilling their desires, and providing an evaluation of law in terms of justice.

Finally, the CLS critique entertains the assumption that there is a necessary relationship between liberalism and capitalism and that liberalism must bear the responsibility for the ills of capitalism. However, it is difficult to accept that liberalism considers market relationships natural or necessary. In fact, some liberals are quite critical of capitalism. Hume, for example, denies that property rights are natural. He considers them a social convention, instead. The liberal support for capitalism had been contingent, only as long as it served the security and welfare interests of ordinary people.

AS TO FUNDAMENTAL CONTRADICTION.—The CLS assertion of fundamental contradiction that all normative concepts contain unresolvable conflicts is too dogmatically made and not proven or argued. It simply is claimed, in the manner of a moral axiom. Moreover, although the term contradiction is used not in the ordinary sense of propositions negating each other but in the dialectic sense of conflicting social forces, any possibility of compromise or adjustment between them is nevertheless denied totally. This is incomprehensible, since the dialectic sense makes synthesis possible, not impossible.

AS TO DECONSTRUCTION.—The use of Derridean deconstruction by CLS ignores the fact that while the technique might be quite suitable for literary or philosophical texts, it may not be appropriate for legal texts. Derrida used his technique on texts of great thinkers that contained elaborate metaphorical structures. These structures provided opportunities for deconstruction. However, judicial opinions are not of this nature. Moreover, a deconstructionist analysis turns out to be less than satisfying since it is more in the nature of an indulgence of the analyst's imagination than a logical argument. Furthermore, since the technique erodes an integrated view of society, it lacks the ability to provide foundations for an alternative social theory.

AS TO INDETERMINACY.—The indeterminacy thesis of CLS argues that law is not independent of the social order and that historical meaning is subjective. It maintains that if there is no clear meaning of the text, i.e., the Constitution, then the rule of law is nothing but a rule of those in power. However, there are problems with this thesis. In the first place, the ideal of the rule of law is just that, an ideal, rather than a specific content. Consequently, the arbitrary or illegitimate nature of decisions might challenge the political and legal order of the society but not the ideal of the rule of law. Secondly, the concept of the rule of law has many aspects, including the laying down of procedural rules safeguarding against the abuse of power. However, the CLS critique has not explored the various aspects of the concept it criticizes. Thirdly, constitutionalism provides checks on the power of the sovereign. CLS rejects constitutionalism but has failed to provide an alternative means for checking this power.

AS TO UNITY OF LAW AND POLITICS.—In this respect CLS betrays an inability to distinguish political reasoning from legal reasoning. While political reasoning is characterized by teleological justification, legal reasoning is characterized by deontological justification. These are two different methods of justification, not, as CLS claims, one and the same.

AS TO SUPPLYING AN ALTERNATIVE.—Finally, CLS has thus far failed to provide an alternative of its own to institute in the place of that which it has set out to destroy.

12

CONCLUSION: WHY HAS IT NOT BEEN POSSIBLE TO DEFINE LAW?

We have examined and criticized various theories about law that have been proposed in an effort to define law. We shall now attempt an explanation of why the enterprise of defining law has not been very successful.

We offer three reasons.[1] One, the theories attempt to define law, claiming to make a universal statement about it, for a universe whose civilizations do not share law as a central principle of social organization. The consequence is that, although the universality of a concept does not require the universality of its existence in space and time, a universal statement about law that exists in actual societies can only be very minimal under these conditions. Two, the persuasiveness of a theory is dependent upon the acceptance of its epistemological premise, but the epistemologies underlying these theories are various. Three, the theories either attempt to make non-ideological statements about the substance of a concept (namely, law) that is inextricably mixed with ideology or they make analytical statements about the form or structure of it, and either alternative hangs on a horn of the definitional dilemma.

1. *Non-universality of law as a principle of social organization:* The method of defining law has been like defining a natural phenomenon that exists everywhere in language that would be valid everywhere. However, law does not exist as a principle of social organization in all civilizations. The same fire may burn in Greece as well as in Persia,[2] but that is not so with the law. Law is a social phenomenon. As such, it has an ontologically mixed structure: it is partly mental insofar as it concerns rules of law, partly psychological insofar as it concerns attitudes, and partly external insofar as it concerns behavior. Thus, it is quite unlike fire or any other phenomenon of nature. As shown in Chapter I, while law has grown into an indispensable principle of social organization in the civilization of the West due to the particular historicity of that civilization, that is not the case with other civilizations whose historicity has produced their own particular principles of social organization wherein law and its concomitant principles, such as equality of humans, are deemed, as in China and Japan, as dehumanizing.

In the face of this situation, the theories about law have indulged into either of the two fallacies. They have either unwittingly assumed that law exists everywhere, or they have ascribed a civilizationally superior status to the Western societies for the fact of being possessed of law.[3] As to the task of defining it, any definition of it can only be very minimal under the circumstances of these civilizations. This procedure may satisfy some sense of having achieved a definition for definition's sake, but the social phenomenon that is law cannot be fully understood by such a minimal device.

2. *Epistemological multiplicity:* Another reason why it has not been possible to define law to the satisfaction of all in the manner of physics' definition of fire is that there are various epistemologies, or theories of knowledge, that underlie the above theories about law. Epistemology is concerned with whether we are justified in claiming knowledge of some whole class of truths or even whether knowledge is possible at all. As discussed in Chapter I, there are three epistemologies that have provided the knowledge-basis for these legal theories: the metaphysical-rational, the idealist, and the empiricist. These theories of knowledge are mutually exclusive and totally irreconcilable. One cannot claim that knowledge is contained in nature discoverable by

reason and, at the same time, that it is gained from an inquiry into the human mind and, again at the same time, that it lies in experience. There does not exist one single unifying concept of what knowledge is that would make one definition of law possible, whereas attempting one definition has been the enterprise of each theory.

It must be pointed out here that the question of the knowledge function of definition, that is to say, whether definition conveys knowledge and of what kind, is quite controversial in philosophy. According to the essentialist account, definitions convey information that is more exact than descriptive statements.[4] According to the prescriptivist account, definitions are symbolic conventions and they do not communicate information.[5] Finally, according to the linguistic account, definitions are empirical reports of linguistic behavior.[6] However, our point here is not to appraise the theories about law in light of the knowledge function that their definitions perform but to make a more fundamental proposition, namely, that the concept of what law is is determined under these theories by their underlying epistemologies that speak to the issue of what proper knowledge is, and these epistemologies are various and irreconcilable, making the task of arriving at one acceptable definition of law impossible.

3. *Value dilemma*: The theater of law is values. It is inextricably related to values in society that are at conflict. It makes a choice from among conflicting values and makes the chosen value imperative. Legal philosophies, in attempting to give a universal definition of law unbound to any particular value, have gone either of two ways. They have either incipiently made an ideological statement or, in the alternative, have merely presented a skeletal (formal or analytical) structure that, bereft of the flesh of values, brings the usefulness of that sort of a definition under question.

Examples of incipience of preferred value abound in the above theories, which we have pointed out in the preceding chapters. For example, the very methodology of natural law lends itself to be used for rationalizing any ideological preference. Or, in Kant we proceed from an inquiry into the human mind for apprehending his philosophy of law and find ourselves drowned in his ideology of maximization of man's freedom through his maxims of moral law. Or, in Hegel we proceed along the unfolding of the Idea through his dialectics and end up with the glorification of the state. Or, in Stammler we are led through an analysis of just law but are simply given his principles of just law dogmatically asserted. Or, in Savigny we follow the empirical method of his historical approach but discover preference for values of conservation rather than change. Or, Marx and Engels condemn ideology but in turn give us their own materialist ideology. Or, Duguit takes us through his scientific positivism but gives us his ideological postulate of social solidarity made up of the dogmas of collectivism, objectivism, and realism. Or, American realism gives us a framework for promoting any preferred ideology and, even at that, it limits the range of permitted ideologues to those who become judges. Or, the phenomelogical theory of surfacing of the immanent values offers a disguise for any ideology. And so on.

On the other horn of the value dilemma, there are theories in the mode of analytical positivism, such as those of Bentham, Austin, Kelsen, and Hart, which provide a definition of law that is so skeletal as to expunge from it law's crucial value element. To the extent these theories deal with that part of the legal phenomenon that interests them, they are not entirely devoid of their truth value. However, they fail in providing a complete grasp of the phenomenon of law.

This value dilemma, thus, is the third reason why it has not been possible to define law satisfactorily. The enterprise of defining law, undertaken by the various theories about law, has attempted to make a universal statement about law in the manner of defining a physical phenomenon of nature. It has not been possible to define law satisfactorily in this manner for the above reasons.

The clarification attempted here has two consequences of far-reaching practical significance. One, the realization that law is not the principle of social organization everywhere on this earth must make us question any professed inevitability for it and must prompt us to reexamine our crusade for law in such delicate movements as, for example, the universalization of human rights.[7] We can then be freed to seeking ways of making these movements more effective than they have hitherto been due partly to the misapprehension that law is a universally existent phenomenon. Two, conflicting values exist in society. A choice between these is made in law and morals. The realization that such choice does not result from philosophy, whose concern is objective truth, must alert us to be on our guard for watching how and by whom that choice is made so that we can put the responsibility for that choice squarely upon its maker and protect ourselves from accepting a philosophical disguise for an ideological choice. Conversely, we can avoid making that confusion ourselves when proferring an ideology. For "[w]hen ideology is disguised as philosophy, philosophy is discredited and ideology is made suspect."[8]

NOTES

Chapter 1

[1]R.T.H. Griffith, trans. and ed., *The Hymns of Rig Veda*, Vol. IV, Book X, Hymn 129, Verse 7 (1892).

[2]H. S. Maine, *Ancient Laws*, (ed. Pollock, 1906).

[3]The term was coined in the 1880s by an English historian.

[4]The term came into vogue in the 1950s.

[5]The word meant peace.

[6]The theories of law mentioned in this section are discussed in the subsequent chapters.

[7]G.W. Leibniz, *Réponse aux réflexions de Bayle*, written 1702, published in C.I. Gerhardt, ed., *Philosophische Schriften* 7 vols., vol. IV, 559–60, 1875–1890, facsimile reprint Hildesheim, 1960–61.

[8]G. Berkeley, *A Treatise Concerning the Principles of Human Knowledge*, 1710, in A.A. Luce and T.E. Jessop, eds., *The Works of George Berkeley, Bishop of Cloyne*, 9 vols., 1948–1957.

[9]I. Kant, *Kritik der reinen Vernunft*, Riga, 1781, trans., N.K. Smith, *Critique of Pure Reason*, 1929.

[10]I. Kant, *Prolegomena zu einer jeden künftigen Metaphysik die als Wissenschaft Wird auftreten können*, Riga, 1783, trans., L.W. Beck, *Prolegomena to Any Future Metaphysics*, 1951

[11]"Like a harlot, nature is at the disposal of everyone. The ideology does not exist that cannot be defended by an appeal to the law of nature. And indeed, how can it be otherwise, since the ultimate basis for every natural right lies in a private direct insight, an evident contemplation, an intuition. Cannot my intuition be just as good as yours?" A. Ross, *Of Law and Justice*, 260 (1958).

[12]S.P. Sinha, "Freeing Human Rights from Natural Rights," 70 *Archiv für Rechts-und Sozialphilosophie*, 342, 378 (1984).

Chapter 2

¹Hindu legal science originated in the theological schools formed to perpetuate the holy text of the Vedas. These schools produced textbooks for their students on the subject of *dharma*, or moral law, in the form of *sutras*, or threads, which are pithy sayings expressing an idea. Four of these Dharma Sutras have been found (attributed to Gautama, Baudhyana, Vasishtha, and Apastamba) and date from between the sixth and second centuries B.C. As the accumulation of Vèdic learning became too vast for a single person to master, specialized schools grew up for various branches of the Vedic study. The Sacred Law thus became a separate science, which produced a new form of literature called Dharma Shastra. Each of the verse-books of Dharma Shastra is probably based on a particular Dharma Sutra. The Laws of Manu (or Manava Dharma Shastra) is the earliest of these books discovered and was composed sometime between the first century B.C. and the second or third century A.D.

Chapter 3

¹It is impossible to date exactly the life of Heraclitus of Ephesus. This work probably dates not before 500 B.C. and not after 460 B.C.

²The Sophists were Greek itinerant teachers of the fifth and early fourth centuries B.C., such as Protagoras, Hippias of Elis, Prodicus of Ceos, and Thrasymachus, all based in Athens. Prior to the middle of the fifth century B.C., the term *sophistes* referred to the seers, prophets, and sages of early Greek communities, such as Orpheus, Musaeus, Pythagoras, and members of the group called the Seven Wise Men.

³These are reprinted here from S.P. Sinha, "Freeing Human Rights from Natural Rights," 70 *Archiv fur Rechts-und Sozialphilosophie* 342, 349–378 (1984). In developing these criticisms, I have gained from the following sources: R. Abelson, "Unnatural Law" in S. Hook (ed.), *Law and Philosophy, A Symposium* 247, (1964); D. Baumgardt, "Natural Law Valid in Itself and Alleged by Relativistic Eudaemonism", in Hook, at 172; E. Bodenheimer, *Jurisprudence: The Philosophy and Method of the Law*. 11 12 (1967); A.B. Bozeman, *The Future of Law in a Multicultural World* (1971); H. Cairns, *Legal Philosophy from Plato to Hegel*, 168 175 (1949); H. Cantril, "Ethical Relativity from the Transactional Point of View", 52 *The Journal of Philosophy* 677 (1952); F. Castberg, "Natural Law and Human Rights", 1 *Revue des Droits de l'homme* 14 (1968); A.H. Chroust, "On the Nature of Natural Law", in Paul Sayre (ed.), *Interpretations of Modern Legal Philosophies, Essays in Honor of Roscoe Pound*, 70 (1947), M. Cranston, *What are Human Rights*, (1962); R.W.M. Dias, *Jurisprudence*, 523 524 (1964); W. Friedmann, "An Analysis of 'In Defense of Natural Law'," in Hook, at 144; W. Friedmann, *Legal Theory*, 12 (5th ed., 1967); C. Kluckhohn, "Ethical Relativity, Sic et Non", 52 *The Journal of Philosophy*, 663 (1955); P. Kurtz, "Law, Decision, and the Behavioral Sciences", in Hook, at 224; J. Ladriere, "Human Rights and Historicity", 10 *World Justice* 147 (1968 69); M. Macdonald, "Natural Rights", 47 *Proceedings of the Aristotelian Society* 225 (1946–47), reprinted

in A.I. Melden (ed.), *Human Rights* 40 (1970); K. Nielson, "The Myth of
Natural Law", in Hook, at 122; K. Nielson, "Scepticism and Human Rights",
52 *The Monist* 573 (1968); F.S.C. Northrop, "Contemporary Jurisprudence
and International Law", 61 *Yale Law Journal* 623 (1952); F.S.C. Northop,
"Ethical Relativity in the Light of Recent Legal Science", 52 *The Journal of
Philosophy* 649 (1955); F. Olafson, "Essence and Concept in Natural Law
Theory", in Hook, at 234; F. Oppenheim, "The Metaethics of Natural Law",
in Hook, at 241; E.W. Patterson, *Men and Ideas of the Law*, 340, 342–343,
352–353, 362–366 (1953); K. Popper, *The Open Society and its Enemies*
(1966); L. Reinhardt, "Comment on Professor Machan's Address", 52 *The
Personalist* 346 (1971); K. Rimanque, "Human Rights", 7 *World Justice* 170
(1965–66); A. Ross, "A Critique of the Philosophy of Natural Law", in M.P.
Golding (ed.), *The Nature of Law*, 68, (1966); A. Ross, *On Law and Justice*,
237–239, 258–267 (1958); B. Russell, *Mysticism and Logic* (1927); K. Stern,
"Either-or or Neither-nor", in Hook, at 247; K. Vasak, "Le droit international
des droits de l'homme", 140 *Recueil des Cours* 332 (1974); J.H.W. Verzijl,
Human Rights in Historical Perspective (1958); R. Wolheim, in 8 *The Encyclopedia of Philosophy*, 450, 451 (1967).

[4]R.M. Hare, "Universalizability", 55 *Proceedings of the Aristotelian Society*
295, 303 (1954–55); R.M. Hare, *Freedom and Reason*, 108 (1963)

[5]Historically, the point of departure must be with Aristotle. See M. Villey,
" 'Sein' and 'Sollen' im Erfahrungsbereich des Rechts. Un point de vue d'historien", 13 *Archives de Philosophie du Droit* 333 (1968).

[6]"I cannot forbear adding to these reasonings an observation, which may,
perhaps, be found of some importance. In every system of morality, which I
have hitherto met with, I have always remark'd, that the author proceeds for
some time in the ordinary way of reasoning, and establishes the being of a
God, or makes observations concerning human affairs; when of a sudden I
am surpriz'd to find, that instead of the usual copulations of propositions, is
and is not, I meet with no proposition which is not connected with an ought
or an ought not. This change is imperceptible; but is, however, of the last
consequence. For as this ought or ought not, expresses some new relations or
affirmation, 'tis necessary that it shou'd be observ'd and explain'd; and at the
same time that reason shou'd be given, for what seems altogether inconceiv-
able, how this new relation can be a deduction from others, which are entirely
different from it. But as authors do not commonly use this precaution, I shall
presume to recommend it to the readers; and am persuaded that this small
attention woul'd subvert all the vulgar systems of morality, and let us see,
that the distinction of vice and virtue is not founded merely on the relations
of objects, or is perceiv'd by reason." D. Hume, *A Treatise of Human Nature*,
edited by L. A. Selby Bigge, 469 470 (1888).

[7]P. Jones, "Another Look at Hume's Views of Aesthetic and Moral Judge-
ments", 20 *Philosophical Quarterly* 53 (1970); G. Taylor, "Hume's View of
Moral Judgements", 21 *Philosophical Quarterly* 24 (1971); A.C. MacIntyre,
"Hume on 'Is' and 'Ought' ", 68 The *Philosophical Review* 451 (1959); R.F.
Atkinson, "Hume on 'Is' and 'Ought': A Reply to Mr. MacIntyre", 70 *The*

Philosophical Review 231 (1961); J.M. Scott-Taggart, "MacIntyre's Hume", 70 *The Philosophical Review* 239 (1961); W.D. Hudson, "Hume on Is and Ought", 14 *The Philosophical Review Quarterly* 246 (1964); W.D. Hudson, "Editor's Introduction: The Is-Ought Problem", in W.D. Hudson (ed.), The Is-Ought Question, 11 (1969); W.D. Hudson, *Modern Moral Philosophy*, 249ff. (1970); G. Hunter, "Hume on 'Is' and 'Ought' ", 37 *Philosophy* 148 (1962); A. Flew, "On the Interpretation of Hume", in Hudson (ed.), *Is-Ought*, 64; G. Hunter, "A Reply to Professor Flew", in Hudson (ed.), *Is-Ought*, 70.

8M. Zimmerman, "The 'Is-Ought': An Unnecessary Dualism", 71 *Mind* 53 (1962); M. Zimmerman, "A Note on the 'Is-Ought' Barrier", 76 *Mind* 286 (1967). For criticism, see K. Hanly, "Zimmerman's 'Is-Is' ": A Schizophrenic Monism" 73 *Mind* 443 (1964).

9A. Gewirth, "Must One Play the Moral Language Game?" 7 *American Philosophical Quarterly* 107 (1970). He makes a disclaimer by saying "I am not claiming that an 'ought'-statement is to be derived from an 'is' statement" [p.109]. It is hard to see the difference between what he disclaims and that which he claims, but if his desired difference is to be respected he must be taken to be making an argument for reduction of *ought* to *is*.

10See, R. Frondizi, "The Axiological Foundation of the Moral Norm", 50 *The Personalist* 241 (1969)

11CF. Sidgwick's point that moral injunctions are not addressed to anyone who has not accepted the end. H. Sidgwick, *The Methods of Ethics*, 6 (4th ed., 1890).

12Black gives the example that "Fischer wants to mate Botwinnik. The one and the only way to mate Botwinnik is for Fischer to move the Queen. Therefore, Fischer should move the Queen." M. Black, "The Gap between 'Is' and 'Should' ". 73 *The Philosophical Review* 165 (1964); G.E.M. Anscombe, *Intention*, 67 (1957); M. Black, "Austin on Performatives", 38 *Philosophy* 217 (1963). For a criticism of Black's specific formulation of the thesis in question, see M.F. Cohen, " 'Is' and 'Should': An Unbridged Gap", 74 *The Philosophical Review* 220 (1965). See also, D.Z. Phillips, "The Possibilities of Moral Advice", 25 *Analysis* 37 (1964 65).

13G.E.M. Anscombe, "On Brute Facts", 18 *Analysis* 69 (1957–58); J.R. Searle, *Speech Acts*, 50 (1959); J.R. Searle, "How to Derive 'Ought' from 'Is' ", 73 *Philosophical Review* 43 (1964).

14J.R. Searle, *supra* note 13: Searle, *Speech Acts*, ch. 8. For criticism, See A. Flew, "On Not Deriving 'Ought' from 'Is' ", 25 *Analysis* 25 (1964); R.M. Hare, "The Promising Game", in Hudson (ed.), *Is Ought*, 144; J.J. Thomson, "How Not to Derive 'Ought' from 'Is' ", in Hudson (ed.), *Is-Ought*, 163; Hudson, *Modern Moral Philosophy*, 288 289; W. D. Hudson, "The 'Is Ought' Controversy", in Hudson (ed.), *Is-Ought*, 168; N. Cooper, "Two Concepts of Morality", in G. Wallace and A.D.M. Walker (eds.), *The Definition of Morality*, 72 (1970); A.C. Genova, "Institutional Facts and Brute Values",

81 *Ethics* 36 (1970); J.M. Zemach, "Ought, Is, and a Game Called 'Promise' ", 21 *Philosophical Review* 61 (1971); H. Ofstad and I. Bergstrom, "A Note on Searle's Derivation of 'Ought' from 'Is' ", 8 *Inquiry* 309 (1965); J.E. McClellan and B.P. Komisar, "On Deriving 'Ought' from 'Is' ", 25 *Analysis* 32 (1964–65); B.T. Wilkins, "The Is-Ought Controversy", 80 *Ethics* 160 (1969–70); M. Stocker, "Moral Duties, Institutions, and Natural Facts", 54 *The Monist* 602 (1970).

¹⁵Searle explains that when a speaker S utters a sentence T in the presence of a hearer H, then, in the literal utterance of T, S sincerely and non-defectively promises that p to H if and only if the following nine conditions obtain: 1. Normal input and output conditions obtain, input being understanding and output speaking. 2. S expresses the proposition that p in the utterance of T. 3. In expressing that p, S predicates a future act A of S. 4. H would prefer S's doing A to his not doing A, and S believes H would prefer his doing A to his not doing A, and S believes H would prefer his doing A to his not doing A. 5. It is not obvious to both S and H that S will do A in the normal course of events. 6. S intends to do A. 7. S intends that the utterance of T will place him under an obligation to do A. 8. S intends (I-I) to produce in H the knowledge (K) that the utterance of T is to count as placing S under an obligation to do A. S intends to produce K by means of the recognition of I-I, and he intends I-I to be recognized in virtue of (by means of) H's knowledge of the meaning of I. 9. The semantical rules of the dialect spoken by S and H are such that I is correctly and sincerely uttered if and only if conditions 1–8 obtain. Searle, *Speech Acts*, 57 61.

¹⁶Searle dropped this *ceteris paribus* clause from his revised formulation of the example because the considerations invoked by it are outside the act of promising and do not bear on the logical relations involved here. See Searle, *Speech Acts*, 179–180.

¹⁷D.B. Lyons, *Forms and Limits of Utilitarianism*. Ch. V (1965); D.H. Hodgson, *Consequences of Utilitarianism*, 31 32 (1967).

¹⁸Stocker suggests that if you freely and knowingly give or get someone to believe that he can count on you to do a certain thing, you have a moral non-institutional obligation to do it, given certain conditions. These conditions are: 1. What you get him to believe you will do must not be immoral. 2. It must not be a matter of threat or indifference to him. 3. Your getting him to count on you must have been free. 4. You may have no moral obligation to do it even if you do some act knowing that your doing it will get others to believe that they can count on your doing it. 5. If you did not know that you were getting someone to count on you, you may well have no moral obligation to it. You may have no moral obligation to do it, even if the other conditions are met, if you were not believed to have meant to get others to count on you. M. Stocker, "Moral Duties, Institutions, and Natural Facts". 54 *The Monist* 602,618 19(1970). *Cf.* Searle's conditions outlined in note 15, *supra*. Stocker maintains that while promising allows his conditions to be met in a compendious and convenient manner, and, therefore, is very useful for letting others know that they can count on us, what it has done is to serve as a means

of placing us under a moral obligation. But there are other means of placing outselves under such obligations. M. Stocker, *supra* this note, at 620.

[19] J.R. Searle, *supra* note 13, at 51, 52. Searle, *Speech Acts*, 196, 197.

[20] *Cf.*, H.L.A. Hart, *The Concept of Law*, 86, 87(1961).

[21] It is important to note that the *ceteris paribus* clause has been deleted from the revised version of the example because its considerations "do not bear on the logical relations I am here trying to spell out . . .", Searle, *Speech Acts*, 180.

[22] *Cf.* J.E. McClellan and B.P. Komisar, "On Deriving 'Ought' from 'Is' ", 25 *Analysis* 32 (1964 65).

[23] "Where the institution of promising is concerned, *ceteris paribus* will have the functions of (a) ensuring that any particular promise was neither coerced nor obtained under false pretensions and (b) raising the question of whether the keeping of any given promise actually violates the provision of [hierarchically precedent moral institution]." B.T. Wilkins, "The Is-Ought Controvesy", 80 *Ethics* 160, 163 (1969 70).

[24] The reason for acting is distinguished here from a motive or a reason for judgment. G.R. Grice, *The Grounds of Moral Judgment*, ch.1 (1967).

[25] G.R. Grice, "Hume's Law", 44 *The Aristotelian Society: Supplementary Volume* 89 (1970).

[26] R. Edgley, "Hume's Law", 44 *The Aristotelian Society: Supplementary Volume* 105, 115–16 (1970).

[27] G.O. Allen, "From the 'Naturalistic Fallacy' to the Ideal Observer Theory", 30 *Philosophy and Phenomenological Research* 553 (1970); G.O. Allen, "The Is-Ought Question Reformulated and Answered", 82 *Ethics* 181 (1972).

[28] W.K. Frankena, "Ought and Is Once More", 2 *Man and World* 515 (1969). *Cf.* A.M. Prior, "The Autonomy of Ethics", 38 *The Australasian Journal of Philosophy* 199 (1960); Prior's criticism in J.M. Shorter, "Professor Prior on the Autonomy of Ethics", 39 *Australasian Journal of Philosophy* 286 (1961).

[29] This is Lon Fuller's theory, which underlies his theory of law. L.L. Fuller, "Human Purpose and Natural Law", 53 *Journal of Philosophy* 697 (1956); L. Fuller, *The Morality of Law* (rev. ed., 1969). For my examination of this approach, see S.P. Sinha, "The Fission and Fusion of Is-Ought in Legal Philosophy", 21 *Villanova Law Review* 839, 848, 854 (1975–76).

[30] G. Ryle, *The Concept of Mind*, 43 (1949).

[31] R.J. Spilsbury, "Dispositions and Phenomenalism", 62 *Mind* 339 (1953).

[32]G. Nakhnikian, "Professor Fuller on Legal Rules and Purpose", 2 *Wayne Law Review* 190 (1956).

[33]E. Nagel, "Fact, Value and Human Purpose", 4 *Natural Law Forum* 26, 28 (1959).

[34]E. Nagel, "On the Fusion of Fact and Value: A Reply to Professor Fuller", 3 *Natural Law Forum* 77 (1958); E. Nagel, *supra*, note 33; S.I. Shuman, *Legal Positivism, Its Scope and Limitations*, 75, 83 (1963). See also J.U. Lewis, "An Analysis of 'Purposive Activity': Its Relevance to the Relation Between Law and Moral Obligation", 16 *The American Journal of Jurisprudence* 143 (1971).

[35]See S.P. Sinha, *supra* note 29, at 855–858. For a survey of these theories, see P. Amselek, "La phénoménologie et le droit", 17 *Archives de Philosophie du Droit* 185 (1972), translated as "The Phenomenological Description of Law," in M. Natanson (ed.), *Phenomenology and the Social Sciences*, Vol. 2, 367 (1973); W. Friedmann, "Phénoménology and Legal Science", *ibid.*, 343, at 346 359.

[36]N. Poulantzas, *Nature des choses et droit*, 82–103, 290, 292 (1964); N. Poulantzas, "Notes sur la phénoménologie et l'existentialisme juridiques", 8 *Archives de Philosophie du Droit* 271, 271–272 (1963); V. Peschka, "La phénoménologisme dans la philosophie du droit moderne", 12 *Archives de Philosophie du Droit*, 259 (1967).

[37]K. Pearson, *The Grammar of Science*, 134 (2d ed., 1900).

[38]*E.g.*, G.E.G. Catlin, *A Study of the Principles of Politics*, 96, 99 (1930).

[39]*Ibid.*

[40]For example, history may be explained not in terms of evolvement of an essence or in terms of concatenation of constituent moments, but in terms of anticipatory action of a telos. J. Ladrière, "Human Rights and Historicity", 10 *World Justice* 147 (1968 69).

[41]U.N.DOC.E/CN4/SR 37, 13–15; CN4/ACI/SR 35, 7-4; *Proceedings of the Third Committee*, 1948, 90–126.

[42]M. Arnold, *Culture and Anarchy* (1869); D. Bidney, *Theoretical Anthropology* (1953); T.S. Eliot, *Notes Towards the Definition of Culture* (1949); A.L. Kroeber, *The Nature of Culture* (1952); A.L. Kroeber and C. Kluckhohn, *Culture: A Critical Review of Concepts and Definitions* (1952); R.M. MacIver, *Society: Its Structure and Changes* (1931); R. Williams, *Culture and Society* (1958).

[43]See S.P. Sinha, "Human Rights: A Non-Western Viewpoint", 67 *Archiv für Rechts-und Sozialphilosophie* 76 (1981).

[44] E. Ehrlich, *Fundamental Principles of the Sociology of Law*, trans. by W.L. Moll, 37 (1936).

[45] C. Kluckhohn, "Universal Categories of Culture", in A.L. Kroeber (ed.), *Anthropology Today*, 507 (1953); A.L. Kroeber, *Configurations of Culture Growth* (1944); A.L. Kroeber, "Concluding Review", in Tax, Sol et al (eds), *An Appraisal of Anthropology Today*, 373 (1953).

[46] C. Kluckhohn, "The Philosophy of the Navaho Indians", in F.S.C. Northrop (ed.), *Ideological Differences and World Order*, 356, 384 (1949).

[47] F.S.C. Northrop, *European Union and United States Foreign Policy, A Study in Sociological Jurisprudence*, 75–137 (1954). See also F.S.C. Northrop, "Contemporary Jurisprudence and International Law", 61 *Yale Law Journal* 623 (1961).

[48] *Infra*, criticism number 9.

[49] A. Edel, *Ethical Judgment*, 30 (1955).

[50] R. Brandt, *Hopi Ethics*, 11 (1954).

[51] R. Benedict, *Patterns of Culture*, 278 (1934).

[52] S.P. Sinha, *supra*, note 43, at 88–90.

[53] A. Maslow, "Psychological Progress in Understanding Human Nature and a Scientific Ethics", 10 *Main Currents* 75 (1954).

[54] Frenkel-Brunswik, "Social Research and the Problem of Values: A Reply", 49 *Journal of Abnormal and Social Psychology*, 466 (1954).

[55] S. Asch, *Social Psychology*, 375–378 (1952).

[56] Kolb, "A Social-Psychological Conception of Human Freedom", 63 *Ethics* 180 (1953).

[57] T. Parsons and E. Shils, *Toward a General Theory of Action*. 171 (1951).

[58] G. Roheim, *Psychoanalysis and Anthropology*, 435 (1950).

[59] G. Murdock, "The Common Denominator of Cultures", in R. Linton (ed.), *The Science of man in the World Crisis* (1945); C. Kluckhohn, "Universal Categories of Culture", in *Anthropology Today* (1953).

[60] I. White, "Energy and the Evolution of Culture", 45 *American Anthropologist* 335 (1943); G. Child, *Social Evolution* (1951). J. Steward, "Cultural Causality and Law", 51 *American Anthropologist* 1 (1949).

[61] I. Boas, *The Mind of Primitive Man*, 195 (rev. ed.,) 1938).

[62]C. Wissler, *Man and Culture* (1923).

[63]A.I. Kroeber, "The Concept of Culture in Science", 35 *Journal of General Education* 188 (1949).

[64]R. Linton, "Universal Ethical Principles: An Anthropological View", in R. Anshen (ed.), *Moral Principles of Action*, 646 (1952); R. Linton, "The Problems of Universal Values", in R. F. Spencer (ed.), *Method and Perspective in Anthropology*, 150 (1954).

[65]P. V. Kane, *History of Dharmasastra*, Vol. II, 244 245 (1946).

[66]G. Dorsey, "Two Objective Bases for a World-Wide Legal Order", in F.S.C. Northrop (ed.), *Ideological Differences and World Order*, (1949); J. Needham, *Human Law and the Laws of Nature in China and the West* (1951).

[67]*Supra.* criticism number 8.

[68]G. Vlastos, "Justice and Equality", in R.B.B. Brandt (ed.), *Social Justice*, 31 (1962), reprinted in A.I. Melden (ed.), *Human Rights*, 76 (1970); R. Wasserstrom, "Rights, Human Rights, and Racial Discrimination", 61 *Journal of Philosophy* 628 (1964), reprinted in Melden, *Human Rights*, 96.

[69]*E.g.*, U.S. Declaration of Independence uses this mode of argument.

[70]T.R. Machan, "A Rationale for Human Rights", 52 *the Personalist* 216 227–232 (1971); T.R. Machan, "Human Rights: Some Points of Clarification", 5 *The Journal of Critical Analysis* 30, 33, 35 (1975). *Cf.* W.I. Blackstone, "The Justification of Human Rights", in G.H. Pollack (ed.), *Human Rights*, 90, 100 (1971). For criticisms, see K. Nielson, "On Taking Human Nature as the Basis of Morality", 29 *Social Research* 159 (1962); I. Reinhardt, "Comments on Professor Machan's Address", 52 *The Personalist* 346 (1971).

[71]For example, in Hindu philosophy there is a strict causal connection between deeds and consequences, but the connection is spread out over a scale of transmigration of the soul from one living form to another, the human form being only one of them.

[72]L.L. Fuller, *Morality of Law*, rev. ed. 155 (1969).

[73]*Id.*, at 157–59

[74]*Id.*, at 159–62.

[75]*Id.*, at 162–167

[76]L. Fuller, "A Reply to Professors Cohen and Dworkin," 10 *Villanova Law Review* 655, 656–59 (1965).

⁷⁷*Id.*, at 660. Some of these points that support the claim of morality are pursued further in Fuller, *Morality of Law*, 200–23.

⁷⁸Mullock, "The Inner Morality of Law", 84 *Ethics* 327, 329 (1974).

⁷⁹This distinction may be similar to that made by Plato and Aristotle between the theoretical (causal, logical) and the practical. See, generally, Aristotle, *Ethica Nichomachea;* Plato, *Statesman.* For an attempt to defend Fuller's theory along these lines, see Mullock, *supra* note 78, at 327–28.

Chapter 5

¹Discussed, below, in Chapter VI.

²Discussed, below, in Chapter VII.

³The question was confronted by the scholars when they began to study law and legal institutions in the African tribal society. See, for example, M. Gluckman, "African Jurisprudence," 18 *Advancement of Science* 439 (1962); P. Bohannan, *Justice and Judgment Among the Tiv*, 4–5, 69 (1957); P. Bohannan, "Differing Realms of Law," 67 *American Anthropologist* 36 (1965); I. Schapera, "Malinowski's Theories of Law," in R. Firth, ed., *Man and Culture*, 139 (1957); A.R. Radcliffe-Brown, *Structure and Function in Primitive Society*, 208, 212 (1952); S.F. Nadel, *The Nuba: An Anthropological Study of the Hill Tribes of Kordofan*, 500 (1947); M.J. Herskovits, *Man and his Works: The Science of Cultural Anthropology*, 345 (1948); E.A. Hoebel, *The Law of Primitive Man*, 28 (1954); R.H. Lowie, *Social Organization*, 156 (1948); I. Schapera, *A Handbook of Tswana Law and Custom*, 37 (2d ed., 1955); B. Malinowski, *Crime and Custom in Savage Society*, 55, 58 (1926); B. Malinowski, "A New Instrument for the Interpretation of Law—Especially Primitive," 51 *Yale Law Journal*, 1243, 1244 (1942); J. Fried, "The Relation of Ideal Norms to Actual Behavior in Tarahumara Society," 9 *Southwestern Journal of Anthropology* 286 (1953); J. Goebel, Jr., *Cases and Materials on the Development of Legal Institutions*, 67–69 (1946); R. Bienenfeld, "Prolegemena to a Psychoanalysis of Law and Justice, Part II—Analysis," 53 *California Law Review* 1329 (1965); K. S. Carlston, *Law and Organization in World Society* (1962); K. S. Carlston, *Law and Structures of Social Action*, 5 (1956); K. S. Carlston, *Social Theory and African Tribal Organization*, 53 (1968); L. Nader, "The Anthropological Study of Law," 67 *American Anthropologist* 3 (1965); L. Pospisil, "Kapauku Papuans and Their Law," *Yale University Publications in Anthropology*, No. 54, 248–272 (1958); R. Pound and T. F. Plucknett, *Readings on the History and System of the Common Law*, 3 (3d ed., 1927); H. Kuper and L. Kuper, "Introduction," in H. Kuper and L. Kuper, eds., *African Law: Adaptation and Development*, 3 (1965); M. G. Smith, "The Sociological Framework of Law," in *id*; 24; T. O. Elias, *The Nature of African Customary Law*, Chaps. 1–4 (1956). *Cf*, J. H. Provinse, "The Underlying Sanctions of Plains Indian Culture," in F. Eggan, ed., *Social Anthropology of North American Tribes*, 341 (2d ed., 1955); R.H. Lowie, "Military Societies of the Crow Indians," 11 *Anthropological Papers of the American Museum of Natural History* 147 (1916); R.H. Lowie, "Hidasta

Men's Societies," *id.*, 225; K. Llewellyn and E.A. Hoebel, *The Cheyenne Way: Conflict and Case Law in Primitive Jurisprudence*, Chap. 5 (1941).

⁴For a rather unfair criticism of Kelsen in this regard, see S. Shuman, *Legal Positivism, Its Scope and Limitations*, 95–119 (1963). For example, Shuman seemingly reads Kelsen's theory as dismissing the apparent need to have men believe in some objective values, and he then questions this proposition. *Id.*, at 100. Also, he interprets Kelsen's statement that "[t]he legal norms enacted by the law creating authorities are prescriptive; the rules of law formulated by the science of law are descriptive," (Kelsen, *General Theory*, 9, at 45) to mean "that scientific laws prescribe nothing while legal norms describe nothing." Shuman, *supra*, at 105. After accepting such an obviously overbroad interpretation of Kelsen's views, Shuman then proceeds to criticize this proposition as well. *Id.*, at 105–19. In the process, he overlooks Kelsen's own distinction between legal and ethical norms. Id., at 107.

⁵This thesis of Henri Poincaré has had far-reaching impact upon the philosophy of science. H. Poincaré, *Science and Hypothesis* (1952). See also E. Nagel, *The Structure of Science*, 293–98 (1961); Bridgman, Determinism in Modern Science, in *Determinism and Freedom in the Age of Modern Science* 43, 57 (S. Hook ed. 1958).

⁶The subatomic phenomenon defies causal explanation altogether, partly due to the uncertainty formula propounded by Heisenberg. According to this theory, the relation between the momentum and the position of a given subatomic particle at a given moment cannot be precisely determined because of the unpredictable variations in the momentum and position of subatomic particles produced by the interaction of these particles with the measuring instruments. W. Heisenberg, *The Physical Principles of the Quantum Theory*, 3 (C. Eckart & F.C. Hoyt transl., 1930).

⁷See, *e.g.*, Nomos VIII, *Rational Decision* (C.J. Friedrich ed. 1962); Berns, "Law and Behavioral Science," 28 *Law and Contemporary Problems* 185 (1963); Kort, "Simultaneous Equations and Boolean Algebra in the Analysis of Judicial Decisions," 28 *Law and Contemporary Problems* 143 (1963); Ulmer, "Quantitative Analysis of Judicial Processes: Some Practical and Theoretical Applications," 28 *Law and Contemporary Problems* 164 (1963).

⁸H.L.A. Hart, "Kelsen Visited," 10 *U.C.L.A. Law Review* 709, 712–13 (1963), wherein he states: "So we would expect the general form of the statements of the normative science of English or California law, if its task is simply that of describing or representing the law of those systems, to be the kind indicated by the following blank schemata:

Section 2 of the Homicide Act of 1957 which provides . . . means that. . . .
Section 18, subsection 2 of the California Penal Code means the same as. . . .

Statements of the form of these two schemata are of course about the rules of English or California law in the sense that they tell us what these rules mean but they are not themselves to be identified with the rules whose meaning they explain. They are jurist's statements about law, not legislative pronouncements of law," *Id.*, at 713.

⁹A. Ross, *On Law and Justice*, 9–10 (1959).

¹⁰Golding, "Kelsen and the Concept of 'Legal System' ", 47 *Archiv fur Rechts-und Sozialphilosophie* 355 (1961).

¹¹*Ibid.*

¹²Kelsen, *General Theory*, at 374.

¹³Id. at 375.

¹⁴Id. at 375–76.

¹⁵Hart criticizes Kelsen for dealing only with the situation where the moral duty and legal duty actually collide within a specific individual, and for ignoring the possibility of the moral criticism of law where the critic, although under no duty imposed by the law, nevertheless objects to that law on moral grounds. See Hart, *supra* note 8, at 724, 726. This criticism, however, seems to be inapposite, since Kelsen's theory appears to apply in both situations.

¹⁶Hart, *supra* note 8, at 725, n26. Criticizing Kelsen, Hart states that the statement that a valid legal rule conflicted with a valid moral rule would not be equivalent to the joint assertion of "A ought to be" and "A ought not to be," which he considers a contradiction; it would be equivalent to the statement about "A ought to be" and "A ought not to be" to the effect that they conflict. This certainly is not a contradiction or logically impossible, though Kelsen would be entitled to argue that it was false. *Id.* at 727. The fallacy of this criticism lies in the very equivocation against which Kelsen warns when he explains that terms like "norm" and "duty" are equivocal. On the one hand, they have a significance that can be expressed only by means of an ought statement (the primary sense). On the other hand, they also are used to designate a fact that can be described by an is statement (the secondary sense), the psychological fact that an individual has the idea of a norm, that he believes himself to be bound by a duty (in the primary sense), and that this idea or this belief (norm or duty in the secondary sense) disposes him to follow a certain line of conduct. It is possible that the same individual at the same time has the idea of two norms, that he believes himself bound by two duties that contradict and hence logically exclude one another. Kelsen, *General Theory*, at 375.

¹⁷A. Ross, *Towards A Realistic Jurisprudence, A Criticism of the Dualism in Law*, 42–44 (1946). Ross also interprets Kelsen as considering morality as a natural order and law as a normative order, and his criticism of Kelsen is based upon that proposition. *Id.*, at 46–48. However, it would appear that Kelsen considers both law and morality as belonging to ideality (not reality) and, therefore, to normative sciences (not natural sciences).

[18]For a searching critique of the basic norm, see H.L.A. Hart, *The Concept of Law,* 245–47 (1961); J. Stone, *Legal System and Lawyers' Reasonings,* 98–136 (1964); J. Stone, "Mystery and Mystique in the Basic Norm," 26 *Modern Law Review* 34 (1963). For Kelsen's response to Stone, see H. Kelsen, "Professor Stone and The Pure Theory of Law," 17 *Stanford Law Review* 1128 (1964).

[19]An example of such procedures would be rules of recognition along the lines of Hart's analysis in *The Concept of Law.*

[20]*Cf.* Hughes, "Validity and the Basic Norm," 59 *California Law Review* 695, 699–700 (1971).

[21]Kelsen explains: "If we attempt to make explicit the presupposition on which these juristic considerations rest, we find that the norms of the old order are regarded as devoid of validity because the old constitution and, therefore, the legal norms based on this constitution, the old legal order as a whole, has lost its efficacy; because the actual behavior of men does no longer conform to this old legal order. . . . The efficacy of the entire legal order is a necessary condition for the validity of every single norm of the order." Kelsen, *General Theory,* at 118–19.

[22]*Cf.* Lauterpacht, "Kelsen's Pure Science of Law," in *Modern Theories of Law* 131 (1933).

[23]*Id.*; Liebholz, "Les tendances actuelles de la doctrine de droit public en Allemagne," 1931 *Archives de Philosophie du Droit et de Sociologique Juridique* 209.

Chapter 6

[1]See, *Supra,* Ch. V, fn. 3.

Chapter 8

[1]For an excellent exposition and a profound analysis of Petrazycki's theory, see A.W. Rudzinski, "Petrazycki's Significance for Contemporary Legal and Moral Theory," 21 *The American Journal of Jurisprudence* 107 (1976). I have gathered from this article certain propositions of Petrazycki's theory that are available only in Russian and Polish.

Chapter 9

[1]M.R. Cohen, *Law and the Social Order, Essays in Legal Philosophy,* 362 (1933).

Chapter 10

[1]H. Spiegelberg, *The Phenomenological Movement: A Historical Introduction,* Vol. II, 659 (1960).

Chapter 12

¹Based on views expressed by S.P. Sinha, "Why Has It Not Been Possible to Define Law," 75 *Archiv für Rechts-und Sozialphilosophie*, (1989).

²Aristotle, *Ethica Nichomachea*, trans. by W.D. Ross in *The Works of Aristotle*, Vol. IX, Book V, 1129b.

³For example, Sir Henry Sumner Maine's theory does that in his concept of progressive societies. His theory has been classified above under historical theories. See *Supra* note 10.

⁴Plato, *The Dialogues of Plato*, trans., by B. Jowett, especially *Charmides, Euthyphro, Meno, Republic, Sophist*, and *Theaetetus*; Aristotle, *Works*, ed. by W.D. Ross (1928), especially *Physics* 192–195, *Metaphysics* 982–984, *Posterior Analytics* 90, Topics; I. Kant, "Introduction," in *Critique of Pure Reason*, trans., by N.K. Smith (1929); E. Husserl, *Ideas*, trans. by W.R. Boyce Gibson, Vol. I (1931).

⁵T. Hobbes, *Leviathan*, Book I, Secs. 3–5; B. Russell and A.N. Whitehead, *Principia Mathematica*, Vol. I (1910); W.V. Quine, "Truth by Convention," in *Philosophical Essays for A.N. Whitehead* (1936); N. Goodman, *The Structure of Appearance*, Ch. I (1951); R. Carnap, *Introduction to Semantics*, Secs. 6, 24 (1942); R. Carnap, "The Two Concepts of Probability," 5 *Philosophy and Phenomenological Research* 513 (1945); C.G. Hempel, *Fundamentals of Concept Formation in Empirical Science*, Ch. I, Parts 2–4 (1952).

⁶J.S. Mill, *A System of Logic*, 72 ff, 436 ff. (1879); G.E. Moore, *Principia Ethica*, Ch. I (1913); G.E. Moore, "Reply to My Critics", in P.A. Schilpp, ed., *The Philosophy of G.E. Moore*, 660–667 (1942); R. Robinson, *Definitions*, (1954); L. Wittgenstein, *Philosophical Investigations*, trans., by G.E.M. Anscombe (3d ed., 1958), Secs. 3, 66–67.

⁷S.P. Sinha, "Human Rights: A Non-Western Viewpoint," 67 *Archiv für Rechts-und Sozialphilosophie* 76 (1981); S.P. Sinha, "Axiology of the International Bill of Human Rights," 1 *Pace Yearbook of International Law* 21 (1989).

⁸S.P. Sinha, "Freeing Human Rights from Natural Rights," 70 *Archiv für Rechts-und Sozialphilosophie* 342, 378 (1984).

SELECTED
BIBLIOGRAPHY

Chapter 1

Abraham, P., *The Mind of Africa*, Chicago, Toronto, London, 1927, 1954.
Abraham, R.C. *The Tiv People*, London, 2d ed., 1940.
Ajayi, F.A., "The Future of Customary Law in Nigeria", in Afrika—Instituut, *The Future of Customary Law in Africa* 42, Leiden, 1956.
Ajisafe, A.K., *The Laws and Customs of the Yoruba People*, Lagos, 1946.
Allott, A.N., *Essays in African Law*, London, 1960.
——. "African Law", in J.D.M. Derrett, ed. *An Introduction to Legal Systems*, New York, 1968.
Anderson, J., *Studies in Empirical Philosophy*, Sydney, Australia 1962.
Anderson, J.N.D., "Customary Law and Islamic Law in British African Territories," in Afrika—Instituut, *The Future of Customary Law in Africa*, 70, Leiden, 1956.
Appert, G. "Un Code de la Féodalité Japonais au XIIIe Siècle," 24 *Nouvelle Revue Historique de Droit* 338 (1900).
Apter, D.E., *The Political Kingdom of Uganda*, Princeton, 1961.
Ashley-Montague, M.F., ed., *Culture and the Evolution of Man*, New York, 1962.
Ayer, A.J., *The Problem of Knowledge*, London, 1956.
Ayer, A.J. and Winch, R., eds., *British Empirical Philosophers*, London, 1952.
Basham, A.L., *Wonder That Was India*, London, 1956.
Baxter, P.T.W. and Butt, A., "The Azandi and Related Peoples of the Anglo-Egyptian Sudan and Belgian Congo," in D. Forde, ed., *Ethnographic Survey of Africa*, 120, London, 1953.
Baynes, N.H., and Moss, H. St. L.B., eds., *Byzantium*, Oxford, 1961.
Beckman, G.M., *The Modernization of China and Japan*, New York, 1962.
Berkeley, G., *A Treatise Concerning the Principles of Human Knowledge*, 1710, in A.A. Luce and T.E. Jessop, eds., *The Works of George Berkeley, Bishop of Cloyne*, 9 vols., London, New York, 1948–1957.
Bodde, D., and Morris, C., *Law in Imperial China*, Philadelphia, 1967.
Bowra, C.M., *The Greek Experience*, New York, 1957.
Boxer, C.R., *The Christian Century in Japan, 1549–1650*, Berkeley. 1951.
Biobaku, S.O., "An Historical Sketch of Egba Traditional Authorities," 22 *Africa* 35 (1952).
Bohannan, L., "Political Aspects of Tiv Social Organization," in J. Middleton and D. Tait, eds., *Tribes Without Rulers: Studies in African Segmentary Systems*, 54, London, 1958.
Bohannan, P., *Justice and Judgement Among the Tiv*, London, New York, Toronto, 1957.

————. *Social Anthropology*, New York, 1963.

————. *Tiv Farm and Settlement*, Colonial Research Studies No. 15, London, 1954.

————. "The Migration and Expansion of the Tiv." 24 *Africa II* 1954.

Bohannan, L. and P., "The Tiv of Central Nigeria," in D. Forde, ed., *Ethnographic Survey of Africa*, western Africa, Part VIII, London, 1954.

Borton, H., *Japan's Modern Century*, New York, 1955.

Bury, J.B., *History of Greece to the Death of Alexander the Great*, London, 3d ed., 1951.

Busia, K.A., "The Ashanti," in D. Forde, *African Worlds*, London, New York, Toronto, 1954.

————. *The Position of the Chief in the Modern Political System*, London, New York, Toronto, 1951.

Buxbaum, D.C., ed., *Traditional and Modern Legal Institutions In Asia and Africa*, Leiden, 1967.

Cagnolo, C., *The Akikiyu: Their Customs, Traditions, and Folklore*, Nyeri, Kenya, 1933.

Carlston, K.S., *Social Theory and African Tribal Organization*, Urbana, Chicago, London, 1968.

Cary, M., *History of Rome Down to the Reign of Constantine The Great*, London 2d. ed., 1954.

Childe, V.G., *The Aryans: A Study of Indo-European Origins*, New York, 1926.

————. *The Dawn of European Civilization*, 6th ed., New York, 1958.

Chu Cheng., *On the Reconstruction of the Chinese System of Law*, Nanking, China, 1947.

Chiu, T., *Law and Society in Traditional China*, Paris, 1961.

Clark, W.E.L. *The Antecedents of Man*, Chicago, 1960.

Cochrane, C. N., *Christianity and Classical Culture*, New York, 1944.

Cohen, J.A., "Chinese Mediation on the Eve of Modernization," 54 *California Law Review* 120 (1966).

Cotran, E., "The Place and Future of Customs in East Africa," in *East African Law Today*, 77 (1966).

Coulson, N.J., *A History of Islamic Law*, Edinburgh, 1964.

Creel, H.G., *The Birth of China*, London, 1936.

Daniel, G.E., *The First Civilizations: The Archaeology of Their Origins*, London, 1968.

Danquah, J.B., *Akan Laws and Customs*, London, 1928.

David, R., and Brierly, J.H.C., *Major Legal Systems in the World Today*, 2d ed., New York, 1978.

Dawson, C., *The Making of Europe*, London, 1932.

DeBary, W.T. Jr., et al, eds., *Sources of Chinese Tradition*, New York, 1960.

————. *Sources of Indian Tradition*, New York, 1958.

Derrett, J.D.M., ed., *An Introduction to Legal Systems*, New York 1968.

————. *Hindu Law Past and Present*, Calcutta, 1967.

————. *History of Indian Law (Dharmasastra)*, Leiden, 1973.

Driver, G.R., and Miles, J.C., *The Assyrian Laws*, Oxford, 1935.

Driver, G.R., *The Babylonian Laws*, Oxford, 1952.

Dundar, C., "Native Laws of Some Bantu Tribes of East Africa," 51 *Journal of the Royal Anthropoligical Institute* 217 (1921).

————. "The Organization of Laws of Some Bantu Tribes of East Africa", 45 *Journal of the Royal Anthropological Institute* 234 (1915).

Elias, T.O., *The Nature of African Customary Law*, Manchester, 1956.

Escarra, J., *Chinese Law: Conception and Evolution, Legislative and Judicial Institutions, Science and Teaching*, 1936, trans, G.R. Browne, Cambridge, Mass., 1961.

Evans—Pritchard, E.E., *Kinship and Marriage Among the Nuer*, Oxford, England, 1951.

————. *The Nuer: A Description of the Modes of Livelihood and Political Institutions of a Nilotic People*, Oxford, England, 1940.

————. "The Nuer of the Southern Sudan," in M. Fortes and E.E. Evans—Pritchard, eds., *African Political Systems*, 272 London, 1940.

————. "The Political Structure of the Nandi-Speaking People of Kenya," 13 *Africa* 250 (1940).

Ewing, A.C., ed. *The Idealist Tradition: From Berkeley to Banshard*, Glencoe, Juniors, 1957.

Fallers, L.C., et al, "Social Stratification in Traditional Buganda," in L.A. Fallers, ed., *The King's Men: Leadership and Status in Buganda on the Eve of Independence*, London, New York, Nairobi, 1964.

Fallers, M.C., "The Eastern Lacustrine Bantu-Ganda, Saga," in D. Forde, ed., *Ethnographic Survey of Africa*, Part XI, London, 1960.

Finley, J.H., Jr., *Four Stages of Greek Thought*, Stanford, 1966.

Forde, D., "The Yoruba-Speaking Peoples of South-Western Nigeria," in D. Forde, ed., *Ethnographic Survey of Africa*, Western Africa, Part IX, 1, London, 1951.

Fortes, M., *The Dynamics of Clanship Among the Tallensi*, London New York, Toronto, 1945.

————. *The Web of Kinship Among the Tallensi*, London, New York, Toronto, 1949.

————. "Ritual and Office in Tribal Society," in M. Gluckman, ed., *Essays on the Ritual of Social Relations*, 1962.

Fortes, M. and Evans—Pritchard, E.E. eds., *African Political Systems*, London, New York, Toronto, 1940.

Forde, D. and Jones, G.I., "The Ibo and the Ibibo-Speaking People of South-Eastern Nigeria," in D. Forde, ed., *Ethnographic Survey of Africa*, Part III, 25, London, New York, Toronto, 1950.

Gernet, J., *Ancient China from the Beginning to the Empire*, London, 1968.

————. *Le monde chinois*, Paris, 1972.

Gluckman, M., *The Ideas in Barotse Jurisprudence*, New Haven, London, 1965.

————. *The Judicial Process Among the Barotse of Northern Rhodesia*, Glencoe, 1955.

————. *Politics, Law, and Ritual in Tribal Society*, Chicago, 1965.

————. ed., *Ideas and Procedures in African Customary Law*, London, 1969.

Gonidec, P.F., *Les droits Africains: Evolution et Sources*, Paris, 1968.

Green, M.M., *Ibo Village Affairs*, London, 1947.

Greenberg, J., "Islam and Clan Organization Among the Hausa," 3 *Southwestern Journal of Anthropology* 193 (1947).

Griffith, R.T.H., trans. and ed., *The Hymns of Rig Veda*, Benares, 1892.

Gulliver, P.H., *Social Control in an African Society, A Study of the Arusha: Agricultural Masai of Northern Tanganyika*, London, 1963.

———. "Structural Dichotomy and Jural Processes Among the Arusha of Northern Tanganyika," 31 *Africa* 9 (1961).

Haas, W.S., *The Destiny of the Mind, East and West*, London, 1956.

Hamlyn, D.W., *Sensation and Perception*, London, 1961.

Hawkes, C.F.C., *The Prehistoric Foundations of Europe to the Mycenean Age*, London, 1940.

Haydon, E.S., *Law and Justice in Buganda*, London, 1960.

Henderson, D.F., *Conciliation and Japanese Law: Tokugawa and Modern*, Seattle, 1964.

Henderson, R.N., "Onitsha Ibo Kinship Terminology: A Formal Analysis and Its Functional Applications," 23 *Southwestern Journal of Anthropology* 15 (1967).

Hodgkin, T., *Nigerian Perspectives: An Historical Anthology*, London, Ibadan, Accra, 1960.

Horten, W.R.G., "God, Man and the Land in a Northern Ibo Village Group," 26 *Africa* 17, (1956).

Howell, P.P., *A Manual of Nuer Law*, London, New York, Toronto, 1954.

Hsu, I.C.Y., *The Rise of Modern China*, New York, 1970.

Huntingford, G.W.B., *The Nandi of Kenya: Tribal Control in a Pastoral Society*, London, 1953.

———. *Nandi Work and Culture*, London, 1950.

———. "Nandi Witchcraft," in J. Middleton and E.H. Winter, eds., *Witchcraft and Sorcery* in East Africa, 175, New York, 1963.

Jain, M.P., *Outlines of Indian Legal History*, Bombay, 3d ed., 1966.

Jones, G.I., "Ibo Age Organization, with Special Reference to the Cross River and North Eastern Ibo," 92 *Journal of the Royal Anthropological Institute* 191 (1962).

Jouon des Longrais, F., *L'est et l'Ouest, Institutions du Japon et de l'Occident europeen. Six etudes de sociologie juridique*, Tokyo, 1958.

Kagwa, A., *The Customs of the Baganda*, ed. M.M. Edel, trans, E.B. Kalibala, New York, 1934.

Kane, P.V., *History of Dharmasastra*, 7 vols., 2d ed., Poona, 1968–75.

Kant, I., Kritik der reinen Vernunft, Riga, 1781, trans., N.K. Smith, *Critique of Pure Reason*, London, 1929.

———. *Prolegomena zu einer jeden kunftigen Metaphysik die als Wissenschaft Wird auftreten konnen*, Riga, 1783, trans., L.W. Beck, *Prolegomena to Any Future Metaphysics*, New York, 1951.

Kenyatta, J., *Facing Mount Kenya: The Tribal Life of the Gikuyu*, London, 1938, 1953.

Koestler, A., *The Lotus and the Robot*, New York, 1961.

Kramer, S.N., *Sumerian Mythology*, Philadelphia, 1944.

———. *The Sumerians: Their History, Culture and Character*, Chicago, 1963.

Kuper, H. and L., *African Law: Adaptation and Development*, Berkeley, 1965.

Lambert, H.E., *Kikuyu, Social and Political Institutions*, London New York, Toronto, 1956.

Leibniz, G.W., Response aux reflexions de Bayle, written 1702, Published in C.I. Gerhardt, ed., *Philosophische Schriften*, 7 vols., Vol. IV, Berlin, 1875–1890, facsimile reprint Hildesheim, 1960–1961.

Leng, S. *Justice in Communist China*, Dobbs Ferry, New York, 1967.

Li Chi, *The Beginnings of Chinese Civilization*, Seattle, 1957.

Li, V., "The Role of Law in Communist China," 44 *The China Quarterly* 66 (1970).

Lingat, R., *Les sources du droit dans le systeme traditionnel de l'Inde*, La Haye, 1967.

Lloyd, P.C., "Agnatic Cognatic Descent Among the Yoruba", 1 *Journal of the Royal Anthropological Institute* 484 (New Series, 1966).

———. "Sacred Kingship and Government Among the Yoruba," 30 *Africa* 221 (1960).

———. "The Traditional Political System of the Yoruba," 10 *Southwestern Journal of Anthropology* 365 (1954).

———. "The Yoruba Lineage," 225 *Africa* 234 (1955).

Macciochi, M.A., *Daily Life in Revolutionary China*, New York, 1972.

Maine, H.S., *Ancient Laws*, 1861, Pollock ed., Boston, 1963.

Mair, L.P., *An African People in the Twentieth Century*, London, 1934.

Majumdar, R.C., and Pusalker, A.D., eds., *History and Culture of the Indian People, I: The Vedic Age*, London, 1951.

Manoukian, M., "Akan and Ga-Adangme Peoples of the Gold Coast," in D. Forde, ed., *Ethnographic Survey of Africa, Western Africa*, Pt. I, London, 1950.

May, R., *Law & Society East and West*, Wiesbaden, 1985.

McAleavy, H., "Chinese Law," in J.D.M. Derrett, ed., *An Introduction to Legal Systems* 115, New York, 1968.

McConnell, "Notes on the Lugwari Tribe of Central Africa," 55 *Journal of the Royal Anthropological Institute* 439 (1925).

McLuhan, H.M., *The Gutenberg Galaxy: The Making of the Typographic Man*, Toronto, 1962.

McNeil, W.H., *A World History*, 2d ed., New York, London, Toronto, 1971.

———. *The Rise of the West*, Chicago, 1963.

Meek, C.K., *Law and Authority in a Nigerian Tribe*, London, New York, Toronto, 1937.

Middleton, J., *Lugbara Religion: Ritual and Authority Among an East African People*, London, 1960.

———. "Some Social Aspects of Lugbara Myth," 24 *Africa* 189 (1954.

———. "The Central Tribes of the North-Eastern Bantu," in D. Forde, ed., *Ethnographic Survey of Africa*, Part V, London, 1953.

———. "The Concept of Bewitching in Lugbara," 25 *Africa*, 525 (1955).

———. "Witchcraft and Sorcery in Lugbara," in J. Middleton and E.H.Winter, eds., *Witchery and Sorcery in East Africa*, New York, 1963.

Middleton, J. and Tair, D., eds., *Tribes Without Rulers: Studies in African Segmentary Systems*. London, 1958.

Morton-Williams, P., "An Outline of the Cosmology and Cult Organization of the Oyo Yoruba," 34 *Africa* 243 (1964).

Murray, G., *Hellenism and the Modern World*, London, 1953.

Nadel, S.F., *A Black Byzantium*, London, New York, Toronto, 1942.

Neufeld, E., *The Hittite Laws*, London, 1951.

Noda, Y., *Introduction au droit japonais*, Paris, 1966.

O'Connor, *A Critical History of Western Philosophy*, New York, 1964.

Oliver, R. and Atmore, A., *Africa Since 1800*, London, 1967.

Ollenu, N.A., *Principles of Customary Land Law in Ghana*, London, 1962.
Oppenheim, A.L., *Ancient Mesopotamia, Portrait of a Dead Civilization*, 3d ed., Chicago, 1968.
Palmer, R.R. and Colton, J., *A History of the Modern World*, New York, 2d ed., 1956.
Partridge, C., "Native Law and Custom in Egbaland," 10 *Journal of the African Society* 422 (1911).
Poirier, J., "L'analyse des especes juridiques et l'etude des droits coutumiers africains," in M. Gluckman, ed., *Idees et procedures dans les systemes legaux africains*, 110 London, 1969.
Prins, A.H.J., *East African Age-Class Systems.*, Groniopen, Djakarta, 1953.
Pritchard, J.B., Speiser, E.A., trans., *Ancient Near Eastern Texts Relating to the Old Testament*, 2d ed., Princeton, 1955.
Pritchard, J.B., ed., Wilson, J.A., trans., *Ancient Near Eastern Texts Relating to the Old Testament*, 2d ed., Princeton, 1955.
Ranger, T.D., ed., *Aspects of Central African History*, London, 1968.
Rattray, R.S., *Ashanti*, London, 1923, 1955.
————. *Ashanti Law and Constitution*, London, 1929, 1956.
Reischauer, E.O., Fairbank, J.K., and Craig, A.M., *A History of East African Civilization, II: East Asia; A Modern Transformation*, Boston, 1965.
Richards, A.I., "Traditional Values and Current Political Behavior," in L.A.Fallers,, ed., *The King's Men: Leadership and Status in Bugunda on the Eve of Independence*, 294, London, New York, Nairobi, 1964.
Roscoe, J., *The Baganda: An Account of their Native Customs and Beliefs*, London, 1911.
Ross, A., *Of Law and Justice*, London, 1958.
Routledge, W.S., and Routledge, K., *With a Prehistoric People: The Akkiyu of East Africa*, London, 1910.
Russell, B., *Human Knowledge*, London, 1948.
————. *The Problems of Philosophy*, Oxford, 1912.
Sanders, N.K., trans., *The Epic of Gilgamesh*, Penguin, 1960.
Sastri, K.A.N., *A History of South India from Prehistoric Times to the Fall of Vijayanagar*, Madras, 3d ed., 1966.
Setalvad, M.C., *The Role of English Law in India*, Jerusalem, 1966.
Schwab, W.B., "Kinship and Lineage Among the Yoruba," 25 *Africa*, 352 (1955).
Singer, C., *A Short History of Scientific Ideas to 1900*, Oxford, 1959.
Sinha, S.P., *New Nations and the Law of Nations*, Leyden, 1967.
————. "Freeing Human Rights from Natural Rights," 70 *Archiv für Rechts und Sozialphilosophie* 342 (1984), summaries in French and German.
————. "Human Rights: A Non-Western Viewpoint," 67 *Archiv für Rechts und Sozialphilosophie* 76 (1981), summaries in French and German.
————. "New Nations and the International Custom," Symposium, Recent Developments in International Law, 9 *William and Mary Law Review* 788 (1968).
————. "Perspectives of the Newly Independent States on the Binding Quality of International Law," 15 *International and Comparative Law Quality* 121 (1965).
————. "Some Reflections on the Impact of New Nations on International Law," 13 *Howard Law Journal*, 349 (1967).

Smith, M.G., *The Economy of the Hausa Communities of Zaria*, London, 1955.

———. "Hausa Inheritance and Succession," in J.D.M. Derret, ed., *Studies in the Laws of Succession in Nigeria*, 230 London, 1965.

———. *Government in Zazzau 1800–1950*, London, New York, Toronto, 1960.

Smith, N.K., *Prolegomena to an Idealist Theory of Knowledge*, London, 1924.

Snell, G.S., *Nandi Customary Law*, London, 1954.

Southwold, M., "Leadership Authority and the Village Community," in L.A. Fallers, ed., *The King's Men: Leadership and Status in Buganda on the Eve of Independence*, 210, London, New York, Nairobi, 1964.

Spear, P., *India: A Modern History*, Ann Arbor, 1961.

Stenning, D.J., *Savannah Nomads*, London, Ibadan, Accra, 1959.

———. "Transhumance, Migratory Drift, Migration; Patterns of Pastoral Fulani Nomadism," 87 *Journal of the Royal Anthropological Institute* 58 (1957).

Tanaka, K., "Democracy and Judicial Administration in Japan," 2 *Journal of the International Commission of Jurists* 7 (1959–60).

Tate, H.R., "The Native Law of the Southern Gikuyu of East Africa," 9 *Journal of the African Society* 233 (1909–10).

Thomas, N.W., *Anthropological Report on the Ibo-Speaking Peoples of Nigeria*, London, 1913, 1914.

Trevor-Roper, H., *The Rise of Christian Europe*, London, 1965.

Tsien, T-H., "La responsibilité civile delictuelle en China populaire," 1967 *Revue international de droit comparé* 875.

Van der Sprenkel, S., *Legal Institutions in Manchu China*, London, 1962.

Verdier, R., "Chef de terre et terre de lignage," in J. Poirier, ed., *Études de droit africain et de droit malgaché*, 333 Paris, 1965.

Villey, M., *Leçons d'histoire de la philosophie du droit*, 2d ed., Paris, 1962.

Von Mehren, A., *Law in Japan: The legal Order in a Changing Society*, Cambridge, Mass., 1963.

Wheeler, R.E.M., *The Indus Civilization*, The Cambridge History of India, supplementary volume, 3d ed., Cambridge, 1968.

Whitehead,. A.N., *Science and the Modern World*, New York, 1925.

Wigmore, J.H., *A Panorama of the World's Legal Systems*, 3 vols., St. Paul, 1928.

Wilson, G., "Introduction to Nyakyusa Law," 10 *Africa* 16 (1937).

———. "The Nyakyusa of South-Western Tanganyika," in E. Colson and M. Gluckman, eds., *Seven Tribes of British Central Africa*, 261, London, 1951.

Wilson, J.A., *The Burden of Egypt: An Interpretation of Ancient Egyptian Culture*, Chicago, 1951.

Wilson, M., *Communal Rituals of the Nyakyusa*, London, New York Toronto, 1959.

———. *Good Company: A Study of Nyakyuna Age-Villages*, London New York, Toronto, 1951.

———. "Divine Kings and the 'Breath of Men' " *Frazer Lecture*, Cambridge, England, 1959.

———. "Nyakyusa Kinship," in A.R. Radcliffe—Brown and D. Forde, *African Systems of Kinship and Marriage*, London, New York, Toronto, 1950.

Woozley, A.D., *Theory of Knowledge*, London, 1949.

Worsley, P.M., "The Kinship System of the Tallensi: A Revaluation," 86 *Journal of the Royal Antropological Institute* 37 (1956).
Zeller, E., *Stoics, Epicureans, and Sceptics*, trans. O.J.Reichel, London, 1892.

Chapter 2

Buehler, G., trans, *The Laws of Manu*, in *The Sacred Books of the East*, vol. 25, Oxford, 1886.
Coulson, N.J., *A History of Islamic Law*, Edinburgh, 1964.
Driver, G.R., and Miles, J.C., *The Babylonian Laws*, Oxford, 1952.
Fyzee, A.A.A., *Outlines of Muhammadan Law*, 2d ed., Oxford, 1955.
Schacht, J., *An Introduction to Islamic Law*, Oxford, 1964.
———. *The Origin of Muhammadan Jurisprudence*, Oxford, 1950.

Chapter 3

Allen, G., "From the 'Naturalistic Fallacy' to the Ideal Observer Theory", 30 *Philosophy and Phenomenological Research* 553 (1970).
———. "The Is-Ought Question Reformulated and Answered", 82 *Ethics* 181 (1972).
Anscombe, G., "On Brute Facts", 18 *Analysis* 69 (1957–58).
———. *Intention*, Ithaca N.Y. 67 (1957).
Amselek, P., "La Phénoménologie el le droit", 17 *Archives de Philosophie du Droit* 185 (1972) trans. as "The Phenomenological Description of Law", in M. Nathanson, (ed.), *Phénoménology and the Social Sciences*, Vol. 2, 367 (1973).
Aquinas, T., St., *Summa Theologica*, trans. by Fathers of the English Dominican Province, London, 1942.
Aristotle, *Ethica Nichomachea*, trans. by W. Ross, in *The Works of Aristotle*, Oxford, London, 1969.
———. *Politica*, trans. by B. Jowett, in *The Works of Aristotle*, translated into English under the editorship of W. D. Ross, London, 1961.
———. *Rhetorica*, trans. by W.R. Roberts, in *The Works of Aristotle*, translated into English under the editorship of W.D. Ross, London, 1946.
Arnold, M., *Culture and Anarchy*, London (1869).
Asch, S., *Social Psychology*, New York, 1952.
Atkinson, R., "Hume on 'Is' and 'Ought': A Reply to Mr. MacIntyre", 70 *The Philosophical Review* 239 (1961).
Barker, E., *The Political Thought of Plato and Aristotle*, New York, 1959.
Basham, A., *The Wonder that was India*, London 1956.
Benedict, R., *Patterns of Culture*, Boston, 1934.
Bidney, D., *Theoretical Anthropology*, New York, 1954.
Black, M., "The Gap Between 'Is' and 'Should' ", 73 *The Philosophical Review* 220 (1965).
———. "Austin on Performatives" 38 *Philosophy* 217 (1963).
Blackstone, W., "The Justification of Human Rights", in G.H. Pollack (ed.), *Human Rights*, 90, 1971.
Boas, F., *The Mind of Primitive Man*, New York rev., ed., 1938.
Bodenheimer, E., *Jurisprudence: The Philosophy and Method of the Law*, Cambridge, Mass., 1967.

Bozeman, A., *The Future of Law in a Multicultural World*, Princeton, 1971.

Brown, S. "Huntsmen: What Quarry?" in S. Hook (ed.), *Law and Philosophy, A Symposium*, New York 177, (1964).

Buehler, G., trans., *The Laws of Manu*, in *The Sacred Books of the East*, Vol. 25, Oxford, 1886.

Cahn, E., *The Sense of Injustice*, New York, 1949.

Cairns, H., *Legal Philosophy from Plato to Hegel*, Baltimore, 1949.

Calhoun, G., *Introduction to Greek Legal Science*, Aaten, W. Germany, reprint of the edition, Oxford, 1944

Cantril, H., "Ethical Relativity from the Transactional Point of View", 52 *The Journal of Philosophy* 677 (1952).

Castberg, F., "Natural Law and Human Rights". *l Revue des Droits del'homme* 14 (1968).

Catlin, G., *A Study of the Principles of Politics*, New York, 1930.

Childe, G., *Social Evolution*, Cleveland, 1963.

Chroust, A., "Natural Law and Legal Positivism", 13 *Ohio State Law Journal* 178 (1952).

————. "On the Nature of Natural Law", in Paul Sayre (ed.), *Interpretations of Modern Legal Philosophies, Essays in Honor of Roscoe Pound*, 70 (1947).

Cicero, Marcus Tulius, *De Re Publica De Legibus*, trans. by C.W. Keys, The Loeb Classical Library, London, Cambridge, Mass., 1952.

Cohen, M., "Law, Morality, and Purpose", 10 *Villanova Law Review* 640 (1965).

————. " 'Is' and 'Should': An Unbridged Gap", 74 *The Philosophical Review* 220 (1965).

Cohen, M.R., *Law and the Social Order, Essays in Legal Philosophy*, New York, 1933.

————. *Reason and Nature, An Essay on the Meaning of Scientific Method*, Glencoe, Illinois, 1953.

Cranston, M., *What are Human Rights?*, New York, 1962.

Dabin, J., *Théorie générale du droit* (1944), translated as General Theory of Law by Kurt Wilk in *The Legal Philosophies of Lask, Radbuch, and Dabin*, 20th Century Legal Philosophy Series, Vol. IV, Cambridge, Massachusetts, 1950.

Dias, R. *Jurisprudence*, London, 1964.

Dworkin, R., "The Elusive Morality of Law", 10 *Villanova Law Review* 631 (1965).

————. "Philosophy, Morality and Law—Observations Prompted by Professor Fuller's Novel Claim", 113 *University of Pennsylvania Law Review* 668 (1965).

Dorsey, G., "Two Objective Bases for a World-Wide Legal Order", in F.S.C. Northrop, ed., *Ideological Differences and World Order*, New Haven, 1949.

D'Entreves, A.P., "The Case for Natural Law Reexamined", 1 *Natural Law Forum* 5 (1956).

Edel, A., *Ethical Judgment*, Glencoe, Illinois 1955.

Edel, M., and Edel, A., *Anthropology and Ethics*, rev. ed., Cleveland, 1968.

Edgley, R., "Hume's Law", 44 *The Aristotelian Society: Supplementary Volume* 105 (1970).

Ehrlich, E., *Fundamental Principles of the Sociology of Law*, trans. by W.L. Mall, Cambridge, Mass., 1936.

Eliot, T., *Notes Towards the Definition of Culture*, New York, 1949.

Emmet, D., *Function, Purpose and Powers*, 2d ed.; with a foreward by Victor Turner, London, *Macmillan*, 1972.

Flew, A., "On the Interpretation of Hume", in W.D. Hudson, ed., *The Is-Ought Question* 64, 1969.

Frankena, W. "Ought and Is Once More", 2 *Man and World* 515 (1969).

Freeman, K., *Ancilla to the Presocratic Philosophers*, Oxford, 1948.

———. *Compassion to the Presocratic Philosophers*, Oxford, 1946.

Frenkel-Brunswick, "Social Research and the Problem of Values: A Reply", 49 *Journal of Abnormal and Social Psychology* 466 (1954).

Friedmann, W., *Legal Theory New York*, 5th ed., 1967.

———. "An Analysis of 'In Defense of Natural Law'," in S. Hook, ed., *Law and Philosophy: A Symposium*, New York, 1964.

Frondizi, R., "The Axiological Foundation of the Moral Norm", 50 *The Personalist* 241 (1969).

Fuller, L.L., *The Morality of Law*, rev. ed., New Haven, 1969.

Fuller, L., "Human Purpose and Natural Law", 53 *Journal of Philosophy* 697 (1956). reprinted in 3 *Natural Law Forum* 68 (1958).

———. "A Reply to Professors Cohen and Dworkin", 10 *Villanova Law Review*, 655 (1965).

———. "Human Purpose and Natural Law", 53 *Journal of Philosophy* 697 (1956).

Genova, A., "Institutional Facts and Brute Values", 81 *Ethics* 36 (1970).

Geny, F., *Méthode d'interprétation et Sources en droit prive positif* 2d ed., English translation by the Louisiana State Law Institute, 1963.

———. *Science et technique en droit privé positif* (4 vols., 1914—24), translated as *Science of Legal Method*, in *Modern Legal Philosophy* Series 35.

Gewirth, A., "Must One Play the Moral Language Game?" 7 *American Philosophical Quarterly* 107 (1970).

Grice, G., *The Grounds of Moral Judgment*, Cambridge, 1967.

———. "Hume's Law", 44 *The Aristotelian Society: Supplementary Volume* 89 (1970).

Guthrie, W.K.C., *History of Greek Philosophy*, Vol. 1, Cambridge, 1962.

Hanly, K., "Zimmerman's 'Is-Is': A Schizophrenic Monism" 73 *Mind* 443 (1964).

Hare, R., "Universalizability", 55 *Proceedings of the Aristotalian Society* 295 (1954–55).

———. *Freedom and Reason*, Oxford, 1963.

———. "The Promising Game", in W.D. Hudson, ed., *The Is-Ought Question*, 163, 1969.

Hart, H., "Positivism and the Separation of Law and Morals", 71 *Harvard Law Review* 593 1958.

———. Book Review, 78 *Harvard Law Review* 1281 (1965).

Hodgsons, D., *Consequences of Utilitarianism*, 1967.

Hudson, W., *Modern Moral Philosophy*, Garden City, New York, 1970.

———. "Editors Introduction: The Is-Ought Problem" in W.D. Hudson, ed., *The Is-Ought Question*, 1969.

————. "Hume on Is and Ought", 14 *The Philosophical Review Quarterly* 246 (1964).

Hunter, G., "Hume on 'Is' and 'Ought' ", 37 *Philosophy* 148 (1962).

————. "A Reply to Professor Flew", in W.D. Hudson, ed., *The Is-Ought Question*, 70, 1969.

Jaeger, W., *Paideia* (Berlin, 1934), trans. by G. Highet, Vol. 1, Oxford, 1939.

————. *The Theology of the Early Greek Philosophers*, Oxford, 1947.

Jhering, R. von., *Law as a Means to an End*, trans. by I. Husik, New York, 1913.

Jones, J.W., *The Law and Legal Theory of the Greeks*, Oxford, 1956.

Jones, P., "Another Look at Hume's View of Aesthetic and Moral Judgments", 20 *Philosophical Quarterly* 53 (1970).

Jones, W., trans., *Institutes of Hindu Law; or, The Ordinances of Manu*, London, 1869.

Kane, P.V., *History of Dharmasastra (Ancient and Medieval Religions and Civil Law)*, Vol. 1, Poona, 1930.

Kelsen, H., *General Theory of Law and State*, New York, 1945.

Kerferd, G.B., "The First Greek Sophists", 44 *Classical Review* 8 (1956).

Kirk, G.S., *Heraclitus, The Cosmic Fragments*, Oxford, 1954.

Kirk, G.S., and Raven, J.E., *The Presocratic Philosophers*, 2d ed., Cambridge, 1960.

Kluckhohn, C., "The Philosophy of the Navaho Indians", in F.S.C. Northrop, ed., *Ideological Differences and World Order*, 356 New Haven, 1949.

————. "Ethical Relativity, Sic et Non", 52 *The Journal of Philosophy* 663 (1955).

————. "Universal Categories of Culture", in A.L. Kroeber, ed., *Anthropology Today*, 507 (1953).

Kolb, "A Social-Psychological Conception of Human Freedom", 63 *Ethics* 180 (1953).

Kroeber, A., *Configurations of Culture Growth*, Berkeley and Los Angeles, 1944.

————. "The Concept of Culture in Science", 35 *Journal of General Education* 188 (1949).

————. "Concluding Review", in Tax, Sol, et al, *An Appraisal of Anthropology Today*, 1953.

Kroeber, A., and Kluckhohn, C., *Culture: A Critical Review of Concepts and Definitions*, New York, 1952.

Kurtz, P., "Law, Decision and the Behavioral Sciences", in S. Hook, ed., *Law and Philosophy, A Symposium*, New York, 1964.

Láo-Tsze, *Treatise on the Law of Nature and Practical Utility*, in J.C.H. Wu, *Juridical Essays and Studies*, Shanghai, 1928.

Ladrière, J., "Human Rights and Historicity", 10 *World Justice* 147 (1968–69).

Laird, "It All Depends Upon the Purpose", 1 *Analysis* 49 (1934).

Lewis, J., "An Analysis of 'Purposive Activity': Its Relevance to the Relation Between Law and Moral Obligation". 16 *The American Journal of Jurisprudence* 143 (1971).

Linton, R., "Universal Ethical Principles: An Anthropological View", in R. Anshen (ed.), *Moral Principles of Action*, 646, New York 1952.

————. "The Problem of Universal Values", in R.F. Spencer (ed.), *Method and Perspective in Anthropology*, Minneapolis, 1954.

Lyons, D., *Forms and Limits of Utilitarianism*, 1965.

Macdonald, M., "Natural Rights", 47 *Proceedings of the Aristotelian Society* 225 (1946–47), reprinted in A.I. Melden, ed., *Human Rights*, Belmont, California, 40, 1970.

Machan, T., "A Rationale for Human Rights", 52 *The Personalist* 216 (1971).

————. "Human Rights: Some Points of Clarification", 5 *The Journal of Critical Analysis* 30 (1975).

MacIntyre, A., "Hume on 'Is' and 'Ought' ", 68 *The Philosophical Review* 451 (1959).

MacIves, R., *Society: Its Structures and Changes*, 1931.

Maslow, A., "Psychological Progress in Understanding Human Nature and a Scientific Ethics", 10 *Main Currents* 75 (1954).

McClellan, J., and Komisar, B., "On Deriving 'Ought from Is' ", 25 *Analysis* 32 (1964–65).

Mead, M., "Some Anthropological Considerations Concerning Natural Law", 6 *Natural Law Forum* 51 (1961).

Mullock, "The Inner Morality of Law", 84 *Ethics* 327 (1974).

Murdock, G., "The Common Denominator of Cultures", in R. Linton (ed.), *The Science of Man in the World Crisis*, New York, 1945.

Nagel, E., "Fact, Value and Human Purpose", 4 *Natural Law Forum* 26 (1959).

————. "On the Fusion of Fact and Value: A Reply to Professor Fuller", 3 *Natural Law Forum* 77 (1958).

Nakhnikian, G., "Professor Fuller on Legal Rules and Purpose", 2 *Wayne Law Review* 190 (1956).

Nielson, K., "On Taking Human Nature as the Basic of Morality", 29 *Social Research* 159 (1962).

————. "The Myth of Natural Law", in S. Hook, ed., *Law and Philosophy, A Symposium*, New York, 1964.

————. "Scepticism and Human Rights", 52 *The Monist* 573 (1968).

Northrop, F.S.C., "Ethical Relativity in the Light of Recent Legal Science", 52 *The Journal of Philosophy* 649 (1955).

————. *European Union and United States Foreign Policy, A Study in Sociological Jurisprudence*, New York, 1954.

————. "Contemporary Jurisprudence and International Law", 61 *Yale Law Journal* 623 (1961).

————. *The Complexity of Legal and Ethical Experience, Studies in the Method of Normative Subjects*, Boston and Toronto, 1959.

Ofstad, H., and Bergstrom, I., "A Note on Searle's Derivation of 'Ought from Is' ", 8 *Inquiry* 309 (1965).

Olafson, F., "Essence and Concept in Natural Law", in S. Hook, ed., *Law and Philosophy, A Symposium*, 234, New York, 1964.

Parsons, T., and Shils, E., *Toward a General Theory of Action*, Cambridge, 1951.

Paton, G.W., *A Text-book of Jurisprudence*, 3d ed., Oxford, 1964.

Patterson, E.W., *Jurisprudence: Men and Ideas of the Laws*, Brooklyn, 1953.

Pearson, K., *The Grammar of Science*, 2d ed., 1900.

Peschka, V., "La Phénoménologisme dans la philosophie du droit Moderne", 12 *Archives de Philosophie du Droit* 259 (1967).

Phillips, D., "The Possibilities of Moral Advice", 25 *Analysis* 37 (1964–65).

Popper, K., *The Open Society and its Enemies*, New York, 1963.

Poulantzas, N., *Nature des Choses et droit*, 1964.

———. "Notes sur la phénoménologie et l'existententialisme juridiques" 8 *Archives de Philosophie du Droit* 271 (1963).

Prior, A., "The Autonomy of Ethics", 38 *The Australian Journal of Philosophy* 199 (1960).

Recasens—Siches L., *Human Life, Society and Law, Fundamentals of the Philosophy of Law*, trans. by G. Ireland, in *20th Century Legal Philosophies Series*, Vol. III, Latin American Legal Philosophy, Cambridge, 1948.

Reinhardt, L., "Comments on Professor Machan's Address", 52 *The Personalist* 346 (1971).

Rimanque, K., "Human Rights", 7 *World Justice* 170 (1965–66).

Roheim, G., *Psychoanalysis and Anthropology*, New York, 1950.

Ross, A., *On Law and Justice*, Berkeley, California, 1958.

———. "A Critique of the Philosophy of Natural Law", in M.P. Golding, ed., *The Nature of Law*, New York, 1966.

Russell, B., *Mysticism and Logic*, London, 1927.

Ryle, G., *The Concept of Mind*, New York, 1949.

Searle, J., *Speech Acts*, London, 1969.

———. "How to derive 'Ought' from 'Is'", 73 *Philosophical Review* 43 (1964).

Selznick, P., "Sociology and Natural Law," 6 *Natural Law Forum* 84 (1961).

Shorter, J., "Professor Prior on the Autonomy of Ethics", 39 *Australian Journal of Philosophy* 286 (1961).

Shuman, S., *Legal Positivism, Its Scope and Limitations*, Detroit, 1963.

Sidgwick, H., *The Methods of Ethics*, 7th ed., reissued, Chicago 1962.

Sinha, S.P., "The Anthropocentric Theory of International Law as a Basis for Human Rights", 10 *Case Western Reserve Journal of International Law*, Human Rights Issue 469 (1978).

———. "Human Rights Philosophically", 18 *Indian Journal of International Law*, 139 (1978).

———. "Human Rights: A Non-Western Viewpoint", 67 *Archiv fur Rechts- und Sozialphilosophie* 76 (1981).

———. "The Fission and Fusion of Is-Ought in Legal Philosophy", 21 *Villanova Law Review*, 839 (1975–76).

Sparshot, "The Concept of Purpose", 72 *Ethics* 157 (1962).

Spilsbury, "Dispositions and Phenomenalism", 62 *Mind* 339 (1953).

Stern, K., "Either-Or Or Neither-Nor", in S. Hook, ed., *Law and Philosophy, A Symposium*, 247, New York, 1964.

Steward, J., "Cultural Causality and Law", 51 *American Anthropologist* 1 (1949).

Stocker, M., "Moral Duties, and Institutions, and Natural Facts", 54 *The Monist* 602 (1970).

Summers, "Professor Fuller on Morality and Law", 18 *Journal of Legal Education*. 1 (1965).

Taylor, "Purposeful and Non-Purposeful Behavior: A Rejoinder", 17 *Philosophy of Science*, 327 (1950).

Taylor, G., "Hume's Views of Moral Judgments", 21 *Philosophical Quarterly* 24 (1971).
Thomson, J., "How Not to Derive 'Ought' from 'Is' ", in W.D. Hudson, ed., *The Is-Ought Question*, 163, 1969.
Vasak, K., ed., *The International Dimensions of Human Rights*, revised and edited for English edition by P. Alston, Westport, Conn., Paris, 1982
Verzijl, J., *Human Rights in Historical Perspective*, 1958.
Villey, M., "Sein' and 'Sollen" im Erfahrungsbereich des Rechts un point de vue d'historien", 13 *Archives de Philosophie du droit* 333 (1968).
Vlastos, G., "Justice and Equality", in R.B.B. Brandt (ed.), *Social Justice*, 31, New Jersey, 1962, reprinted in A.I. Melden (ed.), *Human Rights*, Belmont, California, 76 (1970).
———. "On Heraclitus," 76 *American Journal of Philosophy* 337 (1955).
Waley, A., trans., *The Analects of Confucius*, London, 1958.
———. *The Way and Its Power; A Study of the Tao Te Ching*, London, 1934.
Wasserstrom, R., "Rights, Human Rights, and Racial Discrimination", 61 *Journal of Philosophy* 628 (1964), reprinted in A.I. Melden ed., *Human Rights*, 96, Belmont, California, 1970.
White, L., "Energy and the Evolution of Culture", 45 *American Anthropologist* 335 (1943).
Wilkins, B., "The Is-Ought Controversy", 80 *Ethics* 160 (1969–70).
Williams, R., *Culture and Society*, New York, 1958.
Wissler, C., *Man and Culture*, New York, 1923.
Witherspoon, "The Relation of Philosophy to Jurisprudence", 3 *Natural Law Forum* 105 (1958).
Wolheim, R., 8 *The Encyclopedia of Philosophy* 450 (1967).
Zemach, F., "Ought, Is, and a Game called 'Promise' ", 21 *Philosophical Review* 61 (1971).
Zimmerman, M., "The 'Is-Ought': An Unnecessary Dualism", 71 *Mind* 53 (1962).
———. "A Note on the 'Is-Ought' Barrier". 76 *Mind* 286 (1967).

Chapter 4

Berolzheimer, F., *The World's Legal Philosophies*, Boston, 1912.
Bosanquet, B., *The Philosophical Theory of the State*, 2d edition, London, 1910.
Cairns, H., *Legal Philosophy from Plato to Hegel*, Baltimore, 1949.
Cohen, M.R., *Law and the Social Order, Essays in Legal Philosophy*, New York, 1933.
———. *Reason and Law, Studies in Juristic Philosophy*, Glencoe, Illinois, 1950.
———. *Reason and Nature, An Essay on the Meaning of Scientific Method*, Glencoe, Illinois, 1953.
———. "On Absolutism in Legal Thought", 84 *University of Pennsylvania Law Review* 681 (1936).
Croce, B., *What Is Living and What Is Dead of the Philosophy of Hegel*, translated from the original text of the 3d Italian ed., 1912, by Douglas Ainslie, New York, 1969.

Del Vecchio, G., *Philosophy of Law*, trans. by T.O. Martin, Washington, D.C., 1953.
———. "The Formal Bases of Law", *Modern Legal Philosophy Series*, 1921.
Friedmann, W., *Legal Theory*, 5th ed., New York, 1967.
Friedrich, C., *Philosophy of Law in Historical Perspective*, 2d ed., Chicago, 1963.
Geny, F., "The Critical System (Idealistic and Formalistic) of R. Stammler", in R. Stammler, *The Theory of Justice*, trans. by I. Husik, New York, 1925, Appendix I.
Ginsberg, "Stammler's Philosophy of Law", in *Modern Theories of Law*, 1933.
Hegel, G.W.F., *Philosophy of Right* (1821), translated with notes by T.N. Knox, Oxford, 1958.
Hobhouse, L.T., *The Metaphysical Theory of the State; A Criticism*, London, 1951.
Hussik, I., "Legal Philosophy of Stammler", 24 *Columbia Law Review*, 373 (1924).
Kant, I., *The Philosophy of Law, An Exposition of the Fundamental Principles of Jurisprudence as the Science of Right* (1796), translated from German by W. Hastie, Edinburgh, 1887; reprinted, Ann Arbor, 1966.
Paton, G.W., *A Textbook of Jurisprudence*, 3d ed., ed. by D.P. Derham, Oxford, 1964.
Patterson, E.W., *Jurisprudence, Men and Ideas of Law*, Brooklyn, New York, 1953.
Plamenatz, J., *Man and Society, A Critical Examination of Some Important Social and Political Theories from Machiaevelli to Marx*, London, 1966.
Russell, B., *A History of Western Philosophy*, Book 3, Part 2, New York, 1945.
Sabine, G., *A History of Political Theory*, rev. ed., New York, 1950.
Stace, W.T., *The Philosophy of Hegel, A Systematic Exposition*, London, 1924.
Stammler, R., *The Theory of Justice*, trans. by I. Husik, New York, 1925.
Windelband, W., *A History of Philosophy*, 2d. ed., rev. and enl., New York, London, 1938.

Chapter 5

Austin, J., *Lectures on Jurisprudence*, 5th ed., rev. ed., by Robert Campbell, New York, 1875.
———. *The Province of Jurisprudence Determined and the Uses of the Study of Jurisprudence*, with an Introduction by H.L.A. Hart, London, 1968.
deBary, W.J., Wing–tsit Chan, Watson, B., *Sources of Chinese Tradition*, New York, 1960.
Bentham, J., *Introduction to the Principles of Morals and Legislation*, London, 1970.
———. *The Limits of Jurisprudence Defined*, edited by C.W. Everett, New York, 1945.
———. *The Theory of Legislation*, edited by C.K. Ogden, London, New York, 1931.
Bryce, J., *Studies in History and Jurisprudence*, Oxford, 1901.

Cohen, L.J., "Critical Notices—The Concept of Law by H.L.A. Hart", 71 *Mind* 395 (1962).

Cohen, M., "Idealism in the Law, Limits of Positivism", 27 *Columbia Law Review* 237 (1927).

Dias, R.W.M., *Jurisprudence*, 3d ed., London, 1970.

Duyvendak, J.J.L., trans., *The Book of Lord Shang*, London, Chicago, 1928.

Friedmann, W., "Bentham and Modern Legal Thought", in *Jeremy Bentham and the Law, A Symposium* (1948).

———. *Legal Theory*, 5th ed., New York, 1967.

Fuller, L.L., *The Law in Quest of Itself*, Chicago, 1940.

Golding, M.P., "Kelsen and the Concept of Legal System", 47 *Archiv für Rechts-und Sozialphilosophie* 355 (1961).

Gray, J.C., *Nature and Sources of Law*, 2d. ed., New York, 1921.

Hart, H.L.A., *The Concept of Law* (1961), Oxford, 1967.

———. "Kelsen Visited", 10 *U.C.L.A. Law Review* 709 (1963).

Hughes, G., "Validity and the Basic Norm", 59 *California Law Review* 695 (1971).

Kautilya, *Arthasastra*, in P.B. Kangle, trans., *The Kautilya Arthasastra*, Bombay, 1963.

Kelsen, H., *General Theory of Law and State*, trans. by A. Wedberg, Cambridge, Massachusetts, 1949.

———. "Professor Stone and the Pure Theory of Law", 17 *Stanford Law Review* 1128 (1964).

———. "Pure Theory of Law", 51 *Law Quarterly Review* 517 (1935).

Liao, W.K., trans., *The Complete Works of Han Fei Tzu*, Vol. I, London, 1939, Vol. II, London, 1959.

Liebholz, "Les tendances actuelles de la doctrine de droit public en Allemagne", 1931 *Archivs de Philosophie du Droit et de Sociologique Juridique* 209.

Maine, H.S., *Lectures on the Early History of Institutions*, 7th ed., Port Washington, New York, 1966.

Mill, J.S., *Utilitarianism*, edited by O. Priest, Indianapolis, New York, 1957.

Paton, G.W., *A Textbook of Jurisprudence*, 3d ed., ed. by D.P. Derham, Oxford, 1964.

Patterson, E.W., *Jurisprudence: Men and Ideas of The Law*, Brooklyn, New York, 1953.

Plamenatz, J., *Man and Society, A Critical Examination of Some Important Social and Political Theories from Machiavelli to Marx*, Vol. 2, London, 1966.

Pound, R., "The Call for a Realist Jurisprudence", 44 *Harvard Law Review* 697 (1930–31).

Ramaswamy, T.N., trans., *Essentials of Indian Statecraft, Kantilya's Arthasastra for Contemporary Readers*, Bombay, 1962.

Ross, A., *Towards a Realistic Jurisprudence, A Criticism of the Dualism in Law*, Copenhagen, 1946.

Shuman, S., *Legal Positivism, Its Scope and Limitations*, Detroit, 1963.

Silving, H., "Law and Fact in the Light of the Pure Theory of Law", *Interpretations of Modern Legal Philosophies* (1933).

———. "The Fission and Fusion of Is-Ought in Legal Philosophy", 21 *Villanova Law Review* 839 (1975–1976).

Stone, J., "Mystery and Mystique in the Basic Norm", 26 *Modern Law Review* 34 (1963).
Waley, A., *Three Ways of Thought in Ancient China*, London, 1939.
Watson, B., trans., *Han Fei Tzu; Basic Writings*, New York, 1964.
Wing—tsit Chan, *A Source Book on Chinese Philosophy*, Princeton, N.J., 1963.
Wu, J.C.H., *Juridical Essays and Studies*, Shanghai, 1928.

Chapter 6

Allen, C.K., *Law in the Making*, 7th ed., Oxford, 1964.
Cohen, M.R., *Reason and Nature, An Essay on the Meaning of Scientific Method*, Glencoe, Illinois, 1953.
Dewey, J., *Freedom and Culture*, New York, 1939.
Dias, R.W.M., *Jurisprudence*, 3d ed., London, 1970.
Engels, F., *Herr Eugen Duhring's Revolution in Science [Anti-Dühring]*, trans. by E. Burns, ed. by C.P. Dutt, London, 1938.
Friedmann, W., *Legal Theory*, 5th ed., New York, 1967.
———. "Some Reflections on Status and Freedom", in *Essays in Jurisprudence in Honor of Roscoe Pound*, 222 (1962).
Fuller, L.L., *The Law in Quest of Itself*, Chicago, 1940.
Graveson, R., "The Movement from Status to Contract", 4 *Modern Law Review* 261 (1941).
Jones, J., *Historical Introduction to the Theory of Law*, Oxford, 1956.
Kantorowicz, H.U., "Savigny and the Historical School of Law", 53 *Law Quarterly Review* 334 (1937).
Maine, H.S., *Ancient Law*, Introduction by J.H. Morgan, Everyman's Library, London, New York, 1965.
Marx, K., and Engels, F., *Karl Marx and Frederick Engels, Selected Correspondence*, trans. by I. Lasker, ed. by S. Ryazanskaya, Moscow, 1965.
———. *A Contribution to Critique of Political Economy*, translated by N.I. Stone, 2d revised ed., New York, London, 1904.
Marx, K. and Engels, F., *The Communist Manifesto* (1848), in *The Communist Manifesto of Karl Marx and Friedrich Engels*, with an introduction and explanatory notes by D. Ryazanoff, New York, London, 1930.
———. *The German Ideology*, edited with an Introduction by R. Pascal, London, 1938.
Paton, G.W., *A Textbook of Jurisprudence*, ed. by D.P. Derham, 3d ed., Oxford, 1964.
Patterson, E.W., *Jurisprudence: Men and Ideas of the Law*, Brooklyn, 1953.
Plamenatz, J., *Man and Society, A Critical Examination of Some Important Social and Political Theories from Machiavelli to Marx*, Vol. II, London, 1966.
Prausnitz, O., *The Standardization of Commercial Contracts in English and Continental Law*, London, 1937.
Savigny, F.K., von, *Of the Vocation of Our Age for Legislation and Jurisprudence*, translated by Abraham Hayward, London, 1831.
Stammler, R., *The Theory of Justice*, trans. by I. Husik, New York, 1925.
Symposium on Compulsory Contracts, 43 *Columbia Law Review* 565 (1943).

Chapter 7

Allen, C.K., *Law in the Making*, 7th ed., Oxford, 1964.

Brown, J., "The Jurisprudence of M. Duguit", 32 *Law Quarterly Review* 168 (1916).

Cohen, M.R., *Law and the Social Order, Essays in Legal Philosophy*, New York, 1933.

Duguit, L., *Law in the Modern State* (1913), trans. by F. and H. Laski, New York, 1970.

———. "Objective Law", 20 and 21 *Columbia Law Review* 817 and 1 (1920 and 1921).

———. "Theory of Objective Law Anterior to the State", in *Modern French Legal Philosophy* (1921).

Ehrlich, E., *Fundamental Principles of the Sociology of Law* (1912), trans. by W.L. Moll, New York, 1962.

———. "Judicial Freedom of Decisions: Its Principles and Objects", trans. by E. Bruncken and L.B. Register, in *The Science of Legal Method*, Boston, 1917.

Elliot, W., "The Metaphysics of Duguit's Pragmatic Conception of Law", 37 *Political Science Quarterly* 639 (1922).

Friedmann, W., *Legal Theory*, 5th ed., New York, 1967.

Gény, F., *Méthode d'interpretation et Sources en droit privé positif*, 2d ed., English translation by the Louisiana State Law Institute, 1963.

Heck, P., "The Jurisprudence of Interests", trans. by M.M. Schoch, in M.M. Schoch, ed., *The Jurisprudence of Interests*, 20th Century Legal Philosophy Series, Vol. II, Cambridge, Massachusetts, 1948.

von Ihering, R., *Law as a Means to an End*, trans. by I. Husik, Modern Legal Philosophy Series, Vol. V, Boston, 1913.

Jenkins, I., "Rudolf von Jhering", 14 *Vanderbilt Law Review* 169 (1960).

Kantorowicz, H.U., "Legal Science—A Summary of Its Methodology", 28 *Columbia Law Review* 679 (1928).

Lask, F. and H., "Duguit's Concept of the State", in *Modern Theories of Law* (1933).

Patterson, E.W., *Jurisprudence: Men and Ideas of the Law*, Brooklyn, 1953.

Paton, G.W., *A Textbook of Jurisprudence*, ed. by D.P. Derham, 3d ed., Oxford, 1964.

Pound, R., *Interpretations of Legal History*, New York, 1923.

———. *Jurisprudence*, Vol. 3, St. Paul, 1959.

———. *Social Control Through Law*, New Haven, London, 1942.

———. "Fifty Years of Jurisprudence", 51 *Harvard Law Review* 777 (1937).

———. "Individual Interests of Substance", 59 *Harvard Law Review* 1 (1945).

———. "A Survey of Social Interests", 57 *Harvard Law Review* 1 (1943).

———. "The Scope and Purpose of Sociological Jurisprudence", 25 *Harvard Law Review* 489 (1921).

Chapter 8

Babb, H.W., "Petrazhitski's Science of Legal Policy and Theory of Law", 17 *Boston University Law Review* 793 (1937).

————. "Petrazhitski's Theory of Law", 18 *Boston University Law* 511 (1938).

Langrod, G.S., and Vaughan, M., "The Polish Psychological Theory of Law", in W.J. Wagner, ed., *Polish Law Throughout the Ages*, 229, Stanford, 1970.

Laserson, M.M., "Positive and 'Natural' Law and Their Correlation", in *Interpretations of Modern Legal Philosophies, Studies in Honor of Roscoe Pound*, New York, 1947.

————. "The Work of Leon Petrazhitski: Inquiry Into the Psychological Aspects of the Nature of Law", 51 *Columbia Law Review* 59 (1951).

Meyendorf, A., "The Tragedy of Modern Jurisprudence", in *Interpretations of Modern Legal Philosophies, Studies in Honor of Roscoe Pound*, New York, 1947.

Northrop, F.S.C., *The Complexity of Legal and Ethical Experience (Studies in Normative Subjects)*, Boston, Toronto, 1959.

Petrazycki, L.I., *Law and Morality*, trans. by H.W. Babb, Introduction by N.S. Timasheff, Cambridge, Massachusetts, 1955.

Rudzinski, A.W., "Petrazycki's Significance for Contemporary Legal and Moral Theory", 21 *The American Journal of Jurisprudence* 107 (1976).

Sadurska, R., "Jurisprudence of Leon Petrazycki," 32 *The American Journal of Jurisprudence* 63 (1987).

Timasheff, N.S., "Petrazhitski's Philosophy of Law," in *Interpretations of Modern Legal Philosophies, Studies in Honor of Roscoe Pound*, New York, 1947.

Chapter 9

A. AMERICAN REALISM

Bingham, J.W., "What Is Law?" 11 *Michigan Law Review* 1 and 108 (1912–13).

Cohen, F.S., *Ethical Systems and Legal Ideals*, Ithaca, New York, 1959.

————. "The Problem of a Functional Jurisprudence", 1 *Modern Law Review* 5 (1937).

————. "Transcendental Nonsense and the Functional Approach", 35 *Columbia Law Review* 809 (1935).

Cohen, M.R., *Law and the Social Order, Essays in Legal Philosophy*, New York, 1933.

Dewey, J., *Essays in Experimental Logic*, Chicago, 1916.

————. *Logic: The Theory of Inquiry*, New York, 1938.

————. *Studies in Logical Theory*, Chicago, 1903.

————. "Logical Method and Law", 10 *Cornell Law Quarterly* 17 (1924–25).

Frank, J., *Courts on Trial*, Princeton, 1949.

————. *Law and the Modern Mind*, New York, 1930, Sixth Printing, 1949.

————. "Say It With Music", 61 *Harvard Law Review* 221 (1948).

Friedmann, W., *Legal Theory*, 5th ed., New York, 1967.

Fuller, L.L., *The Law in Quest of Itself*, Chicago, 1940.

————. "Reason and Fiat in Case Law", 59 *Harvard Law Review* 376 (1966).

Gray, J.C., *The Nature and Sources of the Law*, 2d ed., New York, 1921.

Holmes, O.W., Jr., "The Path of Law", 10 *Harvard Law Review* 457 (1896–97).

James, W., *Pragmation: A New Name for Some Old Ways of Thinking*, New York, 1907.

———. *The Meaning of Truth: Sequel to "Pragmatism"*, New York 1909.

———. "Philosophical Conceptions and Practical Results", in R.B. Perry, ed., *Collected Essays and Reviews*, New York, 1920.

Kantorowicz, H., "Some Rationalism About Realism", 43 *Yale Law Journal* 1240 (1933–44).

Llewellyn, K.N., *The Bramble Bush, On Our Law and Its Study*, New York, 1951.

———. *The Common Law Tradition, Deciding Appeals*, Boston, 1960.

———. "On Reading and Using the Newer Jurisprudence", 40 *Columbia Law Review* 581 (1940).

———. "Some Realism About Realism—Responding to Dean Pound", 44 *Harvard Law Review* 1222 (1930–31).

McDougal, M., "Fuller v. The American Legal Realists", 50 *Yale Law Journal* 827 (1940–41).

Mendelson, W., "Mr. Justice Holmes—Humility, Skepticism, and Democracy", 36 *Minnesota Law Review* 343 (1951).

Oliphant, H., "Facts, Opinions, and Value Judgments", 10 *Texas Law Review* 127 (1932).

———. "A Return to Stare Decisis", 14 *American Bar Association Journal* 71 and 159 (1928).

Yntema, H.E., "The Rational Basis of Legal Science", 31 *Columbia Law Review* 925 (1931).

B. SCANDINAVIAN REALISM

Castberg, F., *Problems of Legal Philosophy*, (1939), 2d revised English edition, Oslo, London, 1957.

———. "Philosophy of Law in the Scandinavian Countries", 4 *American Journal of Comparative Law* 388 (1955).

Hagerstrom, A., *Inquiries Into The Nature of Law and Morals*, ed. by K. Olivecrona, trans. by C.D. Broad, Stockholm, 1953.

Hart, H.L.A., "Scandinavian Realism", 1959 *Cambridge Law Journal* 233

Lundstedt, A.V., *Legal Thinking Revisited, My Views on Law*, Stockholm, 1956.

Olivecrona, K., *Law as Fact*, Copenhagen, London, 1939.

Ross, A., *On Law and Justice*, London, 1958.

———. *Towards a Realistic Jurisprudence*, trans. by A.I. Fausboll, Copenhagen, 1946.

Chapter 10

Amselek, P., "La Phénoménologie et le droit", *Archives de Philosophie du Droit*, 185 (1972), translated as "The Phenomenological Description of Law", in M. Natanson, ed., *Phenomenology and the Social Sciences*, Vol. II, 367 (1973).

Bachelard, S., *La logique de Husserl*, Paris, 1957.

Boehm, R., "Basic Reflection on Husserl's Phenomenological Reduction", 5 *International Philosophical Quarterly* 183 (1965).

Cossio, C., *Phenomenology of the Decision*, trans., in *Latin-American Legal*

Philosophy, Twentieth Century Legal Philosophy Series, Vol. III, Cambridge, Massachusetts, 1948.

Downes, C., "On Husserl's Approach to Necessary Truth", 19 *The Monist* 87 (1965).

Farber, M., ed., *Philosophical Essays in Memory of Edmund Husserl*, Cambridge, Massachusetts, 1940.

Friedmann, W., *Legal Theory*, 5th ed., New York, 1967.

———. "Phenomenology and Legal Science", in M. Natanson, ed., *Phenomenology and the Social Sciences*, Vol. II, 343, 346–459 (1973).

Hartmann, N., *Ethics*, London, New York, 1932.

Husserl, E., *Formale und Transcendentale Logik*, 1929, translated by S. Bachelard as *Logique formelle et logique transcendantale*, Paris, 1957.

———. *The Idea of Phenomenology*, (1907), translated by W.P. Alston and G. Nakhnikian, The Hague, 1964.

———. *Ideen zu einer reinen phänomenologie und phänomenologischen Philosophie*, Vol. I, 1913, translated by W.R. Boyce Gibson, as *Ideas—General Introduction to Pure Phenomenology*, London, 1931.

———. "Philosophy als strenge Wissenschaft, 1 *Logos* 289 (1910), translated by Q. Lauer as "Philosophy as Rigorous Science", in Edmund Husserl, *Phenomenology and the Crisis of Philosophy*, New York, 1965.

Maihofer, W., "Die Natur der Sache", 44 *Archiv für Rechts-und Sozialphilosophie* 145 (1958), summaries in English and French.

———. "Le Droit Naturel comme depassement du droit positif", trans. by Poulantzas and Mavrakis, 8 *Archives de Philosophie du Droit* 177 (1963).

Mohanty, J.N., *Edmund Husserl's Theory of Meaning*, The Hague, 1964.

Peschka, V., "La Phénoménologisme dans la philosophie du droit moderne", 12 *Archives de Philosophie du Droit* 259 (1967).

Poulantzas, N., *Nature des choses et droit*, 1964.

———. "Notes sur la phénoménologie et l'existentialisme juridiques" 8 *Archives de philosophie du droit* 213 (1963).

———. "Response à M. Kalinowski", 8 *Archives de Philosophie due Droit* 271 (1963.

Radbruch, G., *Lehrbuch der Rechtsphilosophie*, 3d ed., 1932, translated in *Legal Philosophies of Lask, Radbruch, and Dabin*, in *Twentieth Century Legal Philosophy Series*, Vol. 4, Cambridge, Massachusetts, 1948.

Recasens-Siches, L., *Human Life, Society and Law: Fundamentals of the Philosophy of the Law*, translated by G. Ireland, in *Twentieth Century Legal Philosophy Series, Vol. III: Latin-American Legal Philosophy*, Cambridge, Massachusetts, 1948.

Sinha, S.P., "The Fission and Fusion of Is-Ought in Legal Philosophy", 21 *Villanova Law Review* 839 (1976).

Spiegelberg, H., *The Phenomenological Movement: A Historical Introduction*, 2 Vols., The Hague, 1960.

———. "Toward a Phenomenology of Experience", 1 *American Philosophical Quarterly* 1 (1964).

Thevenaz, P., *What Is Phenomenology? and Other Essays*, 1961.

Villey, "Deux Theses de Philosophie du Droit", 10 *Archives de Philosophie due Droit* 157 (1965).

Chapter 11

Abel, R., ed., *The Politics of International Justice*, San Diego, 1982.

Adorno, T., *Negative Dialectics*, trans. by E.B. Ashton, New York, 1973.

Arato, A. and P. Gebhardt, eds., *The Essential Frankfurt School Reader*, New York, 1978.

Ayer, A., *Logical Positivism*, Westport, CT, 1959.

Balkin, J.M., "Deconstructive Practice and Legal Theory," 96 *Yale Law Journal* 743 (1987).

Barthes, R., *Critical Essays*, trans. by R. Howard, Evanston, IL, 1972.

———. *The Pleasure of the Text*, trans. by R. Miller, New York, 1975.

Benedict, R., *Patterns of Culture*, 2d ed. New York, 1960.

Boliek, Jr., R.G., Commentary, "The Two Worlds of the Trashers and the Locust-Eaters: Flushing Critical Legal Studies From Out of the Bramble Bush," 37 *Alabama Law Review* 89 (1985).

Boyle, J., "The Politics of Reason: Critical Legal Theory and Local Social Thought," 13 *University of Pennsylvania Law Review* 685 (1985).

Brest, P., "The Fundamental Rights Controversy: The Essential Contradictions of Normative Constitutional Scholarship," 90 *Yale Law Journal* 1063 (1981).

Brosnan, D.F., "Serious But Not Critical," 60 *Southern California Law Review* 262 (1987).

Burtt, E., *The Metaphysical Foundations of Modern Physical Science*, Maryland, 1932.

Capek, M., *The Philosophical Impact of Contemporary Physics*, Princeton, N.J., 1961.

Carrington, P.D., "Of Law and the River," 34 *Journal of Legal Education* 222 (1984).

Cassirer, E., *The Philosophy of Enlightenment*, Princeton, N.J., 1951.

Cavell, S., *Must We Mean What We Say?*, New York, 1976.

———. *The Claim of Reason: Wittgenstein, Skepticism, Morality, and Tragedy*, Oxford/New York (1979).

Cornell, D., " 'Convention' and Critique," 7 *Cardozo Law Review* 679 (1980).

Culler, J., *Ferdinand de Saussure*, New York, 1976.

———. *On Deconstruction*, New York, 1982.

D'Amato, A., "Whither Jurisprudence?," 6 *Cardozo Law Review* 971 (1985).

Derrida, J., *Of Grammatology*, trans. by G. Spivak, Baltimore, 1976.

———. *Writing and Difference*, trans. by A. Bass, Chicago, 1972.

de Saussure, F., *Cours de Linguistique Générale* (1915), trans. as *A Course in General Linguistics*, ed. by C. Bally, A. Sechehaye and A. Reidlinger, trans. by W. Baskin Perry, IL, 1959.

Diamond, S., "Not-So-Critical Legal Studies," 6 *Cardozo Law Review* 693 (1985).

Eagleton, T., *Literary Theory: An Introduction*, Minneapolis, 1983.

Feyeraband, P., *Against Method*, London 1975.

———. *Realism and Scientific Method*, New York, 1981.

Finnis, J.M., "On 'the Critical Legal Studies Movement'," 30 *American Journal of Jurisprudence* 21 (1985).

257

Selected Bibliography

Fiss, O.M., "The Death of the Law?," 72 *Cornell Law Review* 1 (1986).

Fischl, R.M., "Some Realism About Critical Legal Studies," 41 *University of Miami Law Review* 505 (1987).

Foley, M., "Critical Legal Studies: New Wave Utopian Socialism," 91 *Dickinson Law Review* 467 (1986).

Forbath, W., "Taking Lefts Seriously," 92 *Yale Law Journal* 1041 (1983).

Freeman, A.D., "Truth and Mystification in Legal Scholarship," 90 *Yale Law Journal* 1229 (1981).

Friedman, G., *The Political Philosophy of the Frankfurt School*, New York, 1981.

Frug, G., "The City as a Legal Concept," 93 *Harvard Law Review* 1057 (1980).

Gabel, P., "Reification in Legal Reasoning," in P. Beirne and R. Quinney, eds., *Marxism and Law*, 262, New York, 1982.

———. "Intention and Structure in Contractual Conditions: Outline of a Method for Critical Legal Theory," 61 *Minnesota Law Review* 601 (1977).

Gabel, P. and D. Kennedy, "Roll Over Beethovan," 36 *Stanford Law Review* 1 (1984).

Geertz, C., *The Interpretation of Cultures*, Santa Barbara, 1973.

———. *Local Knowledge*, Santa Barbara, 1983.

Geus, R., *The Idea of a Critical Theory: Habermas and the Frankfurt School*, New York, 1981.

Gilson, E., *The Spirit of Medieval Philosophy*, Norwood, PA, 1936.

Gilmore, G., *The Ages of American Law*, New Haven, 1977.

Gordon, R.W., "Critical Legal Histories," 36 *Stanford Law Review* 57 (1984).

———. "New Developments in Legal Theory," in D. Kairys, ed. *The Politics of Law: A Progressive Critique*, 281, New York 1982.

Gutting, G., *Paradigms and Revolution*, Notre Dame, IN, 1980.

Habermas, J., *Theory and Practice*, trans. by J. Viertel, Boston, 1973.

Hawkes, T., *Structuralism and Semiotics*, Berkeley, CA, 1977.

Heisenberg, W., *Physics and Philosophy*, New York, 1958.

Hegland, K., "Goodbye to Deconstruction," 58 *Southern Califormia Law Review* 1203 (1985).

Heller, T.C., "Structuralism and Critique," 36 *Stanford Law Review* 127 (1984).

Henle, P., ed., *Language, Thought, and Culture*, Ann Arbor, Michigan, 1958.

Herzog, D., "As Many As Six Impossible Things Before Breakfast," 75 *California Law Review* 609 (1987).

Hirst, P. and P. Jones, "The Critical Resources of Established Jurisprudence," 14 *Journal of Law and Society* 21 (1987).

Horkheimer, M., *Critical Theory*, New York, 1968.

Hunt, A., "The Ideology of Law," 19 *Law and Society Review* 101 (1985).

———. "The Critique of Law: What is 'Critical' about Critical Legal Theory?," 14 *Journal of Law and Society* 5 (1987).

———. "The Theory of Critical Legal Studies," 6 *Oxford Journal of Legal Studies* 1 (1986).

Hutchinson, A.C. and P.J. Monahan, "Law, Politics, and the Critical Legal Scholars: The Unfolding Drama of the American Legal Thought," 36 *Stanford Law Review* 199 (1984).

———. "The 'Rights' Stuff: Robert Unger and Beyond," 62 *Texas Law Review* 1477 (1984).

258

Hyland, R., "A Defense of Legal Writing," 134 *University of Pennsylvania Law Review* 599 (1986).

Jacobson, A.J., "Modern American Jurisprudence and the Problem of Power," 6 *Cardozo Law Review* 713 (1985).

Jameson, F., *The Prison House of Language*, Princeton, NJ, 1972.

Johnson, P.E., "Do You Sincerely Want to be a Radical?," 36 *Stanford Law Review* 247 (1984).

Kairys, D., "Law and Politics," 52 *George Washington Law Review* 243 (1984).

———. ed. *The Politics of Law: A Progressive Critique*, New York, 1982.

Kelman, M.G., *A Guide to Critical Legal Studies*, Cambridge, MA 1987.

———. "Interpretative Construction in the Substantive Criminal Law," 33 *Stanford Law Review* 591 (1981).

———. "Trashing," 36 *Stanford Law Review* 293 (1984).

Kennedy, David, "Critical Theory, Structuralism, and Comtemporary Legal Scholarship," 21 *New England Law Review* 209 (1985–86).

Kennedy, Duncan and K. Klare, "A Bibliography of Critical Legal Studies," 94 *Yale Law Journal* 461 (1984).

Kennedy, Duncan, "Psycho-Social CLS: A Comment on the Cardozo Symposium," 6 *Cardozo Law Review* 1013 (1985).

———. "Form and Substance in Private Law Adjudication," 89 *Harvard Law Review* 1685 (1976).

———. "The Structure of Blackstone's Commentaries," 28 *Buffalo Law Review* 205 (1979).

———. "Legal Formalism," 2 *Journal of Legal Studies* 351 (1973).

Kuhn, T., *The Structure of Scientific Revolutions*, Chicago, 1962.

Lashchyk, E., *Scientific Revolutions: A Philosophical Critique of the Theories of Science of Thomas Kuhn and Paul Feyeraband*, Ann Arbor, Michigan, 1969.

Leitch, V., *Deconstructive Criticism*, New York, 1983.

Levinson, "Escaping Liberalism: Easier Said Than Done," 96 *Harvard Law Review* 1466 (1983).

Levi-Strauss, C., *Structuralism Anthropology*, Vol. I., trans. by C. Jacobson and B. Schoepf, Santa Barbara, 1963; Vol. II, trans. by M. Layton, Chicago, 1976.

———. *The Elementary Structures of Kinship*, (1949), trans. by J. Bell and J. von Sturmer, ed. by R. Needham, Boston, 1969.

McCarthy, T., *The Critical Theory of Jurgen Habermas*, Cambridge, MA 1978.

Marcus, J. and Z. Tar, eds., *Foundation of the Frankfurt School of Social Research*, New Brunswick, NJ, 1984.

Munger, F. and C. Seron, "Critical Legal Studies Versus Critical Legal Theory: A Comment on Method," 6 *Law and Policy Quarterly* 257 (1984).

Nagel, E., *The Structure of Science*, Indianapolis, 1962.

Nagel, E. and J. Newman, *Godel's Proof*, New York, 1958.

Note, "Round and Round the Bramble Bush: From Legal Realism to Critical Legal Scholarship," 95 *Harvard Law Review* 1669 (1982).

Peller, G., "The Metaphysics of American Law," 73 *California Law Review* 1151 (1985).

Pettit, P., *The Concept of Structuralism: A Critical Analysis*, Berkeley, CA 1977.

259

Poincaré, H., *The Foundations of Science*, Washington, D.C. (1982).

Prior, W.J., *Unity and Development in Plato's Metaphysics*, London 1985.

Purcell, E., *The Crisis of Democracy*, Lexington, KY 1973.

Reevald, J., *The History of Impressionism*, Boston, 1961.

Robey, D., ed., *Structuralism: An Introduction*, New York, 1973.

Rorty, R., *Consequences of Pragmatism*, Minneapolis, 1982.

————. *Philosophy and the Mirror of Nature*, Princeton, NJ, 1979.

Sapir, E., *Language*, New York, 1921.

————. *Culture and Personality*, ed. by D. Mandelbaum, Berkeley, CA, 1944.

Schlegel, J.H., "Notes Toward an Intimate, Opinionated, and Affectionate History of the Conference on Critical Legal Studies," 36 *Stanford Law Review* 391 (1984).

Schwartz, L.B., "With Gun and Camera Through Darkest CLS-Land," 36 *Stanford Law Review* 413 (1984).

Singer, J., "The Player and the Cards: Nihilism and Legal Theory," 94 *Yale Law Journal* 1 (1984).

Sparer, E., "Fundamental Human Rights, Legal Entitlements, and the Social Struggle: A Friendly Critique of the Critical Legal Studies Movement," 36 *Stanford Law Review* 509 (1984).

Standen, J.A., Note, "Critical Legal Studies as an Anti-Positivist Phenomenon," 72 *Virginia Law Review* 983 (1986).

Staten, H., *Wittgenstein and Derrida*, Lincoln, NE, 1984.

Steiner, G., *After Babel*, New York, 1975.

Stick, J., "Can Nihilism Be Pragmatic?," 100 *Harvard Law Review* 332 (1986).

Trubek, D.M., "Complexity and Contradiction in the Legal Order: Balbus and the Challenge of Critical Social Thought About Law," 11 *Law and Society Review* 527 (1977).

————. "Where the Action Is: Critical Legal Studies and Empiricism," 36 *Stanford Law Review* 575 (1984).

Turley, J., "The Hitchhiker's Guide to CLS, Unyer, and Deep Thought," 81 *Northwestern University Law Review* 593 (1987).

Tushnet, M., "Following the Rules Laid Down: A Critique of Interpretivism and Neutral Principles," 96 *Harvard Law Review* 781 (1983).

————. "Critical Legal Studies and Constitutional Law: An Essay in Deconstruction," 36 *Stanford Law Review* 623 (1984).

Unger, R., *The Critical Legal Studies Movement*, Cambridge, MA 1986.

————. *Knowledge and Politics*, New York, 1975.

————. *Law in Modern Society: Toward a Criticism of Social Theory*, New York, 1976.

————. "The Critical Legal Studies Movement," 96 *Harvard Law Review* 561 (1983).

Whorf, B., *Language, Thought, and Reality*, ed. by J. Carroll, Cambridge, MA 1956.

Williams, J.C., "Critical Legal Studies: The Death of the New Langdells," 62 *New York University Law Review* 429 (1987).

Yablon, C.M., "The Indeterminacy of the Law: Critical Legal Studies and the Problem of Legal Explanation," 6 *Cardozo Law Review* 917 (1985).

INDEX